'In this captivating and original volume, Charles van Onsele[illegible]ading social historian of the Witwatersrand, brings vividly to life this vanished world of transport riders, gold smugglers, gun-runners, dynamiters, crooked police and highwaymen, for the South African frontier was as rough as any on earth. Even the townscapes, saloons and stage coaches replicated their American archetypes. This was Britain's own "Wild West" …

Van Onselen … relates a remarkable South African history "from below". In the process, he subverts state-centred narratives and illuminates a fascinating chapter of British imperial, Irish and criminal history.'

– DONAL LOWRY, *Times Literary Supplement*

'This book is a mixture of social commentary and ripping yarns about those Irish rogues and vagabonds who looked to banditry, safe-blowing, prison breaks, highway robbery, murder and illicit gold dealing, many in the "other Irish Brigade" in the old Transvaal Republic and colonial Mozambique in the years of the South African gold rush in the last quarter of the 19th-century …

But this is not just a *Boy's Own* page-turner: it is also a serious study of social banditry, so easily thrown up by a gold rush and an ineffective government. It is a story of restlessness, degradation, seedy lodgings and, indeed, loyalty among thieves. But beyond the criminal heroes and anti-heroes there are fascinating studies.'

– DONAL MCCRACKEN, *Irish Times*

'*Masked Raiders* is an indispensable social history. Not only does it reveal a neglected aspect of South Africa's past and develop a cracked, distant mirror of our present, it also takes its place among those studies that demonstrate that individuals and societies emerge along lines of movement that respect neither the convenience of states nor the normative logic of nationalism.'

– MICHAEL TITLESTAD, *Sunday Independent*

'In an age where popular history is "packaged" into manageable bytes suitably sanitised for the heritage industry, and where academic writing's importance is all too often in indirect proportion to its unreadability, it is a joy to find a serious scholar who combines analytical originality with a narrative that has the pace of a thriller. Such an intellectual "social bandit" (in the best Hobsbawmian sense of the term) is Charles van Onselen. His apparently effortlessly executed account of Irish bandits, corrupt cops, inept politicians and displaced Fenians in latter nineteenth century southern Africa is both intellectually thought-provoking and a literary delight.'

– ANTHONY EGAN, *Focus*

'Van Onselen has made sure that we won't forget the Irish brigades, but in doing so, he has reminded us of the true South African history, of a state forever being carved up, exploited and colonised by one group against another for power and greed – and just how displaced ethnic minorities can make that happen.'

– KEVIN RITCHIE, *Star*

# Masked Raiders

# Masked Raiders

*Irish Banditry in Southern Africa 1880–1899*

CHARLES VAN ONSELEN

PROTEA BOOK HOUSE
PRETORIA
2020

*Masked Raiders: Irish Banditry in Southern Africa 1880–1899*
Charles van Onselen

First edition published in 2010 by Zebra Press
Second edition, first impression published in 2020 by Protea Book House
PO Box 35110, Menlo Park, 0102
1067 Burnett Street, Hatfield, Pretoria
8 Minni Street, Clydesdale, Pretoria
info@proteaboekhuis.co.za
www.proteaboekhuis.com

EDITOR: Anzette Williams
PROOFREADER: Morné van Rooyen
BOOK DESIGN AND TYPESETTING: Ada Radford
COVER DESIGN: Hanli Deysel
FRONT COVER IMAGE: Rissik Street, Johannesburg c. 1908.
The Print Collector/Alamy Stock Photo
TYPOGRAPHY: 10.5 on 14 pt ZapfCalligr BT

Printed by ***novus print***, a division of Novus Holdings

ISBN 978-1-4853-1160-7

*For Ian Phimister and Paul La Hausse de Lalouvière*

# Contents

THE SOUTHERN AFRICAN INTERIOR c.1880–1895
0 50 100 150 200 km
0 25 50 75 100 miles
Bulawayo
MATABELELAND
MOZAMBIQUE
PROTECTORATE OF BECHUANALAND
Pietersburg
SOUTH AFRICAN REPUBLIC (TRANSVAAL)
Pitsani
GOSHEN
Mafeking
Rustenburg
Pretoria
Middelburg
Komatipoort
Barberton
Lourenço Marques
Krugersdorp
Johannesburg
Boksburg
Natalspruit
Heidelberg
Mbabane
SWAZILAND
CROWN COLONY OF BECHUANALAND
STELLA-LAND
Vryburg
Potchefstroom
Klerksdorp
Kroonstad
Christiana
ORANGE FREE STATE
GRIQUALAND WEST
Boshof
Kimberley
Griquatown
Bloemfontein
Ladybrand
NATAL
Mokhokong
BASOTHOLAND
Pietermaritzburg
Durban
CAPE COLONY

THE WEST
WITWATERSRAND
AND ITS HINTERLAND
c.1895
0
10
20
km
Rustenburg
Brits
Pretoria
Sterkstroom
MAGALIESBERG
WITWATERSBERG
Magalies R.
Hennops R.
Hex R.
Crocodile R.
Krugersdorp
Witpoortjie
Luipaardsvlei Mine
Roodepoort
Randfontein
Florida
Johannesburg
Champ D'Or Mine
Langlaagte
Boksburg
Mooi R.
Mooirivierloop
Klip R.
Natalspruit
Potchefstroom
Vaal R.

# Introduction

Nationalist mantras, mouthed by Armani-dressed elites on behalf of the ragged-trousered masses, are often as blinkered in scope as they are short on memory. Clinging to what they see as God-given boundaries, those who rule seldom pause to look back on times when complex underlying factors rather than the will of great men defined the fate of swathes of humanity in territories aligned by the impersonal logic of economic forces. For the suited-ones, the outlines of the nation-state are a given just as surely as is the need for 'nation-building' on terms they decide. It is as if God could scribble the outlines of a state in the sand but was wholly incapable of getting his chosen people to work in concert for a blissful future in the promised land. Long on the 'blood of the martyrs' but often short on authentic historical memories, nationalist elites of all stripes find it difficult to think back to an era when others, including immigrants and refugees, helped to define the modern exclusionary 'us' in terms of time, space and identity.

A state for just over a hundred years, and a democracy of sorts for less than thirty, 'South Africa' remains more of a geopolitical description than an organic socio-economic entity. It has long been a playground for self-styled 'nation-builders', each incoming elite putting forward its own ethnic nucleus as the core of a longed-for 'nation' whose birth – ultimately dependent on the goodwill of untrustworthy others – is about to be realised. Amidst such deep, persistent divisions it may seem bizarre to explore the history of one tiny, displaced ethnic minority engaged in banditry over the few decades that pre-dated the birth of the modern Union of South Africa in 1910.

But it is precisely *because* the Irish formed such a small part of the demographic make-up of southern Africa's interior yet were disproportionately active as brigands between 1880 and 1899 that their story is worth telling. With a history of banditry and resistance that derived, in part, from their own experience as a colony in the British Empire, the

Irish were no strangers to tales about outlaw heroes or the doings of secret agrarian societies. Their socialisation in Ireland, or across the Irish Sea as second-generation ethnic Irish in Lancashire during the Industrial Revolution, included reading 'penny dreadfuls' that portrayed the deeds of brigands, highwaymen and pirates in romantic terms. That, along with first-hand experience gained in belt-and-buckle-wielding gangs stalking rough neighbourhoods in cities such as Manchester, primed the imaginations and hardened the bodies of poverty-stricken Irish teenagers for later, more overtly anti-imperial action in the remote parts of an expanding anglophone world.

It is ironic that it was the British Army – in which, as in the church, Irishmen from deprived backgrounds were always over-represented – that did most to bring these exotic, socially marginalised individuals to southern Africa. In the late nineteenth century, Fort Napier, in the garrison town of Pietermaritzburg, acted as an informal College of Banditry for delinquent Irish, teaching them how to negotiate and survive in the southern African interior while out on patrol in Natal or when based in rural Zululand. Like cacti in the desert waiting for a storm to unleash the moisture needed to bloom, all that was required for those of an antisocial disposition to mutate from soldiers into bandits was the emergence of appropriate socio-economic conditions. The tempest came with the mineral discoveries of the late nineteenth century.

The southern interior, with its dry grasslands around the diamond fields of Griqualand West and goldfields of the Witwatersrand, did not offer the classic terrain for brigandage – mountains, caves, ravines and forests. Rather, it was the remoteness of Kimberley in the early 1870s and Johannesburg in the mid-1880s, along with the slow emergence of a fully integrated regional rail network, that appealed most to the earliest highveld highwaymen. Isolation and underpopulation afforded masked raiders the opportunity to live off the earnings of African migrant workers traversing the countryside on foot, or to fleece better-off whites negotiating sandy tracks on horseback. More ambitious robbers plundered bullion or gemstones destined for export from coaches undertaking the long journey to coastal cities. Consisting for the most part of isolated loners and strongly bonded pairs, many such gunmen based themselves in mining towns where, when not out robbing, they led a robust quasi-urban existence.

What is significant, however, is that when the first cases of organised brigandage by whites on a meaningful scale emerged they were not on the highveld, but in the eastern lowveld, where mountainous terrain and valleys offered bandits the natural fortresses best suited to their adopted profession. When those at Fort Napier with ambivalent feelings about the British Empire learnt about gold discoveries in the De Kaap Valley and the Witwatersrand in the mid- and late 1880s, they deserted by the score to make their way inland. Lacking resources, they took to banditry. Barberton was their first port of call and there they either called themselves – or were soon dubbed – the 'Irish Brigade' by vulnerable and resentful English-speakers.

In 1886, Irish Brigade coach robbers, burglars, store-breakers and highwaymen pillaged and terrorised small mining centres in the De Kaap Valley before they were expelled and moved east to find contract work, as navvies laying track on the east-coast railway line. In Lourenço Marques, in 1887, they again demonstrated their antisocial and anti-imperialist propensities by deliberately embarrassing the British government when they sacked a Portuguese gunboat lying at anchor in Delagoa Bay. In the months that followed, still manifesting the cohesion associated with rural bandits on horseback, the brigands plundered their way back across the highveld before staging a dramatic weekend entry into Johannesburg in February 1888 that was marked by extensive disruption, tension, theft and murder.

Urban living, unsupported by the discipline rooted in the army barracks or the interdependence encouraged by rural operations, corroded social bonds within the Brigade and encouraged individualism. On the highveld, the Irish Brigade, cohering loosely as an ethnicised rather than a purely ethnic 'gang', split up into smaller, specialised units that exploited the longevity of a 'horse economy', a by-product of the regional political contestations that slowed the arrival of the railway north of the Vaal River.

Between 1888 and 1895, when Johannesburg was at last fully integrated into the regional rail system, members of the Irish Brigade – as burglars, bank robbers, highwaymen and safe-robbers – raided not only the central mining districts and broken country around Krugersdorp on the West Rand, but nearby prosperous farming centres such as Potchefstroom and Rustenburg. Demonstrating remarkable adaptability that drew on their prior history of displacement, migrancy and long-distance travel on the one hand, and the social cohesion that derived from military discipline on the other, they plied their trade as urban gangsters and rural bandits with equal ease. Their basic repertoire was extended to take in the robbing of government buildings and the offices of mining commissioners in towns where an absence of banks occasioned an unusual build-up of cash in safes; the sacking of postal carts along well-established routes; and the theft of gold amalgam or payrolls from mine properties noted for their inadequate security systems.

Neither Afrikaner republicans nor insurgent British imperialists, Irishmen sought out targets for their economic rather than their political significance, drawing no distinction between publicly or privately owned property. But, as capital tightened its grip on the burgeoning industry in the late 1880s, attempting to squeeze greater value from its semi-skilled white labour force by means of wage regulation, the mines were increasingly perceived by workers as being essentially British-owned and sympathetically aligned with imperial interests.

This at first inchoate perception by English-speaking underclasses on the highveld was drawn into sharper focus by the onset of a depression in late 1889 that persisted into 1892. As the emerging mining houses paused to consolidate their holdings and became increasingly monopolistic, thousands of disillusioned diggers and white miners lost their livelihoods. In this new social climate, where the banks, mines and state were believed to be uncaring about – even hostile towards – the interests of ordinary working men, the activities of the Irish Brigade took on added and unforeseen political significance.

It was the depression of 1890–92 that did most to turn popular perception of the Irish Brigade as a wholly criminal organisation into something that contained within it anglicised individuals who, by identifying the rich and powerful as their targets, were more akin to 'heroic criminals', 'outlaw legends' or 'social bandits'. Men such as the McKeone brothers and 'One-Armed Jack' McLoughlin – bank robbers, highwaymen and safe-lifters raised on Victorian literature that celebrated the virtues of 'manliness' – were suddenly divested of Irish identities and recast in press and pub as English folk heroes like Robin Hood and Dick Turpin. Fact and fiction were soon elided as charismatic figures drawn from the criminal underworld staged dramatic escapes from prison and fled to neighbouring territories, or sought refuge in strong African polities actively resisting absorption into developing colonial, or independent republican, states.

Southern Africa never produced a fully fledged Ned Kelly capable of contributing significantly to a founding myth for the supposedly white 'nation' that emerged after the advent of Union in the early twentieth century. It did, however, experience its own brief Ned Kelly-like moment in the late nineteenth century, when the southern highveld witnessed the emergence of criminal heroes and outlaw legends; men who – at the time – transcended the importance of the now better-remembered 'Scotty Smith' or, much later still, that of the other Irish-Kimberley offshoot, the Foster gang, whose members expired in another moment of high nationalist confusion in 1914.

In the course of these majestic criminal flights and swoops across the boundaries of a subcontinent riddled with smaller geopolitical entities, members of the Irish Brigade and other miscreants set loose other, countervailing thinking in the minds of local elites. Police and prison administrations – the skeletal framework necessary for all aspiring states – were beefed up to cope with new challenges. Formal extradition treaties and informal agreements between states to deliver fugitives to law-enforcement agencies operating in other jurisdictions primed the pump for pleas for a single 'South African' legal system twenty years before the formation of Union. Although an unintended consequence and one hardly born of strength, small bands of insurgent Irishmen engaged in criminal activity helped foster thinking about regional cooperation and regional integration. 'Nation-building' – ancient or modern – has never been the exclusive preserve of the suited-ones, some of whom themselves manifest alarming criminal tendencies seldom acknowledged fully by their followers.

In this contested and troubled environment, where the criminal was increasingly read as political, the difference between the two was further blurred when, in 1895, discontented mine owners attempted to stage their own bandit-like incursion to effect a *coup d'état* in the South African Republic (ZAR). When the Jameson Raid failed, the political was rendered criminal. The subsequent attempt by the Kruger government to reform but simultaneously resist any future British military challenge attracted the admiration and interest of a small but influential group of advanced Irish nationalists in Dublin.

In 1896–97, half a dozen Fenians, members of the Irish Republican Brotherhood (IRB) – including John MacBride, who was to lead a second, 'political' Irish Brigade into battle on the Boer side in the South African War of 1899–1902, and Arthur Griffith, who went on to found Sinn Féin and become the first president of the Irish Free State in 1922 – left Ireland unexpectedly to find employment on the Witwatersrand. It is uncertain what the real purpose behind their visit was. It may have been a public attempt to mobilise their countrymen to support the cause of Irish nationalism that went well beyond the prevailing plea for 'home rule', but it may also have been part of a secret mission to raise funds – from legal and illegal sources alike – for cultural and political projects back in Dublin.

With the eclipse of the horse economy – occasioned by the extension of the railway network – ensuring the gradual demise of the first 'criminal' Irish Brigade, the arrival of the advanced nationalists assumed added importance for those interested in ethnicised crime. By 1898, MacBride and Griffith, quintessentially literate, middle-class activists, were both working at tasks more manual than mental, and close to, or in, the reduction works of the Robinson Mine in Johannesburg. Their proximity to refining processes came at a time when the theft of gold amalgam had assumed epidemic proportions. It also coincided with the emergence of a criminal syndicate led by a certain 'Dr. Kelly'. 'Kelly' was said to have purchased an abandoned, uninsured ship in Delagoa Bay for the export of illegally acquired gold, which, amidst renewed national and international interest in official quarters about Fenians on the Witwatersrand, was lost in a storm off the Zululand coast. More importantly, it came at a moment when those charged with the security of amalgam at a leading mining house pressed the state to arrange for the entrapment and arrest of a certain 'Mr. A. Griffiths', said to be a leading member of a syndicate devoted to the illicit sale of gold.

Despite the fact that Arthur Griffith met members of the old Irish Brigade in the eastern Transvaal goldfields on at least one occasion, there appears to have been no systemic link between the first, pre-1895 Irish Brigade and the advanced nationalists of the late nineties who went on to help launch the second, 'political' Irish Brigade. There was no natural evolution or linear development from the proto-nationalism of men cast as 'criminal heroes' or 'social bandits' by jaded journalists and disillusioned workers on the Witwatersrand during a sustained economic depression, to the actions of the later, advanced nationalists who helped pave the way for an independent, republican Ireland. That said, it is unlikely that members of the IRB would have taken as great an interest as they did in southern Africa and its mines had they not first heard the myths and realities that swirled in the wake of the first Irish Brigade's criminal actions.

History seldom offers straightforward 'lessons' of the sort beloved by some armchair critics, journalists and politicians. It does, however, occasionally make room for interesting and instructive comparisons that can broaden our perspective and deepen our understanding of the present. For those who follow armed conflicts and wish to trace the role of deserting or demobilised soldiers in the 'crime waves' that sometimes engulf modern societies, there may be some purpose in pausing to reflect on the rise and decline of the Irish Brigade. And, for those interested in 'the nation' and in the suited-ones promoting 'nation-building' in complex multiracial settings, there may be a point in trying to explore more intently the role that displaced ethnic minorities, seeking refuge from hostile environments, can play – directly or indirectly – in shaping the host societies. A probing of the history of Irish banditry in southern Africa throws light on how 'we' and 'they' were constructed and reminds 'us' just how contingent, stubborn and troublesome such categories can be. For the moment, there is a need to distinguish between the authentic and the Armani. Inclusive, tolerant communities are the precursors and building blocks of 'nation-states', whose own roles are becoming increasingly puzzling and problematic in a globalising world.

# 1

# From Agrarian Ireland and Industrial Lancashire to Natal's College of Banditry

> God made the country, and man made the town.
>
> – William Cowper, *The Task*

> Ireland has revenged itself upon England, socially – by bestowing an Irish quarter on every English industrial, maritime or commercial town of any size, and politically – by furnishing the English Parliament with an 'Irish Brigade'.
>
> – Karl Marx, *Neue Oder-Zeitung*, 16 March 1855

Ireland was the first, certainly the most consistently troublesome and, in the shape of Protestant enclave Ulster, arguably also one of the longest lived of England's many colonies. The conquest of Gaelic Catholic Ireland in 1690 ushered in not only a period of profound religious persecution that ended formally only with the repeal of the Penal Laws in 1793 and Catholic emancipation in 1829, but also hundreds of years of agonisingly slow political, economic and social change. In 1801, the Act of Union forced a marriage between the United Kingdom and Ireland – a development prompted by the Irish Rebellion of 1798, itself inspired by the French Revolution.[1]

The advent of the nineteenth century saw further intensification of the long-standing struggle for Irish national self-determination, starting with Daniel O'Connell's movement for the repeal of the Act of Union in the 1830s. Efforts strengthened with the emergence of the Young Irelanders in the wake of the European uprisings of 1848 and, in the 1860s, the Irish Republican Brotherhood – the Fenians – revolutionaries who drew substantial support from Irishmen abroad, including those in the United States of America.[2] In addition to these focused, overt forms of political opposition, however, Irish politics was characterised by innumerable other popular religious, social and economic movements expressing communal, interfamilial, territorial or sectarian conflict in rural settings.

The political contours of these diverse national, regional and local movements were partially shaped and often sharpened by underlying changes in the agrarian economy during the late eighteenth and early nineteenth centuries. This exacerbated culturally sanctioned acts of violence undertaken by individuals, small bands of men or even entire clans of Irishmen. Thus, aside from the usual brawls, formal duels and fist fights taking place between individual men or small groups, rural Ireland was famous for large-scale, bloody faction fights fuelled by alcohol. Sticks were used to great effect to settle family feuds, inter-village rivalries or sectarian differences.[3] At dusk, and more especially so in the south and west of the country, highwaymen took to the roads, giving rise to a local romanticised tradition rivalling that of its more famous English counterpart.[4] By night, oath-bound members of secret societies across the island, some manifesting overtly anti-clerical sentiments, and led by self-appointed 'captains' bearing names such as Burnstack, Cropper and Fearnot, undertook acts of arson, damage to property, theft and the mutilation of animals. These defiant exploits were intended to challenge the hold of landlords or their agents in a rural society wracked by division and inequality.[5] Intra- and inter-communal violence provoked by injustice on the land fed the contempt that many, if not most, Irishmen held for laws and policing that were seen as alien, as 'English'.[6]

The gradual shift from pasturage to tillage in late-eighteenth century Ireland helped give rise to monocrop production. But while the cultivation of potatoes underwrote the continued viability of subsistence farming in the medium term, it left the population vulnerable to long-term natural disaster. The appearance of blight in the potato crop precipitated the disastrous Great Famine of 1847–52, in which a million people starved to death, and prompted subsequent land clearances as better-off farmers sought to revert to more balanced forms of agricultural production. This helped spark the bitterly contested Land War of 1879–82, which saw another million and a half Irish – men and women – leave the country of their birth. Between the years of the Famine and the conclusion of the Land War, the population of Ireland as a whole declined by a full 20 per cent.[7]

Emigration pre- and post-dated the Great Famine, but mass starvation primed the pump for this unprecedented exodus of men, women and children to distant America, Australasia and Canada, or just across the Irish Sea to England and Scotland.[8] By the mid-nineteenth century, Glasgow, Liverpool and Manchester all boasted substantial immigrant communities of Irish Catholics. But for those adults who were Manchester-bound and set to start families, things improved at the pace of an Irish ox as irony and tragedy continued to shape their lives. Having fled the devastation of the economic hurricane that had hit their rural homeland, they sought refuge in urban Lancashire, right in the teeth of the social gales unleashed by the Industrial Revolution.[9]

Manchester's fame as a manufacturing centre that dictated emerging patterns of global trade in the Victorian era was founded on textile production, but, in truth, its economic profile was always more diversified than that. In addition to the 'dark Satanic' cotton mills of historic and literary significance, Manchester boasted substantial chemical works, iron foundries, machine manufactories and metal works. A dedicated system of canals, docks and railways fed industry but also served an enormous commercial and retail sector linked to markets, shops and warehouses. Thus, while pre-Famine Irish immigrants were prominent as workers in the cotton industry, after 1850 they spread out to take up a host of other positions as construction workers, factory hands, hawkers, general labourers, porters, shop assistants and warehouse men in a complex urban economy.[10]

While Manchester's population rose steadily from 243 000 in 1841, to 300 000 in 1851, and then up to 350 000 by 1861, the trajectory of its economic growth was not as smooth. The Cotton Famine of 1861–65, caused by a disruption in trade when the North blockaded the South during the American Civil War, proved a setback but was soon followed by a boom that lasted most of the 1870s. In 1884, however, the economy collapsed into a serious depression.[11] Amidst all this, impoverished Irish 'deckers' who had 'come over with the cattle' and 'micks' who were 'just off the bog' were subjected to sustained prejudice that reached a high point in the 1860s.[12] While retaining distinctive identities as both Irish and Catholic, the new immigrants did not retreat into fully fledged ghettos; they settled instead into heavily ethnicised neighbourhoods in the city, such as Ancoats, Angel Meadow and Collyhurst.[13]

For those in the Irish minority unfortunate enough to live in the slum-ridden surrounds of the cotton mills in which they worked, the very same mills investigated by Engels, the unfamiliar, regimented working environment could be every bit as alienating as Marx portrayed it.[14] This fed into the revolutionary politics of the Fenians – which culminated in the hanging of the 'Manchester Martyrs' in 1867 – almost as readily as it did into the social pathologies of the poor. Dysfunctional working-class habits, some of them informed by, if not derived from, experiences in Ireland, marked most of these deprived communities, including assaults on constables, other disorderly behaviour and drunkenness.[15]

But if these were familiar patterns among Irish-born male and female immigrants, then there were also new, in some ways even more alarming, manifestations of gross antisocial behaviour in many of their Lancashire-born children. Adolescents between the ages of puberty and about twenty, overwhelmingly male but not excluding a significant number of females, drew on elements of Irish rural culture – including faction fighting, notions of honour, oath-taking and secret societies – and combined them with some of the most problematic features of modern urban slum life – distinctive flashy attire and uniform hairstyles, ready use of the knife or the buckle at the end of a belt, and sexual precociousness – to create the violently territorial street-based gangs that dominated working-class Manchester and Salford between circa 1870 and 1890. These gangs of 'scuttlers' were part of a pan-tribal 'youth cult' rather than any distinctively Irish or Catholic group. But to the extent that those based in certain neighbourhoods *were* 'Irish', they were part old, part new, part rural, part urban and wholly feral.[16]

It is the youngsters in this cohort of post-Famine Irish and Manchester-Irish scuttlers – those born in the decade between 1855 and 1865 – imperfectly schooled and brought up, in part, on 'sensational novels' whose heroes were often 'highwaymen, pirates or brigands' who 'openly defied authority and revelled in bloodshed', who should be of some interest to the historians of 'social banditry' in southern Africa.[17] It was these unruly-boys-turned-anarchic-young-men who, between the ages of twenty and thirty, seized the chance to convert the adolescent social fantasies and rebellious politics of their nineteenth-century cult of Irish masculinity into something approximating lived reality.[18]

The Kruger government provided scores, nay, hundreds of dislocated Irishmen and Manchester-born Irish scuttlers with their hour in the sun when, in the early 1880s, it decided to prolong the life of the horse economy in the largely agrarian South African Republic. It did so in a bid to regulate and slow the advance of the twinned horrors of British imperialism and untrammelled industrial capitalism. It was a scenario and a political project that, for most Irishmen, was as natural as mother's milk. It offered a brief moment of opportunity set in a far-off land drenched in tales of gold and diamonds, and it just happened to come at a time when they were entering their mental and physical prime. For these rebellious young men, who were unpersuaded that law and justice were ever in perfect alignment, all that was needed for wish to become reality was for an institution to whisk them off to the far end of the world.

Many scuttlers were halfway to the army even before they encountered the regimental sergeant major. Armed with leather belts wound tightly around wrists and whirring metal buckles directed at the heads of rivals, they were seasoned practitioners of set pieces involving either spontaneous ambushes or pre-arranged, bloody street battles. The outbreak of the Franco-Prussian War in 1870 excited ethno-religious imaginations and spawned a small 'civil war' lasting several weeks in Ancoats, Angel Meadow, New Cross and Collyhurst, as youngsters between the ages of ten and eighteen organised themselves into 'French' and 'German' factions using knives, iron swords and firearms in hand-to-hand fighting. A local commentator, born in 1860, noted that 'many scuttlers joined the army', adding that 'almost without exception they made the best of soldiers'.[19]

## The British Army and its Nineteenth-Century Trojan Horses

Centuries-long British rule of the Irish economy, always overwhelmingly dependent on agriculture, gave rise to widespread resentment and insecurity among a broadly impoverished population. It also helped shape an emerging culture in which politics and religion became particularly closely intertwined and, beyond that, fed into a subculture of vibrant but vulnerable masculinity. All this in a country where opportunities for meaningful employment of sons, beyond small-scale farming, were few and far between.

This toxic country brew did not always settle easily with those men – or women – already burdened with other problems deriving from alcohol abuse and diet, or others with a genetic propensity to mental instability. These factors, too, played themselves out amidst the subculture of masculinity, bedevilling relations between men and women and complicating issues of gender, morality, sexuality and work.[20] The 'Devotional Revolution', led by Archbishop Cullen after the Great Famine, urged a cohort of men already inclined towards the single life into chaste service within the priesthood, and is likely to have influenced others, too. As late as 1911, over a quarter of all Irish-born men were unmarried, while many delayed marriage until after the age of thirty.[21]

For those younger sons who saw no future for themselves on the land, the priesthood offered an all-male religious pathway out of the mainstream of nineteenth-century Irish culture, drawing them towards the image of the Madonna. Life in the church provided a career that, although not without problems, was relatively low on inner political contradictions and tensions. The priesthood was a famously – or notoriously – powerful vector of Irish nationalism. For other sons – more numerous by far – an alternative route out of the mainstream was the British Army; another all-male but secular exit that, more often than not, led to the Whore. Serving in the British Army, however, was a career that for Irish Catholic, Protestant and non-believer alike was fraught with political angst. How could one simultaneously bend the knee before a British queen or fight for empire *and* remain loyal to Mother Ireland?

Both escape routes encouraged misperceptions of women, explicitly excluded or undermined 'normal' heterosexual relationships within marriage and, on occasion, gave way to forms of male bonding that went beyond the bounds of conventional sexual morality at the time. At least some priests and some soldiers – a minority of Irishmen who found the Madonna and the Whore equally elusive – must have shared secrets that in mid-Victorian times were best left buried in the barracks or the monastery. For the majority of priests and soldiers, however, there were other forces at play. Priests, devoted to life and the afterlife, and soldiers who had to confront death in the here and now, did not always see eye to eye. And, in a world where sinners outnumbered saints, there were always going to be more soldiers than soul-savers.

''Tis Ireland gave England her soldiers, her generals too,' remarked novelist George Meredith.[22] They joined in droves. In 1831, a staggering

42 per cent of all men in the British Army were Irish-born. By 1861 that number had dropped sharply to 28 per cent but, by 1871, amidst the rapid radicalisation of Irish politics at home and abroad, it was still 25 per cent.[23] As a mop for structural unemployment, the army retained its functionality well into the latter half of the nineteenth century. For this it had the Cardwell Reforms of 1870 to thank. Cardwell reduced the period of enlistment from ten years in the infantry and twelve years in the artillery, cavalry or engineers, to six years in the artillery, cavalry or engineers followed by six years in the reserves.[24] If this halving in the period of enlistment held some appeal for those Irish-born drawn from a slow-moving agrarian economy, it held even more for those young Lancashire-born Irish based in the great urbanising nodes of the Industrial Revolution who were seeking to retain some flexibility in planning a career in their rapidly expanding world.

With one in five recruits Irish-born and a good number of others drawn from Irish enclaves in London, Manchester and other urban centres in the 1870s, the army could hardly avoid taking in Fenians bent on revolution as well as their fellow travellers of various stripes. It took in, too, a significant number of erstwhile scuttlers prone to antisocial behaviour even if they were not particularly politically conscious. Not all of these potentially volatile elements were necessarily hostile to, or suspicious of, the imperial project. A northern minority, faithful to the Orange of Protestant Ulster, was poorly disposed towards the Catholic Greens of the south and stayed loyal to the Crown. Despite these cross-tensions, however, most Irishmen had strong reservations about British politics.

Although arguably more pony than horse while posted around the United Kingdom, regimental Trojans were recognisable – and partly visible – during the troublesome 1860s and '70s. In Ireland, the 27th Inniskilling Fusiliers, based in the north-west, was known to contain both Green and Orange sympathisers. These low-key tensions were carried over into the enlarged Royal Inniskilling Fusiliers when, in 1881, the 27th was amalgamated with the 108th Regiment of Foot, formerly of Madras.

Predictably, in England itself, Trojans – ranging from revolutionary Fenians to merely unruly scuttlers – clustered in and around Manchester. The 64th Lancashire Rifle Volunteers – an outfit centred on Liverpool rather than Manchester – termed the 'Irish Brigands' by its opponents, hosted many known Fenians and, by 1869, 'it was said that enlisting in a volunteer unit was a prerequisite for joining the Irish Republican Brotherhood in Lancashire'.[25] Similar tensions were evident in 2nd Somerset Regiment of Foot and 82nd Regiment of Foot, which, in 1881, amalgamated to form the South Lancashire Regiment (The Prince of Wales' Volunteers) based at Werrington in Cheshire. If the Royal Inniskillings and the 64th Lancashire Rifle Volunteers got the cream of Ireland in the form of a number of Fenians and their sympathisers, then the South Lancashires had to be content with some of the scum in the shape of Manchester-born criminals or former scuttlers.

By 1881, the British Army had at least two regiments containing Trojans. Irish- or Lancashire-born troops, single young men with varying degrees of political consciousness, were culturally predisposed to alienation and disaffection and prone to romantic visions, the products of a lost agrarian world. Their dreams did not exclude images of a life of brigandage, informed by the idea of being 'hard men', which made it difficult for them to relate to women in ways that included marriage. Here then, if ever, was the raw material for banditry. When the wonderfully named War Office decided to send first the South Lancashires and then the Royal Inniskillings to southern Africa, it hoped both to bolster the British presence in a zone of imperial ambition and to increase the *esprit de corps* of these two newly formed, untested regiments. It was, however, also despatching scores of soldiers to the frontiers of a mineral revolution, to the borders of another disappearing rural universe, where progress towards a great state-in-the-making was being thwarted by a seemingly feudal republic clinging to the last vestiges of an antiquated horse economy.

## Fort Napier: A College of Banditry, 1883–1888

From the late eighteenth century throughout the turbulent nineteenth century, the pre-eminent, growing challenges to the strengthening British imperial presence in southern Africa lay to the north and east of the region. The Boers, north of the Vaal River, and to the east of that the Zulu kingdom stretching beyond the Tugela, demanded a permanent British military presence. This need, long met via Fort Napier, the garrison town at Pietermaritzburg, and the adjacent Indian Ocean port of Durban, was underscored by the Anglo-Zulu War of 1879 and the Boers' First War of

Independence in 1880–81. For decades prior to this, British regiments had rotated through Fort Napier on an overlapping basis, an average tour of duty lasting from three to five years.

By the early to mid-1880s, when the two 'new' post-Cardwell Irish and Anglo-Irish contingents, the 2nd South Lancashire Battalion (1884–87) and the Royal Inniskillings (1886–88), reached Fort Napier, their commanding officers were confronted with a set of contradictory demands. It was an underlying, unstated conflict that became even more pronounced once the 'Irish' were joined, in 1887, by the 64th Regiment, the North Staffordshires, whose tour lasted till 1890. On the one hand, troops deployed in enlarged regiments but untested in battle under new colours needed forging into an entity displaying the unity and the loyalty of purpose that made for successful engagements in the field. On the other, ongoing tensions within Zulu politics required that troops be split into companies and smaller patrols offering a regular, visible presence in potential trouble spots. Centripetal forces called for the barracks, the parade ground and the city to build regimental pride, but realities on the ground made for centrifugal tendencies that pushed men out into the countryside.[26]

In theory, it was possible to strike a balance between these demands, enabling them to feed into one another in ways that were complementary rather than competitive. In practice, the propensity to fragmentation and disintegration became at least as – perhaps even more – pronounced than did the tendency to build regimental pride. In the case of those regiments straddling the 1880s – the Inniskillings, South Lancashires and North Staffordshires – it helped change the nature of the time spent at Pietermaritzburg, giving rise to an unintended consequence. For those antisocial and hard-drinking individuals drawn from the urban areas of the Industrial Revolution – youngsters already familiar with the parameters of institutional life as lived in school, reformatory, factory or prison – Fort Napier offered an additional, transforming experience; it became a virtual College of Banditry. Lengthy spells in the bush, broken by short interludes in the garrison, provided those of a criminal bent with opportunities to form small, close-knit, all-male bands of brigands with all the skills necessary for a life of rural banditry.

Life on patrol in the broken and diversified bush conditions of the Natal and Zululand countryside exposed the much-admired 'hard men' of the Industrial Revolution's urban underbelly to horses and life on horseback.[27] It also taught them a great deal more. They discovered how and where to find water, as well as how to hunt the small and larger game necessary for survival. They learnt to 'read' the region's topography and identify those physical features best suited to the needs of attack or defence by small groups of mounted men. They grew to understand the possibilities and problems of moving by day or by night and, by following the escapades of gunrunners, cattle rustlers and horse thieves, familiarised themselves with not only facets of rural crime but – as importantly – how the police sought to track and apprehend such offenders. Postings in the Zulu heartland were arduous and very unpopular with the troops, but bush patrols increased the independence, self-confidence and self-reliance of the men.[28]

For the more intelligent antisocial characters among the troops, including a few who were clearly psychopathic in an age before psychopathy was generally recognised, there were other – potentially vital – skills to master, or at least mimic in passable fashion, while moving among the natives, black and white. Acquiring the rudiments of rural etiquette, mastering a few phrases in the vernacular or, better still, learning a language, could all be of incalculable value when dealing with awkward people or nasty situations. The bearing and demeanour of ordinary Afrikaner folk or individual African men and women had to be decoded as a prelude to dealing with them in as friendly a manner as possible in what was, in essence, a post-war climate.

Shared experiences of rural deprivation and hardship increased camaraderie and intimacy among some men just as surely as it was considered to be detrimental to overall regimental discipline.[29] Regiments prided themselves on providing troops with 'a male family', social units almost devoid of women in which members of the opposite sex, other than prostitutes, were often viewed with contempt or suspicion. Even while in barracks men undertook many chores that would otherwise be considered 'female' – cleaning, cooking, ironing, washing and repairing. The exchange of small favours in some cases encouraged even deeper bonds that could, on occasion, culminate in the 'unnatural vices' of masturbation and homosexuality.[30] If these were 'problems' in zones of high visibility, such as in the city or Fort Napier – and they were – how much more so would they have been out on patrol where there were greater opportunities for privacy? It is significant that some African boys around Pietermaritzburg claimed later to have been subjected to homosexual rape by British troopers.[31]

But, regardless of whether sexual encounters in the bush were consensual or forced, they could only have added to the social tensions soldiers had to manage on their return to the city. These returns, especially when coupled with military pay days, were marked by predictable bouts of excessive drinking, fighting, gross indiscipline and whoring in the city's few brothels. Bouts of severely disorderly behaviour, reminiscent of rural bandits invading small towns while out on drinking sprees, were often the precursor to individual or collective acts of desertion.[32]

In the case of the 'Irish' and other regiments at the time, these customary pathologies played themselves out against the distant backdrop of the enticing frontiers created by the mineral revolution of 1870–86, and contributed, albeit indirectly, to other criminal activities, riotous incidents and mutiny. In 1885, a small number of Argyll and Sutherland Highlanders marched, in menacing formation, towards the police station. They were eventually successfully dispersed after their commotion outside the house of a woman – who, they claimed, was a prostitute – had led to the arrest of one of their number. In 1886, at a time of deep discontent among a few young Mancunians in the South Lancashires, a set of rifles – eventually traced to Basotholand by the police – was stolen from the garrison armoury. The very next year, 1887, saw a drunken brawl-cum-mutiny involving, it would seem, Green and Orange elements from the Inniskillings, that resulted in the hanging of Joseph McCrea.[33]

Deeply suspicious of Britain's imperial ambitions and by then, arguably, trained and equally qualified to embark on a life of urban crime or rural banditry, the Irish began to desert in droves. They were not the first, or the last, to desert from Fort Napier. Indeed, men from the potteries – the North Staffordshires – were equally prone to abandoning army life and seeking out pastures new before the completion of their contracts. Nor did the men from Erin enter only the ranks of criminals. As in nineteenth-century Australia, the Irish were over-represented in law-enforcement agencies. An examination of the records of the Cape or Natal Mounted Police, or even the much-derided ZAR police and prison services, reveals the presence of a disproportionate number of Irishmen, not excluding deserters.

That said, Irish names are particularly prominent among those who took to organised crime – including bank, highway and safe-robbery – during the lingering period of the horse economy that marked the birth of industrialising southern Africa. Sadly, the War Office failed to record systematically the relevant details of all those recruited into the British Army, let alone the names of every individual who deserted. Yet, even among the surviving documents it is possible to ferret out the names of a few who went on to achieve notoriety on the gold and diamond fields.

In the late 1870s and early '80s, Kimberley and the surrounding diamond fields were among the first ports of call for many deserters-turned-bandits. A squiggly mess of nearby borders, including those with the Orange Free State, the ZAR and the short-lived republics of Goshen and Stellaland that were, in many ways, states founded primarily as a result of Boer bandit and mercenary action, made it ideal terrain for rapid movement and rural crime. Locally based, pioneering 'social bandits' included George Lennox – 'Scotty Smith' – a serial deserter seen by many as 'South Africa's Robin Hood', and the less social Irish highwayman H.J. 'Jack' O'Reilly.[34] In the early 1880s, the oyster of opportunity for banditry creaked open a few degrees more with the discovery of gold in the eastern Transvaal lowveld – remote hilly country conveniently close to Natal, Swaziland and Mozambique. Barberton offered a wonderful field for early practical experience for deserter-bandits. By the time the Witwatersrand fields opened in 1886, there was a seasoned cohort of robbers who, depending on changing economic microclimates determined by the ruling prices of gold or diamonds and the professionalism of local police forces, could move with relative confidence between Barberton, Johannesburg and Kimberley, practising their ever-mutating black arts. For all its adaptability and diversity, however, the core component of the highveld's 'social bandits' continued to be drawn largely from the College of Banditry and its intake from the fringes of Manchester 'scuttling' subculture.

# 2

# Deserters and Navvies: Birth of an 'Irish Brigade'

> Exile immobilises to some degree the minds of those who suffer it. It imprisons them for ever within the circle of ideas which they had conceived or which were current when their exile began.
>
> – Alexis de Tocqueville

Perhaps it is precisely because Ireland itself is so poorly endowed with natural mineral wealth that its folklore is beset with alluring tales of leprechauns guarding crocks of gold at the end of rainbows. The opening of the Rand goldfields triggered the curiosity of men from many nations, but it appears to have done something special to the imagination of the Irish and Manchester-Irish in Fort Napier. In just sixteen weeks, between September and December 1886, close on fifty privates deserted from the South Lancashires alone.[1] Others, albeit in smaller numbers, abandoned the Argyll and Sutherland Highlanders, the Inniskilling Fusiliers and the 6th Dragoons.

Among the earliest deserters, in April of that year, were J. McCann, who abandoned the Inniskillings for Kimberley, and W. Kelly of the Argylls, who probably made his way to Barberton. But, in that crucial final quarter, it was the South Lancashire Battalion that lost P. Carroll (1 December), J. Dwyer (14 September), J. Hutchings (6 November), J. McLoughlin (unknown), J. O'Brien (16 October) and J. Wiggins (28 October). Members of the latter grouping, almost without exception, saw the road to rainbow's end – believed to be around Johannesburg – as twisting through Swaziland and then winding on to the booming goldfields of the eastern Transvaal. Between them, these few Irishmen alone were sentenced to scores of years in prison; three were extradited from adjacent states; one was killed while attempting to escape from prison; and another was later hanged for murder.

The natural-born leader, formerly of the South Lancs, was John Hutchings, a man seemingly Irish-born and certainly deeply inspired by agrarian secret societies, who later took the aliases 'Hutchinson' and 'Muldoon'. In and out of the guard room and military prison throughout his career, Hutchings and John O'Brien – an impulsive man from a Mancunian family with strong Fenian sympathies – had both been recruited in Devonport and shared berths on the same navy vessel that brought them south.[2]

Hutchings' unofficial second in command was a cunning, hard-drinking, laconic native of Manchester raised quite literally in the shadow of the mills. John McLoughlin, aged thirty, was a short, powerfully built man who had joined the South Lancs during the depression year of 1884 having just returned to Lancashire from a noteworthy career of crime in Australia. A man capable of developing the closest bonds imaginable with loyal mates, he possessed most Irishmen's hatred of police informers or those he thought guilty of treachery. His relationships with women, if not wholly misogynistic, were purely functional. He had little time for females of European descent, either colonial or metropolitan, confining the transient relationships that he did have to African women in peasant societies or 'coloured' prostitutes in mining towns. The product of a broken, drunken Irish family, he had been brought up in extreme poverty in the heavily Catholic neighbourhood of Ancoats. Although contemptuous of priests, McLoughlin held few overtly expressed political convictions, but nevertheless had an almost instinctive distrust of Englishmen and an eye for some targets that many poor working men and women would have condoned – bookmakers, mines, pawnshops, publicans and storekeepers.[3]

Within weeks of deserting, in late 1886, several South Lancs appeared in and around Barberton, then just coming out of a remarkable boom and starting that slow slide into a recession from which it never recovered. Within weeks this motley crew of no fixed abode was dubbed the 'Irish Brigade'. Whether this nomenclature was self-generated, in which case it may have harked back to the 64th Rifles, notorious for its Fenian sympathies, and pointed to a low level of anti-English sentiment, or whether the epithet was simply pinned on unruly Celtic soldiers by unhappy mainstream Englishmen is unknown. It may well have been more of the latter than the former – the Brigade appears to have been more ethnicised than fully ethnic. Either way, it was only days before this band of wild Irishmen became actively involved in local crime.

## The De Kaap Valley, 1886–1887

John 'James'/'Jim' O'Brien was a Mancunian who, posing as a man down on his luck, would gain the trust of professionals such as doctors and priests as a prelude to robbing them. It was a technique that minimised the need for violence and could, drastically modified, be extended to exploit African victims. After deserting from Fort Napier, O'Brien made a quick foray into the eastern Cape, robbing a priest in Grahamstown before re-joining his compatriots in the north. Less than twenty-four months later, posing as a faithful servant of the church, he, with the help of McLoughlin, robbed a second priest, in Potchefstroom.[4]

In the De Kaap Valley in late 1887–88, O'Brien was said to have joined the police force and, like many others who lacked a uniform and so simply presented themselves as plain-clothes 'detectives', took to the most popular confidence trick of the horse-economy era – intercepting African migrant labourers making their way on foot to Swaziland, Mozambique or elsewhere, demanding their passes and then relieving them of their wages. In this way, it was claimed later, O'Brien was capable of raising £30 a day.[5] It was a ploy that spoke volumes about the arbitrariness of power and the underlying, frequently coercive function of the police in an industrialising state based on cheap black labour.

It is impossible to determine to what extent the confidence man, O'Brien, was interacting with others in the Irish Brigade who, by late 1886, spent much of their time in camps around Barberton. If he was seeing them socially, at the town's many watering holes, then he may well have been one source of information about the movement of stagecoaches bringing in cash or moving out bullion through the De Kaap Valley. Be that as it may, there were two coach robberies during the period, each involving more than a thousand pounds. These heists were said to have been staged by Irish highwaymen who, in romanticised eighteenth-century fashion, it was claimed, did not accost or interfere with the passengers.[6]

Bored and perhaps down to the last of the coach-cash, it was not long before members of the Brigade gravitated towards the richest area of all in the De Kaap goldfields: the broken but far more densely settled terrain around the Sheba Mine. Here, the never-ending thunder of blasting reverberated through the surrounding hills. Several of the brigands obtained casual work as miners and one or two, including McLoughlin, were inspired by the destructive power of dynamite.[7] Regular employment, however, was not their *métier*. During late 1886 and early 1887, several men negotiating the road between Barberton and Eureka City – the mushrooming hamlet that had sprung up to the north-east of the fields – were held up at gunpoint around Elephant's Creek. This tax collection in the countryside by bush-based highwaymen was a prelude to sprees of the sort that were to occur regularly when the troops returned to Pietermaritzburg.

In the third week of February 1887, a contingent of Lancashire-born brigands led by McLoughlin moved into Eureka City, terrorising its inhabitants and the wider neighbourhood. Assaults, barroom brawls, damage to property, theft and threats to retailers marked a week of mayhem. There was no organised resistance. Then, towards the end of the week, the shutters of the shop belonging to the Justice of the Peace, T. Neale, were removed in preparation for an attempt at store-breaking. Neale, eschewing help from locals, rode to Barberton to summon the mounted police as the brigands disappeared into the bush.

Those Manchester-Irish responsible took refuge at a nearby mining encampment, where, almost immediately, a gold watch went missing. The following morning, Monday, they invaded the miners' kitchen, appropriated and scoffed breakfast prepared for the miners and, when challenged, turned as one on a worker and 'almost smashed his head in'. It was collective, feral behaviour of the kind more readily associated with teenaged scuttlers than with soldiers. 'Not satisfied with hammering him with their fists,' it was reported, 'they actually threw him down and jumped on his head, and other parts of his body.' They then disappeared.[8]

Neale and the troopers hunted them down in the surrounding bush and, a few days later, McLoughlin, Carroll (alias 'John Berry'), William Smith and John Dwyer (alias 'Jones') appeared before the local landdrost charged with various contraventions of Article 69 of the South African Republic's constitution.[9] McLoughlin and Dwyer were found guilty and each sentenced to six months' hard labour and 'upon expiry of such sentence to be sent back to their respective corps, from which they are believed to have deserted'. The latter never happened. Before they left the court, however, Dwyer could not resist a further piece of trademark working-class bravado. He directed an 'insulting expression' at the presiding officer 'for which he was brought back and sentenced to some days' spare diet and solitary confinement'.[10]

The removal of two of the leading brigands was not enough to reassure the inhabitants that they had seen the last of the Brigade. In the end it took a contingent of mounted police stationed at Eureka City to hold off the invaders and encourage them to move on. Pushed by the police presence and pulled by news of the frontier moving east, the vanguard of the Irish, under Hutchings, abandoned the goldfields and made their way to the border, where they crossed into Mozambique. Barberton merely provided the Irish Brigade with a South African apprenticeship.

## Delagoa Bay and the Komatipoort Railroad, 1887

Irish navvies were almost synonymous with construction work in the United Kingdom during the first half of the nineteenth century.[11] For decades Irishmen, whose education was often as weak as their bodies were strong, were sought after to work as manual labourers on the canals, roads and railways that helped spread the economic benefits of the Industrial Revolution.

In the South African Republic the dream of linking the highveld to the nearest point on the coast by rail dated back to the 1870s, but it was only in 1887 that Edward MacMurdo, the American who owned the concession to operate the railway line in Portuguese territory between Delagoa Bay and Komatipoort, sold his rights to the London-based Delagoa Bay and East African Railway Company.[12]

The company awarded the contract for constructing the line to the famous Pauling Brothers, who appointed an Englishman, Sir Thomas Tancred, as chief engineer. Tancred then assembled the necessary accountants, engineers and clerical staff to service the project. Among the latter was a former Dubliner, journalist and soldier, Barry Roonan, who took a keen interest in the lives of the navvies. The subcontractors, including the unnamed revolver-toting brute who eventually assembled the Irish contingent, had originally hoped to make extensive use of cheap African labour, but found it to be of such poor quality that they were forced to take on more navvies than anticipated. In the end, about 200 navvies and 3 000 African labourers were employed. The navvies, as in Britain, were split into working groups by nationality. The numerically preponderant Irish were led by Hutchings of the South Lancs, now calling himself 'Muldoon', while the English were led by an equally formidable murderous former soldier, 'Kentish Jim'. These two platoons of godless, hard-drinking fighting-workers were supplemented by a third group, the 'Salvation Army', under one Buck Williams, who, it seems, may have had the misfortune of being a practising Christian in addition to being an American.[13]

Out of the Barberton bush and back in what were, in effect, mobile barracks, the Irish Brigade armed themselves with the handles of pickaxes as, presumably, did the members of other work gangs. The Portuguese authorities, for their part, called in a few additional police from metropolitan Lisbon and buttressed them with a larger number of untutored African policemen drawn from West Africa. A modest local economy suddenly experienced boom-town conditions as publicans, liquor stores and retailers at both the Lourenço Marques and Komatipoort ends stood to profit from navvies moving up and down the line of rail on pay days. With the ingredients for serious on- and off-the-job conflict in place, construction commenced in mid-1887.

Employed by an English company, overseen by an English engineer and competing with at least one other team made up entirely of Englishmen, Muldoon's thirty to fifty men might as well have been back in Ireland, or Lancashire. On every front they were faced by the olde enemy shielded by the Portuguese, who presided over a manifestly weak state. Within weeks of the works commencing, Muldoon, like many a good commanding officer, set about remoulding former South Lanc troopers into a more cohesive 'Irish' unit that included older deserters from other regiments and a few Mancunians who had abandoned the increasingly monopolistic regime on the distant Kimberley diamond fields. The sudden appearance of a Portuguese gunboat in the bay sparked Muldoon's imagination. The quasi-military project he devised, the way it was planned and then implemented, along with consequences he must have partly anticipated, were designed to embarrass, if not humiliate, the British and Portuguese.

Taking on the honorific rank of choice of many an eighteenth-century highwayman, and drawing on the terminology of Irish agrarian secret societies, Muldoon recast himself as 'Captain Moonlight'. He then penned an insulting letter, written in 'eccentric English on beer-stained paper', to the Governor of the small enclave. According to Roonan, it read: 'The Hirish savages hup the Line will bust your fort and your tin-pot gunboat tomorrer Nite. Lock up your greasy reis [milreis, the local currency] and keep away from [our] headquarters at Berg's Hotell. Capt. Moonlight.'[14]

Forewarned was forearmed. The Governor mobilised all available police, soldiers and sailors and staked out the Hotel Allemande in the hope that, once the Brigade had finished a typical evening of pay-day carousing, it would be easy to arrest the inebriated Irish before they could embark on any foolish escapades. Moonlight, however, was up to the challenge. Into the hotel he poured his troops, who – with the exception of three left to create a sustained, mock-drunken diversion within the pub – immediately exited the premises via a window at the hotel's rear. While the Portuguese continued to guard what in effect was now Hotel Hollow from a safe distance, Moonlight's men assembled on the beach, rowed out to the undermanned gunboat, overpowered the skeleton crew and imprisoned them. The Irish then worked their way through the contents of the wine locker. By the time they left, the gunboat 'wore an unkempt look, the flag of Portugal was reversed from the bowsprit stays, and diverse articles of wearing apparel were protruding from the muzzles of the guns, from which the tompions had been removed'.[15] The rout was complete when the Governor's men eventually entered the hotel only to discover a decoy consisting of just three men.

The weaker the victim of a practical joke, the greater the humiliation and subsequent umbrage. The Portuguese lodged a formal protest with the British authorities, who promptly despatched HMS *Raleigh* and *Swift* from Simon's Town to pursue the Irish. By then, Moonlight and his men had retreated temporarily to a distant inland redoubt beyond the reach of naval bombardment. The incident eventually disappeared from sight beneath a blizzard of diplomatic notes between London and Lisbon while the bandit-pirate chief, Muldoon, boasted that, on the night in question, he could have taken the entire city had he so wished.[16]

The terrain over which the railway was constructed was simultaneously blessed and cursed. The flat, swampy coastal plain hosted squadrons of mosquitoes whose airborne attacks ensured that malaria made death and burial a daily occurrence. It was said later that there was a body beneath every sleeper on the line between Lourenço Marques and Nelspruit. The navvies wilted just as surely as the railway itself sprinted across level countryside, leaping over sluggish streams ambling coastwards.

By mid-December 1887 the formal handing-over ceremony at Komatipoort loomed large. By chance, Muldoon overheard plans being made for catering at the festivities up the line. Moonlight saw the opportunity to reward the Brigade with a party of their own at the expense of the English contractors and Portuguese dignitaries. On the designated day the Irish gave notice of their intentions when they boarded an early up-train taking Sir Thomas Tancred to the border and effectively commandeered a hogshead of beer, which they proceeded to demolish there and then. This was followed by the hijacking and looting of the following train, the one bearing the bulk of the supply of imported alcohol and food intended for the luncheon to mark the official opening. When the newly emptied train limped into Komatipoort a furious Tancred rushed a telegram to Lourenço Marques demanding that the bandits be arrested and prosecuted. That, too, never happened.[17]

The boarding of the gunboat and hijacking of the train bore the imprimatur of outright contempt for Britain and her oldest ally, Portugal. But if these pranks nevertheless displayed a residual measure of political consciousness of the sort more frequently seen in the actions of 'real' social bandits, then there was nothing at all 'social' about the rest of the activities of the Irish bandits. Without the presence of the more sympathetic anglophone working-class men occasionally encountered on the diamond or goldfields, their predations were seen as being wholly criminal. Roonan viewed the brigands as irredeemably antisocial ruffians and his characterisation of them as men capable of 'anything from robbing a church to manslaughter without provocation' is telling. By the time they left Lourenço Marques for the last time, two African policemen had been murdered – allegedly by the bandits – and, as they retreated towards the ZAR border, bound for Johannesburg, they robbed individuals and held up storekeepers in remote settings at will.[18]

## The Witwatersrand, 1888

Fresh from the countryside but penniless after an epic journey chasing the rainbow across the highveld, the ragbag 'Irishmen' staged an entrance into the eighteen-month-old mining camp – situated in the heart of the newly proclaimed fields – dramatic enough to grace a Brechtian opera. It might be significant that, yet again, before the opportunity for any self-identification arose, the press designated them as members of the 'Irish Brigade'. They appeared suddenly, towards the end of the second week in February, and in large numbers of anything between twenty and fifty men. Splitting into individual detachments, each pursuing its own operational objective, they took control of Johannesburg and laid the frontier settlement to waste.

On Friday afternoon, 10 February, the reconnaissance parties went to work. According to one report, 'Loafers entered private boarding-houses and other similar establishments, and on the plea of asking for help, were no doubt "spying out the land" for further burglarious operations.' Other private dwellings and homes were subjected to similar scrutiny.[19] On that and the following evening, as dusk slowly settled, small bands of highwaymen three- to four-men strong took up positions on the approaches to the town. There they held up travellers foolish enough to be caught moving at night and relieved them of substantial sums of cash. The main assault, however, commenced on Saturday, under cover of heavy cloud, when a thunderstorm and unusual darkness enveloped the town.

The mining camp witnessed assaults, burglary, theft and random violence on a scale unprecedented. In a brazen frontal attack the Central Hotel was invaded; two gold watches and £15 in cash went missing. But it was only when the sun rose the following morning that the full price of the pillage became apparent. The body of Joseph Graham, one-armed billiard marker at the Kimberley Bar last seen drunk at the races, was found close to the Roman Catholic church. His head had been crushed and his throat slit. Within a few hundred yards of Graham's body two more corpses were discovered – one of a Baster and the other of a Zulu – both knifed to death with pockets turned out, suggesting that they had been robbed.[20]

It was the classic spree, writ large – in blood – for all to see. Mining men, several of whom had just fled the fast-waning eastern Transvaal goldfields, recognised it as such at once. It bore the trademark of the Brigands of Barberton. All frontier towns demanded justice, but Johannesburg was not little Eureka City or sleepy old Lourenço Marques. 'The wildest talk was indulged in everywhere, and the massacre of the loafer-class, who were regarded as the culprits was openly advocated,' reported the *Standard and Transvaal Mining Chronicle*.[21] At the public meeting that followed hours later, attended by over 500 men, the virtues of the American frontier and Judge Lynch were again praised. Such talk could not be dismissed as mere barroom braggadocio. (Indeed, only a few months later there *was* a lynching, albeit along classic racial lines, by English immigrants in the small gold-mining hamlet of Steynsdorp in the Komati Valley.)[22]

A Vigilance Committee was elected and the state, sensing the dangers of street justice, offered a reward of £100 for the apprehension of the murderer or murderers – a sum that was trumped almost at once when the Committee raised the stakes to £500.[23] Nothing happened; every lumpen Irish lip, sealed by oaths of loyalty and silence, held firm. Eight unnamed invaders, members of the Brigade, were taken into custody and held briefly on charges of vagrancy. Two more post-weekend arrests followed. O'Leary and William Kelly, formerly of the Argyll and Sutherland Highlanders, men said to be closely associated with the Brigade, were caught while breaking into an office.[24] But on the main matter – the murders – the police moved at the pace of Mr Plod, and the public fumed.

The police lacked forensic capacity, and it took close on two weeks to arrest a suspect, James Butler, a former tailor from Galway. Butler, however, claimed that at the time of the killings he had been out drinking with James Sullivan and Thomas Reilly, and nothing came of the arrest. The police then delved into another informer's garbled tale, arresting William Kelly, Michael Frere and George Banks, but that story, too, led only up the garden path. The night of mayhem produced no legal consequence and the reputations of the local law-abiding and insurgent, law-evading Irish suffered alike.[25]

Respectable, middle-class Irishmen and the town's two or three Catholic priests, already shamed by the manner in which the previous year's St Patrick's Day celebrations had culminated in a drunken riot, were particularly distressed by the appearance of the Brigade.[26] They and others argued for the establishment of a focused, professional detective force. The organising committee for the 1888 St Patrick's Day festivities was at pains to distance itself from any unwelcome 'relics of Donnybrook', and the celebrations on 17 March, held in the presence of several ladies and amidst banners trumpeting 'Home Rule', 'O'Connell' and 'Parnell', went off well. When the mining commissioner, Carl von Brandis, rose to propose a toast, declaring that 'the Irish were just as law-abiding as any other nation', the guests responded with an inner sigh of relief and prolonged applause.[27]

Pressure to restructure the police continued, and eventually a measure of relief was obtained when, a week later, it was announced that a dedicated detective unit was to be established that would fall under the direction of Robert Ferguson, an Irishman already serving with the Zuid Afrikaansche Republiek Politie: the 'ZARPs'.[28] Quite fortuitously, the Irish Brigade had ushered in Johannesburg's first detective detachment, and had given Ferguson his first command. More Irish ironies followed. It was the same pioneering former South Lancs brigand, John McLoughlin, who, six years later, proved to be the nemesis of Ferguson. The commander of Johannesburg's inaugural detective unit was, in turn, replaced by yet another Irishman, Andrew Trimble, an even earlier deserter from the 6th Dragoons who was rumoured to have a criminal record.[29]

The emergence of the detective division did not, in itself, herald the dissolution of the bandit corps. Never formally constituted, the Irish Brigade could not be formally dissolved.[30] The invasion of the Witwatersrand in 1888 did, however, mark the end of an era for graduates of Fort Napier. Smelted together in the roaring furnace of the British Army, raw Irish and Lancastrian elements had been recast as roughly hewn, mobile, rural brigands. Members of a regiment filled with criminal intent and low on political consciousness, they could afford to ignore largely the travails of white workers in the eastern Transvaal and Mozambique and treat black peasants with utter contempt.

The Rand, however, called for new, creative and adaptive strategies if erstwhile rural brigands were to transform themselves successfully into something more akin to urban gangsters who would, on occasion, be forced to seek refuge in the black countryside. In Pietermaritzburg, it had been the rural-born Irish, such as 'Captain Moonlight', who had been at an advantage while acquiring the skills of banditry and learning how to live off the veld. In Johannesburg – the 'University of Crime', as Cape Premier John X. Merriman later dubbed it – it was the Mancunians, the former scuttlers, the bastard children of the Industrial Revolution, who led the way. For them, the shift from countryside to city was more like a homecoming. The Witwatersrand offered them a familiar anglophone, working-class culture replete with blood sports, gambling, pubs and prostitutes. On the Rand the Irish fell under the sway of McLoughlin, a highly adaptive, quintessentially urban creature.

Under McLoughlin's charismatic, secretive leadership the Brigade split into smaller, more specialised, overlapping criminal companies. Although unambiguously urban-based, these Irish brigands never quite lost their affinity for the remote hills and valleys that had seen their conversion from petty to more serious crime. This new oscillation, between a sprawling east-west urban complex and the remote countryside, was effected largely on horseback and lasted for approximately half a decade, from 1888 to the completion of the railway revolution in 1895. Few phenomena could have illustrated more clearly the ongoing shift away from an overwhelmingly rural to an increasingly urban economy.

## Rural Brigands to Urban Gangsters, 1888–1895

The outcrop of reef gold found on the Witwatersrand in 1886 was, for some eighteen months, easily mined. The oxidisation of the ore-bearing reef, occasioned by weathering, allowed the mineral to be recovered with relative ease, and the mines prospered throughout the year the Irish Brigade invaded Johannesburg – 1888 – and for the first few months of the following year. By mid-1889, however, the industry found itself mired in a growing crisis: gold locked into reef high in pyrite content became ever more difficult to retrieve during amalgamation. This problem was eventually only fully overcome in 1891, by the widespread adoption of the MacArthur-Forrest process. The technique utilised cyanide to extract gold from reef recovered from greater depths, which contained high levels of unweathered pyrite. The length and scale of the intervening recession – starting in late 1889 and reaching its nadir in 1890–91 before yielding to better times in 1892 – remains one of the least explored or understood events by historians of South Africa.[31]

The crash of 1890 saw the collapse of share prices and the eclipse of hundreds of diggers, prospectors and small mining syndicates who were forced to sell their holdings to larger, well-heeled companies better able to ride out the storm.[32] The newly formed Chamber of Mines coordinated a programme to reduce the wages of white miners – a development that, at the Anglo-Tharsis Mine, produced a response akin to that of the 'Molly

Maguires' in the United States, when unhappy workers used dynamite to blow up the house of the mine manager.[33] The downturn in the fortunes of the mining industry had a knock-on effect as suppliers of mining equipment, wholesalers and small shopkeepers found it more difficult to obtain credit.

The grand founding illusion that envelops all frontier towns – that every man has an equal chance of success and can rise above the odds to make his fortune – evaporated faster than drizzle on sun-baked paving stones. Scores of small businessmen and hundreds of anxious white miners sensed that the lubricant of their dreams, cash, was in ever-shortening supply. Money was controlled by large impersonal institutions to which they had no direct access and, by the mid-1890s, the banks and great mining finance houses effectively controlled the new Witwatersrand economy. Anger, frustration and disillusionment produced a groundswell of discontent; it prompted the need to think of self-help organisations and was a forerunner to the establishment of Friendly Societies, political movements and, eventually, 'a union for white mineworkers'.[34]

But the crash of 1890 did more than stimulate the climate of populism informing anglophone immigrants, who were intent on forging a battery of new associations ranged largely against the Kruger state and partly against the mining houses. It contributed to a growing sense of *Schadenfreude* in which ordinary men and women derived a certain pleasure from any misfortune that befell the emerging Randlords and corporations that prospered as the populace at large struggled to make ends meet. It gave rise to an atmosphere in the pubs, which eventually sifted out into the streets, in which bank robbers, safe-crackers and, to a lesser extent, highwaymen received sullen approval, if not outright support. The importance of such moments in the generation of 'criminal heroes' is captured perfectly by Paul Kooistra:

> At times when large numbers of people have had their sense of order and security disrupted, particularly by economic upheavals such as depressions, then a legitimation crisis occurs. Widespread portions of the public feel 'outside the law' because the law is no longer seen as an instrument of justice but as a tool of oppression wielded by favoured interests. Social justice and state law are in antithesis, and people turn to symbolic representations of justice outside the law such as the Robin Hood criminal.[35]

For its part, the Kruger government experienced the effects of the downturn in the economy and the upturn in crime in ways that were as embarrassing as they were vexing. The convict population, held in the inadequately designed and constructed small-town jails that were suddenly called upon to restrain real desperadoes, including members of the Irish Brigade, swelled to bursting point. The problem was exacerbated by the absence of a reasonably remunerated, professionally trained corps of prison officers; the existing prison personnel were, in hard times, more susceptible to corruption than usual. The result was predictable – an upsurge in the number of escapes by high-profile criminals. By 1889–91, the government was engulfed by a wave of criticism about the inadequacies of its prison administration and jails.

The state responded as best it could, beefing up prison security. Dangerous convicts were later transferred to outlying areas, such as Barberton, where money for bribery was harder to come by and the jails were supposedly more secure. Incompetent or corrupt officials, including the head of the Pretoria prison, were fired and new personnel were appointed, including Thomas Menton, an Irish deserter from the British Army during the First War of Independence who was appointed to head up the prison at Barberton and, later, Johannesburg. Despite a counteroffensive by the state, some of the most notorious convicts of the day continued to escape, or attempt to escape, from prisons. It was not just the last gasp of the pre-railway era, the closing years of the horse economy, that helped make the late 1880s and early 1890s halcyon days for bank robbers, highwaymen and safe-crackers, but a climate of public opinion that, thanks to an unexpected economic downturn, became progressively more resentful towards the rich and powerful on the one hand, and the government and its law-enforcement agencies on the other. President S.J.P. Kruger, as we shall have occasion to note later, responded by making his dislike of the increasingly lawless immigrant population on the Witwatersrand abundantly clear. It was also a climate in which the criminal became ever more 'political' and, by 1895–96 – with the coming of the Jameson Raid led by certain of the mine owners – the 'political' ever more criminal.

3

# Bank Robbers in the Kingdom of the Imagination

> What is robbing a bank compared with founding a bank?
> – Bertolt Brecht, *The Threepenny Opera*

Johannesburg – all mining camp beneath newly sprouted town feathers – experienced a spate of bank robberies commencing in 1889 and continuing, with less frequency, to the distant boom year of 1895 and beyond that.[1] No consistent pattern is to be detected in these early robberies or ready conclusion to be drawn from the fact that, in one instance, the principal perpetrator seems to have been named Kelly. Not surprisingly, few observers at the time saw, let alone suspected, any hidden links between Ireland, Lancashire, the Industrial Revolution and the Witwatersrand's emerging underworld.

What several authors and journalists *did* see, however, was a pattern of lawlessness along the line of the reef that was akin to that of 1850s' gold-rush California as portrayed by novelist Bret Harte.[2] They may not have been alone. If some of the Manchester-born scuttlers who went on to shape the Irish Brigade had been raised partly on melodramatic novels about a bygone era of highwaymen and pirates, then other, equally impressionable young men may have been influenced by more pertinent tales of the 'Wild West'. What is certain amidst all this conjecture is that the bank robbery that did most to capture the imagination of the public at the time – that of the Standard Bank in Krugersdorp, in 1889 – had all the ingredients of the later, classic western movies that drew on Harte's novels. The deeper roots of that robbery did not, however, lie on the Witwatersrand goldfields, but further south, on the diamond fields of Griqualand West, and with one family: the McKeones.

Although most of the McKeone clan have their origins in the west of Ireland, around Galway, John McKeone Snr was born into a Catholic family in Ulster, in 1834. After a lengthy illness he died of malaria in 1894 at the age of 59, in Barberton.[3] He met his wife, Mary – whose maiden name remains unknown despite the considerable press profile she later enjoyed – in the Cape Colony in about 1863–64.[4] After their union, the McKeones appear to have moved around southern Africa a great deal, creating the type of unsettled childhood for their offspring that is thought to contribute to the development of if not fully antisocial then deeply disturbed personalities.[5]

By 1865 the McKeones were, it seems, trading in western-central Basotholand, as that is where their eldest son, John Louis, is said to have been born. Shortly thereafter, the couple had a second son. His name, too, remains a mystery, and he died of unknown causes in Johannesburg in 1890. Martha, the McKeones' only daughter, was born in Basotholand in the year diamonds were discovered in the interior – 1867. At this point the family appears to have acquired its habit of following southern Africa's swiftly unfolding mining frontiers. Hugh James, the couple's fourth child, was born in 1871 at Hopetown, and their fifth and last, Bernard, in 1873. The promise of the diamond fields, however, never materialised, and the McKeones returned to Basotholand in 1876, where they made their living trading – perhaps even selling – firearms before the outbreak of the Basotho Gun War in 1880 sent them scurrying back to Kimberley. Back on the diamond fields the McKeones cohered as a family only until 1885. John Snr, who towards the end of his life seems to have been without a profession and of no fixed abode, departed for the goldfields at Barberton, leaving his wife to deal as best she could with a confused and increasingly disturbed brood of teenaged adults.

Abandoned by her spouse, it would appear that Mary McKeone tried her best but then lost the way. The eldest lad, John Louis, known to everyone as 'Jack' (so as to resonate with 'Mac'), was pulled out of school and promptly sent out to work, as was Hugh. What exactly Jack did to help the family remain afloat is unknown, but Hugh worked as an assistant to a photographer for about a year. At that point something went badly wrong, and mother and the younger children retreated to family in Cape Town for a few months before returning to Kimberley, where they were all reunited with Jack, who had stayed behind.

With Jack prematurely thrust into the adult masculine role of father, Hugh was apprenticed to a local blacksmith. That, too, however, proved to be an unsuccessful recipe; having worked for a while at Varry & Rogers, he left for MacHaftie's shop. The family struggled both to make ends meet and to settle, and, at about this time – late 1887 – in order to help ease the pressure, it was decided to explore one of the oldest Irish routes out of poverty. Martha either chose or her eldest brother pushed her to take orders as a nun back in Basotholand with the French Catholic missionaries who had taught her as a child. But, almost at once, news of the discovery of gold on the Witwatersrand unhinged the rest of the family McKeone. Early in 1888, Mrs McKeone and her three sons moved to Krugersdorp.[6]

By then Jack and Hugh, twenty-three and seventeen years old respectively, were perfectly fashioned for a life of brigandage. A boyhood spent in the broken mountain terrain of Basotholand at a time of war had equipped them with the basic skills required of a modern highveld bandit. In certain respects the lads were indistinguishable from most young Basotho warriors of their cohort, but they were also shaped by powerful notions dictating the need to manifest 'manliness' of the kind expected of most Victorian males. They behaved accordingly, the societal expectations having been cemented and refined during their time in Kimberley. The brothers – and more especially so Jack – spoke fluent Afrikaans-Dutch, English and Sesotho, and numbered a Basotho chief among their personal friends. They had a love of the outdoors, knew how to live off the countryside, could use revolver or rifle to good effect and, like most Basotho, were excellent horsemen. Jack's love of horses was legendary: he was closer to Brian Boru, his famous black steed named after a tenth-century founding king of Ireland, than he was to any man or woman.

But the older McKeone brothers were possessed of much more than just the physical strength and skills needed to become successful bandits. Like many of those in the Irish Brigade who happened to have arrived at the Rand at the same time – almost to the month – as the McKeones in 1888, the brothers carried within them that smouldering discontent about the injustices of the world that is the hallmark of social bandits everywhere. As part-products of the diamond fields that had seen the black flag of anarchy raised in the rebellion of 1875, they had been told and had witnessed how large corporations and financiers entrenched giant monopolies that sounded the death knell for diggers and independent operators. Their hapless father had run before that economic storm, and the dysfunctionality of their own family was partly attributable to the same stark, downward trajectory. Jack, it was said, was a dreamer who entertained strange ideas about property and wealth, while it was claimed that his brother Hugh had socialist ideas.

Having been forced to use their fists and fend for themselves in rough mining towns from an early age, the brothers would quickly turn belligerent when pushed. The boys were also entrepreneurial in ways that were not necessarily always legal. Indeed, before he turned twenty, Hugh and a friend were accused of passing off polished glass as diamonds to greedy but unsuspecting customers in Harrismith in the Orange Free State.[7] In body, mind and spirit the McKeones were ideally prepared for life on the new goldfields, and Krugersdorp, situated amidst rich outcrops that formed a natural gateway to even more broken countryside to the immediate west, was well suited to hosting brigands.[8]

Mrs McKeone, pursued by poverty, hired a house in one of the less salubrious parts of the town and, doing as many a woman without a spouse did at the time, let a few rooms to lodgers to make ends meet. With his heart set on finding gold, Jack McKeone found himself a friend and together they spent most, but not all, of their time prospecting around the Oakley Company Mine. Hugh McKeone, taking a leaf out of his eldest brother's book, also found an employer and persuaded the formidable Barsdorf Syndicate to take on him and a friend as prospectors working near the old road leading to Krugersdorp.[9] But they, too, appear not to have worked full time at mineral exploration. Amidst the boom of 1888, even young Bernard succeeded in finding a job in town, and the partners of the two older brothers quickly moved into the McKeones' family home.[10]

Mary McKeone, as some mothers are wont to, ran what was, in essence, a boarding house for bandits. Her son Jack's slightly younger partner, Joseph Stevens, was a lad of Irish descent who made no secret of his true calling and was known to all, including the Witwatersrand police, as 'Dick Turpin'. Hugh's friend, about whom we shall learn more shortly, was a tall, slightly older fellow of Irish descent who – also a highwayman – had taken the name 'William Cooper'. The four young men got on well and never wanted for other company. The surrounding mines and pubs were well stocked with semi-employable Celtic marginals, deserters from the British Army who may have introduced the foursome to the 'hard men' of the Irish Brigade, including Jack McCann and John McLoughlin, who frequented the reef between Langlaagte in the east and Luipaardsvlei in the west.[11]

As proved by experiences in Australia, where the Irish were equally represented in the ranks of the law-enforcement agencies as they were among the bushrangers, Jack McKeone's basic training could be adapted as readily to a career in the police force as it could to a life of banditry. Sergeant F. de Wit Tossel, the officer in charge of the Krugersdorp district – supposedly American-born because of the accent he affected but confidently claimed by others to be a Devon man – spotted something special in McKeone early on. He saw Jack as a young man who, although of a rather 'romantic disposition', had a 'determined look' that would supplement his excellent skills as horseman and linguist. Tossel invited him to join the police, but McKeone, set on acquiring a fortune while the mining economy was booming, turned down the offer.[12]

A few months later, however, as deeper-level, unweathered reef became more resistant to existing gold-extraction processes, the economy slowed down, reducing both the prospects of the industry and the amount of cash in circulation. There was markedly less money in the pockets of workers – not good news for highwaymen who preyed on black migrant labourers. On 27 May 1889, Jack McKeone went to the mining commissioner's office to have his digger's licence renewed. It was one of those moments when, as one analyst of the rise of outlaw traditions notes, the law and justice took leave of one another.[13] The clerk, McKeone later insisted, demanded £2 more than the fee prescribed by law. Unwilling to pay the bribe, an argument ensued. It ended with McKeone's arrest for 'attempted fraud' and for 'using abusive language'. The young prospector was unperturbed. The charges were trivial, trumped up and would be dismissed when he appeared in court; at worst he would be liable for a fine.[14]

But on the goldfields, where mines were more numerous than churches, mining commissioners were as close to God as most men got. The landdrosts, acting as magistrates, tended to support the pivotal role commissioners played in bringing shape and order to highly contested claims and mining operations. To his amazement and disgust, Jack McKeone was sentenced to three months in prison without the possibility of a fine. It was to be a life-changing incident, one that Ned Kelly and legendary outlaws around the world would have understood only too well.[15]

But, even at that late stage, the consequences of any perceived injustice could have been contained had fate contrived to be kinder to McKeone. The wound, however, turned septic. He lost his position as prospector almost at once and, a fortnight or so later, yet more devastating news arrived. At the time of his arrest the police had impounded two of his horses. When nobody had come forward with cash to feed the animals, the horses had been summarily shot.[16] McKeone was a changed, if not deranged, man and argued his case so forcibly from the cells that 'the very men who got him into prison exerted themselves for his release, regarding his punishment as too severe'.[17] McKeone was released, he later claimed, as a result of the intervention of no lesser a person than 'His Honour, the President'.[18] There is no surviving record of any such intervention on the part of S.J.P. Kruger. It may have been another of those visions derived from the dream world of social bandits in which the king, as opposed to his misguided agents, was inherently good and therefore always blameless.

It was, in any case, too little too late. Every night during his prison term, 'as he reposed on the hard prison bed, he questioned himself why he should be punished thus against the law of man and of God'.[19] McKeone felt that he was entitled to compensation. Upon asking, however, he was told that the State Attorney was away from the capital and unable to address his request. In his mind's eye McKeone saw the landdrost's office and, close by it, the Krugersdorp branch of the Standard Bank. Reasoning that all gold in circulation was the property of the government, which minted sovereigns from the efforts of ordinary folk, he decided to rob the bank. The embodiment of capital that was ranged against the small man all along the reef, the bank, he reckoned, was 'a body that could stand it'.[20]

It is impossible to identify the deepest sources from which McKeone dredged up his idea for the robbery. It had more than an element of the Wild West to it even though it pre-dated 'the Daltons, Bill Doolin, Tom Horn, Butch Cassidy and the Wild Bunch', who became the benchmark for banditry in America in the 1890s.[21] He put a plan to Turpin, but since they were uncertain of how best to dispose of the loot after the robbery or where to hide if necessary, they looked around for professional help. It may have been a McKeone brother, the one who died in 1890 but was still living in Johannesburg at that stage, who introduced them to Patrick Carroll.[22]

Carroll, better known on the eastern Transvaal goldfields as 'John Berry' from the time that he, John McLoughlin and other Irish Brigaders had spent a week trashing Eureka City, was drawn into a new plan grafted onto the original idea. Jack McKeone, who by now saw his life as a story in which justice would prevail and all would end happily, was moving freely across mental terrain in which there were few boundaries between fiction and fact, while his partner modelled himself freely on an eighteenth-century English highwayman. What followed was pure West Rand, from the world's newest mining frontier.

It really *was* a bone-dry day in late winter, with regulation dust swirling, when, at about 9.45 a.m. on 29 August 1889, McKeone and Turpin rode up to the Standard Bank in Krugersdorp and tethered their horses. They strode into the lobby, observed the manager and the accountant, pushed the door closed behind them, produced revolvers and sang out: 'We are Americans! We have come to take your money. If either of you raise an alarm, we will shoot you both. Give up your keys.' After a short struggle the employees were overpowered, bound and gagged and, while Turpin trained a six-shooter on them, McKeone rifled through the safe. There was a brief interruption when a bank clerk who had been out on a chore attempted, unsuccessfully, to re-enter the premises. The robbers split the proceeds, stuffing about £2 000 in notes and £1 500 in gold sovereigns into a few bags, and walked out of the bank. Mounting their horses, they cantered gently down the main street in the direction of Johannesburg; when they reached the town's perimeter, they spurred their mounts into a gallop.[23]

The hotel proprietors across the road from the bank, at long last convinced by a tremulous clerk that the branch had indeed been robbed, ran over and freed the manager and the accountant. By then someone had dashed to the police station and found Tossel, mounted but not yet changed into his uniform for the day. Tossel gave chase only to find himself eating dust, the bandits fading from sight. The self-styled 'American' crooks, on 'first-class' mounts, broadened the gap between them and a lone 'American' cowboy who, seeing his horse tiring, commandeered another steed from a passing rider. Still the distance between the parties widened. But Tossel, a man with frontier experience in hunting down cattle rustlers in Stellaland and horse thieves deep in Scotty Smith country, was already formulating a plan to run down the bandits.[24] As he approached the hotel at Witpoortjie, he leapt from the saddle and requisitioned Mr Boyd's well-known racer 'Atlas' and, leaving instructions for the owner and the policemen following him, resumed his pursuit.[25]

As he rejoined the chase, Tossel noticed a horse-drawn cart driven by two men of 'bad character' – Carroll and 'Crooked Nose' Jackson – making its way slowly in the opposite direction, towards Krugersdorp.[26] In retrospect, this seemingly chance encounter assumed greater significance, but at the time Tossel, all-American marshal, remained focused only on the robbers. 'Atlas', coming into his own, closed the gap and, beyond Wall's Hotel, Tossel rode down the crooks. Sensing that the chase was over, McKeone and Turpin turned their horses off the road and assumed defensive positions behind a rocky ledge. Undaunted, their 'plucky' pursuer followed. Shots were exchanged: McKeone was wounded in the upper part of his right arm. When the posse of policemen that had been following appeared, young Dick Turpin suddenly thought better of the entire business and threw his revolver into the air. The bandits surrendered.[27]

But when the two robbers were frisked, all that the police could find were the highly portable banknotes and a couple of pounds in silver. One thousand five hundred pounds in heavy gold coin had evanesced. The suspects were taken into custody and escorted back into town while a detachment of police was sent ahead to intercept and search the horse and cart Tossel had spotted just beyond Boyd's stables. Jackson and Carroll were discovered at a Krugersdorp hotel; their cart, excluding the 'dogbox' at the rear of the vehicle, was searched and found to contain nothing. Turning back towards Witpoortjie, the search party passed yet another small cart making its way to Johannesburg, but it, too, was ignored.[28]

The sovereigns had been switched; once, perhaps twice. McKeone knew where the coins were hidden – he later boasted that he would be using the money to start a new life once he was clear of prison. Under the circumstances, the small Krugersdorp force did the best it could and asked the Chief Detective in Johannesburg to keep the additional suspects under surveillance. But Irish Bob Ferguson, famous for being a friend of the lads in the pub and, much later, notorious for an unwillingness to confront the formidable John McLoughlin personally, placed only Jackson under observation, who showed no altered patterns of spending. Carroll was ignored.[29]

In Johannesburg, which was drifting slowly into the economic doldrums, the bank, leader-writers and state had eyes only for the brave sergeant and the missing money. The bank offered a £150 reward for the recovery of the coins, yet, despite numerous official and private searches all along the turnpike and surrounding veld, the gold was never found. Privately, it was accepted that the cash was probably being held in trust somewhere in Johannesburg. The Kruger government, under pressure from its critics for the poor performance of the police and the lawlessness that pervaded *Duiwelsdorp* – Satan City – responded as expected. Tossel was elevated to the rank of lieutenant, and given a bonus of £50.[30]

But out on the open oceans of history, surface and deep-water currents often flow in opposite directions. So, while the ruling classes above sailed off in one direction, the masses below were pulled in another. Disgruntled diggers, prospectors and small syndicate owners who had had bad experiences at the hands of mining commissioners or with the state machinery, identified all too readily with the bank robbers. And when McKeone was forcibly held down so that he could be given chloroform prior to having the bullet removed from his arm, awaiting-trial prisoners and convicts alike identified with him almost as easily as did ordinary labouring men contemplating a bleak future. More sympathy was forthcoming when, for a few days prior to the trial, McKeone was placed in the stocks to prevent his escaping.[31]

Charged with robbery and attempted murder, the bank robbers appeared on 7 October 1889 in the Circuit Court in Johannesburg before the newly appointed Justice Ameshoff. The accused, unrepresented, pleaded guilty to the charge of robbery but not guilty to charges of attempted murder. From the outset of the proceedings it was evident that McKeone was aware of a groundswell of opinion in his favour outside the courthouse. It was also clear that, like the outlaws of legend, he would use the opportunity to challenge the authorities publicly, defend himself as a victim of injustice, dispute any intention to kill, protect his younger accomplice and, if need be – like some outlaw hero of the Old American West – be willing to 'die game' if sentenced to death.[32]

It was a *tour de force*, the courtroom used as theatre in classic Victorian mode. McKeone argued that, as he and Turpin saw it, they were pursued unexpectedly by an unknown civilian who eventually cornered them and then suddenly opened fire. Only then did they return fire, hoping to shoot out the horse from beneath their assailant rather than kill an out-of-uniform policeman whom they could scarcely have been expected to recognise in the heat of the moment. Any violence on the part of the bandits was restrained, appropriate to circumstances forced upon them.[33] McKeone was also quick to draw attention to the fact that the same Tossel, now so hostile to the two accused, had once sought to recruit him into the police force.

His argument failed to move the jury, which brought in a verdict of guilty on the charges of attempted murder. Ameshoff asked the accused whether they wished to make a plea in mitigation. Jack McKeone did. In an 'excited tone', he made a statement from the dock 'so that all men might know' the injustices to which he had been subjected, and so that they may be conveyed 'to all the world in the papers'.[34] His plea might have reached a smaller audience than intended, but it would have echoed in the minds of all who subscribed to codes of honour – including members of the Irish Brigade – and in the hearts of virtually all gold-diggers and working men on the Witwatersrand who had fallen foul of mining commissioners. He outlined the origins of his grievances with some eloquence and then, seeking to save his partner from the death sentence, assumed sole responsibility for planning the robbery and for drawing Turpin into the operation.

But the defendants were up against a puisne judge, a man only just appointed to the bench amidst some controversy. Ameshoff was intent on making his mark: he sentenced them to twenty-five years each with hard labour. Lesser men would have buckled but McKeone, drawn from a religious family in a country notable for its missionaries of all stripes, had no intention of leaving court without underscoring the fact that the judge, too, was but an agent of man rather than God, and that the injustices were mounting still. Before he could be led away, he rose and said: 'Thank you, My Lord, may you be judged by your judge in your day, and may your sentence be less than mine.'[35]

The news of the older McKeone's conviction was greeted by a disturbance outside the courthouse. In a sign of things to come, his brother Hugh – another youngster in search of a cause – was arrested, sentenced to a fine of £1 by Landdrost De Beer, and then released.[36] Jack McKeone, villain of the court, was a hero of the cells. A pattern now emerged that, in different combinations, played itself out on more than one occasion during the brief six-month period that he was the guest of the government. McKeone already occupied the moral high ground in the eyes of the common man and his Irish gangster associates, but he also enjoyed indirect access to 750 gold sovereigns, something that helped to persuade those harder of hearing. He was, in short, ideally placed to subvert the Kruger state's rickety police and prison services, which, despite having beefed up regulations governing its jails the previous year, continued to leak high-profile prisoners in startling numbers, including Irish Brigade members such as little Jack McCann.[37]

Within days of being sentenced, McKeone was discovered by a warder with his chains sawn through. His assistant in this venture appears to have been Charles Day, a thirty-eight-year-old American 'locksmith' doing a three-year stretch for theft. The first really broad-based challenge to the prison system, however, came just weeks later when several convicts, with the assistance of two other warders, conspired to allow the chains of Day and yet another highwayman, George Smyth, to be modified in such a way as to set them free – a prelude to an escape attempt by McKeone and Turpin. The plot was foiled, but it nevertheless succeeded in creating a tense stand-off between prison authorities and convicts. The sequel was brutal. Four prisoners were sentenced to a thrashing, including McKeone and Turpin, who received twenty-five and ten lashes respectively. The two warders lost their positions and for several days the prison was protected by a special detachment of armed policemen.[38]

In mid-November 1889, with the Johannesburg jail effectively in administrative and disciplinary ruin, the authorities decided to separate the bank robbers. Turpin was sent to Barberton, where, within weeks, having secured the cooperation of corrupt turnkeys, he escaped in the company of a cross-border cattle rustler named Smythe. The two fugitives made their way through Swaziland hoping to reach the safety of Lourenço Marques before attaining the freedom of the distant Indian Ocean world. Badly misreading the extent of the popular support they enjoyed, however, they confided their true identity to two hoteliers near Komatipoort, which promptly led to their rearrest by the police.[39]

Jack McKeone was moved to the state's premier holding facility in nearby Pretoria. But the staff at the state prison were almost as cosmopolitan as those on the Rand. Given the meagre salaries, the prison was subject to a high turnover in personnel, and many staff members were at least as venal as their Johannesburg counterparts. The weakness of the system was evident to everybody, including McKeone's increasingly alienated younger brothers back on the Witwatersrand.

Shortly after Jack McKeone was sentenced, or so the ubiquitous Mary McKeone claimed later, Hugh and Bernard were summarily dismissed from their places of employment in Krugersdorp. It was only at this point, as the depression began to bite, that the two younger brothers were forced to take to a life of crime. It was, the mother suggested to all who would listen, a survival strategy.[40] It was also at about this time – November 1889 – that Hugh McKeone and his highwayman friend William Cooper set out for the lowveld, probably in the hope of linking up with John McKeone Snr, who was most likely prospecting – if so, unsuccessfully – in the De Kaap Valley.

It was one of three such epic, money-raising expeditions that the highwaymen undertook over a twelve-month period, all of which they were later unwilling to talk about in any detail. What *is* known is that on the way there, somewhere between Middelburg and Barberton, Cooper, with or without Hugh McKeone, somehow became directly or indirectly involved in a murder, presumably of a black man since the identity of the victim was never revealed. The murder was unsolved but remained the subject of official interest for several years thereafter, Cooper always closely linked to subsequent enquiries.[41]

'Cooper' – his real surname has yet to be uncovered – was born of Irish parents in Southampton on 31 December 1865 but, like the McKeones, whom he greatly admired, seems to have led an unsettled existence. In his teens he worked as fireman on the London and South-West Railway Line for about four years, after which he made his way south, to Cape Town. In the colony he was employed by the Cape Western Railways for three years, he said, before going back to England for a time. But he soon returned to work for the Midland Railways out of Port Elizabeth in the early 1880s. It was reported that, under normal circumstances, Cooper was nonchalant in manner and had the disconcerting habit of staring out into the distance when addressing people. The tale of his life prior to meeting the McKeones, however, is so blurred and the available chronology so imperfect that it suggests he may have spent several years in prison for crimes unknown. That, in turn, may have contributed to a vocabulary of cursing and swearing that, when fully roused, was capable of attracting the attention of a barroom full of sailors on the first night of shore leave. A surly, unattractive brute, Cooper had by the late 1880s taken to the life of a highwayman, donning a huge sombrero, Mexican-style, and a bright, flaring necktie.[42]

It was while the highwaymen were on the roads in the Barberton district that Hugh McKeone or, more likely, Cooper came up with the idea of springing Jack McKeone from jail. The plan, designed to exploit the weaknesses of an antiquated state prison system overrun with urban criminals operating along the mining frontier, was simplicity itself: Cooper would join the prison service to help Jack escape.

In January 1890, Cooper took up his duties as warder in the state prison at Pretoria under his adopted name. It took him a few weeks to set up a plan capable of exploiting fully the racial preoccupations underpinning the system. On 3 March, while the white prisoners were in the courtyard attending to their ablutions, Jack McKeone slipped into the shadows, blackened his face and hands, changed garb and, muffling the sound of his chains, inserted himself into the party of black convicts moving night soil into the gardens adjoining the complex. When the tight-lipped African prisoners, persuaded by his fluent Sesotho, returned, he remained hidden in the adjacent gardens. Some say he hid beneath the very platform of the state gallows that his younger brother was to contemplate from close quarters just months later.[43] In the late afternoon he was collected by Cooper, who, by the time darkness had fallen, had failed to collect his wages or report for night-shift duty.[44]

McKeone, well equipped for forays across cultural boundaries in colonial settings where flawed social vision often picked out only the crassest distinctions between black and white, made his way on foot across thirty-five miles of open countryside to Johannesburg, where he was joined by Cooper. This dangerous diversion into the urban centre, the primary purpose of which, presumably, was to re-establish contact with his brothers, Carroll, 'Crooked Nose' Jackson or whoever else it was in the Irish Brigade who had helped the switch of the sovereigns on the road from Krugersdorp, became almost instantly the subject of intense mythmaking and speculation.

For a day or two, he was seen here, there and everywhere. Working men on the Rand were unwilling to betray his presence to embarrassed ZAR authorities. 'Many queer stories have been current as to his impudence,' one frustrated journalist noted, 'but they are probably greatly exaggerated.'[45] McKeone's horse, too, suddenly became an object of wonderment as it underwent an ethnic transformation from the Irish 'Brian Boru' to 'Black Bess', the mount of eighteenth-century English highwayman Dick Turpin.[46] All along the dusty roads linking the mining capitals of the interior, the mind of the public became inflamed with tales of bank robbers and highwaymen. In Kimberley, the animal trainer and circus owner Frank Fillis put on a performance of the life of Dick Turpin, replete with a Black Bess.[47] By now fact and fiction were dancing so close together that some, observing from a distance, were having difficulty telling them apart.

McKeone, a South African-Irish-Mosotho, was, however, about to give a few additional twists to an already extraordinary tale in which 'American' bandits out of Bret Harte country somehow met up with Dick Turpin in colonial southern Africa. Sneaking back into Krugersdorp one night, he collected a slightly out-of-condition Brian Boru and, together with Cooper, set out for the mountain kingdom of Basotholand. After visiting McKeone's sister Martha at the convent, they planned to link up with Hugh, already there, and seek refuge at Mokhokong, home of Chief Maama. The chief was a graduate of the prestigious Zonnebloem College, Cape Town's elite school for the sons of native chiefs, and a family friend.[48] But the Boers were not to be underestimated. Before long, the erstwhile boarding-house bandits were being pursued by a posse of determined ZAR police supported by counterparts drawn from across the Vaal.

Over a three-day-long chase across the highveld in the second week of March, the fugitives struggled to keep ahead of their tails, who changed horses frequently, commandeering fresh mounts whenever they needed them. But the Free State police were apparently no more capable of seeing beyond crude racial distinctions than were their ZAR counterparts. On one memorable occasion, Jack McKeone persuaded a family of Sesotho-speakers to conceal them in a mud hut while the pursuing force of police, in full flight, sailed past the African homestead not 150 yards away.[49]

But, only hours later, beyond Kroonstad, with their horses blown, the bandits were run down on the banks of the Rhenoster River. 'Had Brian

[Boru] been in better condition,' McKeone later lamented in a letter to Bernard, youngest of the brothers, 'the day should have been ours.'[50] What happened at the river was later relayed to avid newspaper readers in Johannesburg by a journalist who either received an embellished account from an overexcited police informant or had himself indulged in too many Bret Harte novels:

> What was [the pursuers'] surprise, however, when they saw McKeone leap his horse down the twenty foot bank into the river, swim across and when he saw Cooper's horse would not follow came back, and reaching out, pulled Cooper's horse down by the bridle and dragged him through.[51]

Flourishes of this sort by reporters were not unusual in late-nineteenth-century America, where telling a good yarn was often considered to be at least as important as getting the facts straight. In an era when chapbooks were a primary constituent of the diet of working-class readers, such accounts, notes a modern analyst, often contributed to the initial 'fashioning of heroic criminals'.[52]

Jack McKeone, capable of excesses of his own, failed to record the action in such vivid terms, merely noting, 'Our horses being done, we off-saddled and went to meet them. They were armed with rifles which was presented at us, so we had to surrender, as discretion was the better part of valour.'[53] But even at that late hour, or so it was alleged in a popular history written six decades later, Jack McKeone demonstrated conduct becoming of an officer and gentleman – or an outlaw legend. 'Unwilling to see his beloved horse shot dead beneath him', McKeone jumped from his mount, 'removed the saddle and stood patting the horse gently until the police arrived and took him prisoner'.[54] It was the stuff of legends, manufactured in, and for, a frontier society.

Two weary republican policemen – 'ZARPs' – eventually emerged from the bush to join the Free State officers in escorting the prisoners and their horses back to the Kruger republic. Without resting, the policemen set off for the border. Forty-eight hours later and having still not slept, the exhausted escorts decided to take a break, locking their prisoners in a roadside hut. Presently, the guards decided, peculiarly, to take a 'nightcap' – McKeone later claimed to have slipped them a few sovereigns. 'At about two in the morning our guards were driving pigs to market,' he wrote, 'and we, like good fellows, took our walking ticket.'[55] Having dug through the mud wall of their makeshift prison, the fugitives set out again, this time on foot back across the Free State. They eventually stole two horses for the triumphant last-leg ride across the border and into the mountain kingdom of Basotholand, where they met the waiting Hugh McKeone. Back in Johannesburg, the errant ZARPs were summarily dismissed, prosecuted and fined £5 each.[56]

The bandits' hopeful retreat into the Maluti Mountains, briefly viewed as but a prelude to their departure for more distant parts of the globe, proved problematic from the outset. Martha McKeone, despatched to the supposed sanctuary of the convent by her mother and brothers, proved to be as independent-minded and unpredictable as her siblings. Within hours of the McKeone boys appearing at the convent, they were told that their sister, having tired of life in the nunnery, had left to become Chief Jonathan Molapo's eleventh wife. It was a major social transgression, something so far beyond the bounds of colonial convention that even Jack McKeone, the most Sotho-ised of the family, was shocked. He tracked Martha down and tried to persuade her to return home, 'but it is useless, she refuses'.[57]

Still acting *in loco parentis*, Jack felt it incumbent upon him to inform Mary McKeone about the 'painful domestic romance', as the Rand press was about to term it. Indeed, Martha's marriage became the subject of instant male, colonial mythmaking, hopeful racial purists claiming that Jack had done the decent thing and given his sister an ultimatum – she was either to leave her black lover within twenty-four hours or risk being shot.[58] In fact, McKeone's view of his sister's supposed misdemeanours was closer to a plea of 'guilty but insane', and was hardly devoid of understanding. He attempted to convey to their mother some of the social complexities attending the case via a letter sent to his brother Bernard. Along with other correspondence, the letter was intercepted by the authorities, who had been tipped off about the bandits' unexpected appearance in the Malutis:

> It is an awful scandal, and as far as I have found out, she is the most to blame. Anyhow do not Judge her too rashly: Yet it is an Awful thing.
>
> And I firmly believe she is not in her right senses. She did not know of my affair [the bank robbery] untill Hugh told her.

> But, Bernard, cheer mother up; stand to her in all her trials; and get yourself in no trouble, for God knows her trials are great. Yet she has been the best of mothers to us all, and nothing that has happened is like the present affair of Martha's. Fancy your sister being the wife of a native chief! What has induced her to such a purpose I know not, for he is far from being a good looking native.
>
> His wealth must have been the object. She is making her own bed, and so will have to lie on it: for I do not see that Jonathan is to blame. A man must receive some incouragement from a woman. I say she is to blame. Of course the priests or nuns might have tried to stop the matter as soon as their suspicions were aroused, for a preventative is better than a cure. But now it is clear they did not.
>
> And I cannot relish her taste, or choice, but she fancies she knows best. She is determined in her choice.
>
> So what are we to do. But I am going to see her again and I will do my best in the matter.[59]

What Jack McKeone did not expand on directly at the time of writing, however, was just what an enormous emotional toll Martha's decisions had exacted on her. The Catholic clergy in charge of the convent, normally supportive and understanding of African marriage customs, had noted with some alarm, towards the end of the previous year, that Martha McKeone's preferences had produced 'bitterness' in certain circles. This unhappiness could, in its turn, have contributed to what appears to have been a further, religious transgression of the times: an attempt at suicide by Martha at a moment of seasonal stress – the New Year festivities of 1890.[60]

With Martha firmly in the glare of the colonial spotlight and seemingly intransigent on the subject of her marriage, the McKeone brothers and Cooper set off for Chief Maama's stronghold at Mokhokong. In a letter to Jack, Martha reiterated her position in moving terms that depicted her attachment to Jonathan and her new, ever more reclusive lifestyle:

> My very dear Brother,
> I was very glad to hear that you arrived safe at your destination [Maama's], and as the boy is going back I write a few lines to show you that I do not forget you; also to tell you that I am ever thinking of what you told me. Only, my brother, speaking plainly, and telling you the truth, I must say that I cannot make up my mind to leave

> here as I told you. I feel too much attached to Jonathan now; you must not say I am selfish, for I can't really help it. Perhaps in one or two years' time I might be disgusted with this quiet and lonely sort of life, but I doubt it. I am now so used to it that I feel it hard to change.
>
> Oh! my brother, I know that as you said to me this will be a cause of sorrow to you all, but what can I do; I cannot for an instant think of leaving, therefore I can only say forgive me for the pain I cause you, and then forget me altogether. God knows where I will end, for I don't know.[61]

It was a letter to melt the heart of a bandit, one who was himself something of a romantic and capable of being as brutal with a policeman as he was benign with a pony. It softened his soul.

Maama, his uneasy Protestant host, was in a difficult position. Basotho politics had become increasingly complex and divided along resistance-collaborationist lines after the Basotho Gun War. Maama's father, Letsie, who favoured him over his elder brother Lerotholi, was attempting to groom Maama to succeed the parmountcy. This made for an awkward relationship with the new British Resident Commissioner, Marshal Clarke. It is plausible – as later claimed by one author – that it was Maama who betrayed the bandits' presence to Clarke in the hope of advancing his position.[62] But it is far more likely to have been poor Jonathan, alarmed by Jack McKeone's insistent attempts to persuade his sister to leave him in order to regain control of her, who revealed the presence of the fugitives to the Commissioner.[63]

Jack McKeone, always dreaming, appeared by then to be entertaining the idea of settling down to a life of cattle rustling on the plains of the eastern Free State and, when the occasion demanded it, retreating into the hills. Had he managed to effect this transition, he would have become a classic rural 'social bandit' of the sort first espoused by Hobsbawm rather than the type of heroic criminal or outlaw legend championed by those who see such bandits operating in many other contexts. It would have been an independent, manly career well suited to a white Mosotho, and one followed by many others on the fringes of Basotho society. In his earlier letter to Bernard, Jack had asked for the address of his old Krugersdorp prospecting patron, Barsdorf, and to be advised 'what good slaughter oxen fetch in the Rant'.[64] He was running short of funds and no longer had easy access to his share of the proceeds of the bank robbery, which, presumably, had been left on the Rand.

But another part of the dreamer was perfectly sober and he understood that, in the real world, removed from reverie, all that he could look forward to was a life on the run, and that officers of the Kruger republic would, with the support of their Orange Free State cousins, never stop searching for him, making a life of cattle rustling difficult. So on the very day that he wrote to Bernard, he forwarded his brother a second letter written from 'Whereabouts Anonimous', to be sent to the State Secretary of the ZAR proposing that they reach an accommodation. Lest this letter be interpreted as a sign of weakness in his dealings with the Afrikaner administration, Jack reminded Bernard privately: 'The letter I send to the Government is but a blind, for I hate the Dutch dogs as I hate hell: yet post it.'

> Sir,
>
> This is to inform you that I the undersigned, a prisoner at large, seek to come to terms of peace with the Government of the South African Republic. It is clear up to the present I have proved myself up to the mark. So I would ask your Government to consider, that I have comitted myself but once while in your state and up to that time bore a good character: testimonials of which I can still produce and if my case is clearly looked into you will find that I comitted myself from a spirit of revenge. I also ask you to see the manner my crime was done in. Was there any want of manliness? Again, I would ask, how it is that most men that have a hand in arresting me regret their share in so doing almost as soon as they come to know me. Now, since I am out of your State, why not leave me in peace; providing I bind myself never to enter the South African Republic again. For, bear in mind, if I am to be hunted about everywhere, and am ever to be on the alert for fear of capture; I might as well retaliate, for if I cannot settle down it stands to reason that it would be as well for me to return to your state, and comit a series of crimes, if for nothing else but to be avenged and get a notorious name.
>
> But such is not my ambition and thus I ask you to consider that any man is liable to make a false step. But why for one false step is a man to be punished all his life? Is it not better to give him an opportunity to reform, and is it likely that 25 years imprisonment can reform a man?

So I ask you kindly to consider my case well, and will await and expect an answer through the *Government Gazette* within twenty-four day[s] from afore written date, and should your Council come to the conclusion of leaving me at peace, I would beg you to consider the case of my companion Joseph Richard Terpend. Now, having laid my views fairly before you, having stated the afore-written to the best of my ability, and trusting you will consider the matter well, awaiting your reply,

I Remain Your humble,
A Prisoner at large,
JOHN LOUIS MCKEONE.[65]

But there was no response forthcoming to the great peace proposal, and McKeone's presence at Maama's village had already been made known to the Resident Commissioner. Clarke did what he had to do and the 'Dutch dogs' lay in wait. Ironically, it may have been Jack's desire to maintain correspondence with various people and to keep track of the press coverage of his dramatic escapes that led to his undoing. When he, Hugh and Cooper ventured over the border into the hamlet of Ladybrand, around 17 April, the Free State police pounced. McKeone was arrested carrying a sheaf of letters notable for their 'pious tone' justifying his actions in ways familiar to heroic criminals.[66] Cooper and Hugh McKeone fled to live off the countryside. We shall encounter them again in due course, as highwaymen.

This time, the ZAR authorities left nothing to chance. By late May 1890, Jack McKeone was back in chains and behind bars.[67] But he was also in Pretoria, within reach of those brigands holding his share of the Krugersdorp robbery money. And, as the recession deepened and stamp batteries along the reef fell silent, so the siren call of gold sovereigns could be heard echoing across the highveld. It took McKeone less than a month to deal a second, harder blow to Kruger's ramshackle prison administration. On this occasion, however, he left less to chance, using coded notes to communicate with unknown accomplices who undertook much of the preparatory work necessary to effect a successful escape.

On 18 June, a convict in a work party by the name of Peel, feigning illness, was sent back to the prison. There he handed McKeone, held in manacles in an isolated cell, a steel file. With the prison almost empty mid-afternoon, McKeone first filed through his chains and then through the hinges of the cell door. He, Peel and a third inmate, Watson, then clambered over the prison walls at a point where they knew they would find bundles of clothing left by outside collaborators. They changed outfits and went their separate ways. McKeone, confident about the popular support he enjoyed, again made his way south.

A full month after McKeone's disappearance the police finally pieced together what had happened next. In Johannesburg, McKeone had a drink with a certain 'Fuchs' and was handed £250 as well as a range of hats, false beards and other items for use on a journey to the coast. He was then taken to the stables at Alexander's Coaches, where, so it was claimed, 'two Jews' saw him off, suitably disguised, on a departing coach. He was last sighted east of Kroonstad, making his way, it was believed, to Bloemfontein, and from there on to Durban. A few weeks later McKeone was allegedly spotted in two small towns in the eastern Transvaal, supposedly on his way to Delagoa Bay en route to Mauritius. They were plausible enough explanations but, in truth, McKeone was never again seen.[68]

The wrath of the administration now descended squarely upon the staff at the Pretoria prison, who had, within a matter of months, twice witnessed the escape of the country's most wanted man. Yet again, however, those in authority read events through racially bifurcated spectacles, seemingly oblivious to the possibility that black warders and inmates were independent actors, at least as capable of implication in McKeone's escapes as were their white counterparts. But, if whites only were capable of foresight and rational thought, then only they could be held to account. In September 1890, Governor J. van Reenen and several white warders lost their positions.[69] And, somewhere out there on the ocean, on board a ship headed for the already shrinking world of the Australian bushrangers, a white Mosotho bandit probably smiled and took out his pen.

# 4

# Coach Robbers and Highwaymen in the Pre-Rail Era

And still on a winter's night, they say, when the wind is
in the trees,
When the moon is a ghostly galleon tossed upon
cloudy seas,
When the road is a gypsy's ribbon looping the
purple moor,
The highwayman comes riding –
Riding – Riding –
The highwayman comes riding, up to the old inn-door.
– Alfred Noyes, 'The Highwayman'

From their inception in 1886 the landlocked, rail-free Witwatersrand mines were faced with problems stemming from the flow of gold of two colours – black and yellow. In the case of cheap African labour, the lifeblood of a nascent industry, one of the earliest challenges arose when inward-bound migrants were intercepted by Boer farmers or labour touts from competing mines, who forced would-be workers into cheap, disadvantageous contracts by deflecting them from better- to worse-paying employers.[1] For migrant labourers the very journey to the fields of employment was hazardous.

But if inward-bound black workers were robbed of time and the marginal differences in meagre wages, then outward-bound migrants were subjected to more brutal and direct assaults. Scores of highwaymen, of both colours, relieved parties of returning African migrants of their savings. While individually modest, these sums could, collectively, add up to hundreds of pounds – amounts that would have taken a skilled white worker years to accumulate by dint of hard work. On the highveld around the Witwatersrand, well-orchestrated forays into the ranks of the returning black workers – like sharks descending upon the sardine run –

reached a peak in the thirty-six months leading up to the great 'Kaffir Boom' in the value of mining stocks in 1895. Thereafter, as the main routes were better policed, and when rail travel slowly became more attractively priced for hard-pressed black migrants, there was a noticeable falling-off in highway robbery.[2]

Predictably, it was the plight of the inward- rather than the outward-bound black workers that first excited the Chamber of Mines, which used the consequent interruptions in labour supply as part of a buttressing argument in its pleas for a regionally integrated rail system. In the medium term, however, the mine owners were forced to concede that it was the systematic plundering of black workers moving in *both* directions that imperilled the industry. In 1894, by which time the problems had been manifest for half a decade, the Chamber responded by establishing labour depots along the Zoutpansberg road, which led from the far north.[3]

But it was the millions of ounces of yellow metal that had to be transported from southern Africa to the United Kingdom that presented mining companies with their most serious problem. Gold production increased from a nominal amount in 1886 to about 35 000 ounces in 1887, and then rose to 231 000 ounces in 1888. By 1889, it was put at an estimated 379 000 ounces. Thereafter, output increased by an astonishing 50 per cent per annum until the outbreak of the South African War in 1899. From the moment gold-rich ore was brought to the surface on the Rand to the point that bars of bullion were stashed away in the vaults of the Bank of England several thousand miles away, the precious metal – always subject to the official gaze – was liable to invoke charges from banks, coach-line operators, governments in search of tariffs and predatory shipping lines.

These state-licensed revenue-collecting agents – authorised highwaymen, if you will – levied fees for safe handling and movement of the metal. It was a premium that relied, in part, on a continuous threat being posed to the security of gold consignments by other, informal agents – amalgam thieves in mine reduction works, bank robbers, safe-crackers and coach robbers.[4] Banditry in the age of the horse economy tended therefore to cheat companies of profits not only directly, through outright robbery, but indirectly in the form of other charges and the cost of insurance. As Marx once reminded his disciples, the 'real' and underworld economies are always inextricably intertwined.

In the pre-rail era, gold-mining companies sought to contain costs arising from both the shipment of the metal and the attendant risks in two ways. In 1889, in the first full year of operation as the authoritative voice of the emerging industry, the Chamber of Mines made it clear that it considered the safe transport of gold to be the responsibility of the Kruger administration and the road tariffs to be excessive. By 1891, it had pressed the government into entering into a contract with Heys & Co. for the armed escort of twice-monthly shipments of gold to Kimberley. In the same year, gold-mining companies, working through the Chamber, persuaded the Union and Castle Lines to reduce their freight charges to Southampton by 10 per cent.[5]

## Coach Robbers

With specie constantly on the road from Kimberley to banks in Johannesburg, and gold bullion moving in the opposite direction, stagecoaches were vulnerable to armed robbers, especially in and around the area where the borders of the Zuid Afrikaansche Republiek, Orange Free State and Cape Colony converged.[6] Masked brigands, some of whom were either Irish-born or Lancashire-Irish, intercepted coaches imported from the same firm that had supplied coaches for the famous Californian gold runs – Abbot, Downie & Co. of Concord, New Hampshire.

H.J. 'Jack' O'Reilly, friend of the McKeone brothers, was one such coach robber. In 1893, emerging from the bush about eight miles north of Christiana on the road to Kimberley, he and a partner shot dead one of the lead horses before approaching the heavily armed coach driver and his assistant. With his hat 'pulled low over his eyes' and the 'lower part of his face covered with a bandana handkerchief', O'Reilly proceeded to speak in an 'unmistakeable Irish brogue'. But the ensuing dialogue was not particularly fruitful for the bandits: the coach was carrying only mailbags. The robbers removed £600 and retreated to the Vaal River, where they swam 'their horses into the Free State and made good their escape'.[7]

The mining companies experienced several more such costly hold-ups on the road to Kimberley but, in general, the much-criticised Kruger administration did an excellent job of ensuring the safe transport of gold across state lines.[8] It is noteworthy that, throughout the pre-rail era, the Chamber of Mines – always a ready critic of republican shortcomings – never separately itemised coach robberies as an impediment to the profitability of the industry. Indeed, many highwaymen appear to have shied away from the dangerous business of attempting to steal gold bullion from heavily guarded, state-protected coaches.

Irish Brigade members active in the eastern Transvaal's De Kaap Valley in the late 1880s, including Jack O'Reilly in the west, preferred robbing unguarded yet profitable mail coaches. When several of their number, led by John McLoughlin, moved out of Johannesburg and into the western Transvaal countryside around Rustenburg in mid-1890, during the worst months of the recession, an enormous safe belonging to a retail store was soon stolen and blown open, government offices were burgled and two coaches were relieved of several thousand pounds.[9]

In other, more remote rural areas such as the north-eastern Transvaal, where relatively small mines remained unconnected to the rail system for years, the theft of bullion from horse-drawn coaches continued for at least a decade, perhaps longer. In 1897, half a dozen armed men emptied the mail coach of bullion worth £12 000 near Lydenburg. Just two years later, in 1899, the highwaymen who robbed a stagecoach at Pilgrim's Rest of gold worth £20 000 fled into neighbouring Mozambique. They then presumably did as many others did and continued their journey on to Lourenço Marques, gateway to the Indian Ocean and, beyond it, Australia.[10]

Most highwaymen, however, eschewed the well-guarded yellow metal as a primary source of income, settling instead for the safer and steadier earnings stream to be derived from the black gold flowing incessantly across the face of the central plateau. Robbing unarmed African migrant labourers, who were in constant fear of being stopped by white men demanding passes, obviated needless professional dangers and enabled these highwaymen to lead more settled lives than their coach-robbing cousins. Like pirates on tropical islands waiting for the trade winds to blow heavily laden schooners across their paths, all they had to do was to lurk in the bush beside the dusty tracks leading from the diamond fields or the Witwatersrand.

## Highwaymen

Unlike bank robbers and safe-crackers, who preferred working at night to avoid unnecessary confrontations with the staff of the faceless corporations that they plundered, highwaymen could not avoid personal contact with victims, who were occasionally well armed and willing to defend their property. Like most sensible professionals, highwaymen and so-called 'noble robbers' sought to circumvent unpleasant problems. 'Moderation in killing and violence,' Hobsbawm reminds us, is part of 'the image of the social bandit'.[11] It was probably the same reason – the desire to minimise danger to life and limb – that many famous highwaymen around the world developed a reputation for being courteous, gentlemanly and well disposed towards women.[12] Again, this should not surprise us unduly, since the deep roots of everyday etiquette lie in ritualised attempts to avoid conflict. That said, few if any southern African highwaymen fell easily into the category of 'social bandits': they induced too much fear in the populace at large to justify that often problematic classification. And, if the same was partly true of highwaymen in societies that were culturally homogenous, it had an added pertinence in a multicultural environment where underlying suspicions were fuelled by a toxic mixture of class and race prejudice.

In the heyday of the horse economy, highway robbery offered a sufficiently steady occupation for some brigands to adopt a peri-urban, if not suburban, lifestyle. It was a mode of living that, in a colonial setting, could be sustained with the help of servants or, occasionally, even white women. As already noted, Jack McKeone's mother, Mary, ran a boarding house for bandits in Krugersdorp. And 'Nongoloza' Mathebula's four white employers hired a house with adjoining stables, at first retaining him only for his on-site services as a groom. But, as the young man soon noted, 'After breakfast the four men would go out at about 8.00 or 9.00 a.m. on their horses and would return at midday for dinner and remain at home until it was dusk. They would then go out again and not return until about midnight. They always seemed to bring some money with them and I used to see them counting it at night.'[13] It was not long before the young isiZulu-speaker was invited to join Tyson, McDonald and the others at their 'work', becoming part of a racially integrated band of brigands capable of being more readily understood when intercepting migrant labourers, and thereby minimising misunderstandings. Mathebula, a native black man, might have been among the first home-grown bandits, but he most certainly was not the only one.

In African migrant labour systems, as with water seeking an outlet to the ocean, wages flow to seas of poverty. The most direct route from the

Rand to the labour reserves of the north-east (Mozambique, Swaziland and the Zoutpansberg) presented one obvious channel. De Koker and Van Greuning, who operated in the Middelburg district in the closing year of the depression – 1892 – may, for example, have been the younger sons of Boers who either saw no future for themselves on the land or who were going through hard times. And let us not forget that the 1890s, taken as a whole, were potholed with rural disaster for Afrikaner farmers in the form of drought, locusts and the cattle disease rinderpest. Unusually, in the case of De Koker and Van Greuning, one of them was said to be engaged to be married at the time of his arrest.[14]

Given the Boer propensity for intercepting black labour making its way *to* the goldfields, it may have been a natural step up for hard-pushed or marginalised Afrikaner farmers to stop, search and strip returning African migrant labourers of their wages. Indeed, for African mine workers making their way home from Johannesburg, the first point of danger to be negotiated was Natalspruit, along the eastern approaches to the town, where white highwaymen of the suburban variety were believed to be a particular danger.[15]

Further afield, the Afrikaner farming community produced several horse thieves, including the criminally versatile and extraordinarily mobile Jacob van de Venter. Van de Venter probably knew the McKeone brothers. He certainly considered Jack McKeone's partners, William Cooper and Stevens (alias 'Turpin'), to be among his close associates. As noted for his cheek as for his gentlemanly manners, Van de Venter led a life every bit as interesting as that of his more famous southern counterpart, that horse thief Scotty Smith.[16] Given the complex freebooting origins of Stellaland and Goshen, many such Afrikaner marginals should be removed from the obvious and tired context of the rise of narrow ethnic nationalism and studied instead as fascinating cases of indigenous brigandage in their own right.

If and when such a more encompassing history is forthcoming, it will be noted, albeit in passing, that not all Afrikaner brigands were drawn from obscure families. 'Groot Adriaan' de la Rey, the nephew of the Boer general most famous for his innovative fieldcraft during the South African War, J.H. 'Koos' de la Rey, was sufficiently well known for his extra-legal adventures to be described as a 'filibuster' by one prominent observer, who himself had more than passing knowledge of the Irish Brigade.[17]

Working in the same, admittedly exceedingly thin, vein, it might be asked whether, on the outer margins, some of the much-vaunted Boer genius for guerrilla warfare did not in some cases derive from prior experience of brigandage.[18]

Established Afrikaner farmers, however, also knew what it was like to be victims of crime. Boers, having sold their grain or livestock at the Johannesburg market, were obvious targets for confidence tricksters, urban footpads and white highwaymen.[19] In 1890, with jobs in the mining industry being shed faster than cat fur in summer, three armed Europeans staged a raid on the farmhouse of Cornelis Smit, a wealthy elderly Boer in the Krugersdorp district. They were repelled only when his sons arrived to drive off the invaders with rifles. Nor were immigrant white miners exempted from the attention of their British highwaymen cousins. Just days after the attack on the Smit homestead, in the same district 'three white men met a European miner, knocked him down off the highway, took everything from him, cracked him over the head and threw him into a cutting for dead'.[20]

The southern corridor of great white theft, leading north- and south-east out of Kimberley towards Basotholand, Natal and the Transkei territories, was, however, both older and potentially more lucrative than its northern counterpart.[21] From the 1870s, returning black labourers and not a few white travellers making their way across the Orange Free State carried illegally acquired diamonds as well as salaries or wages about their persons. Even before the economic downturn on the Rand in 1890, the channel constituted an irresistible temptation for immigrant fortune-seekers, not excluding the Lancashire-Irish.

J.W. Brown (b. 1857) was the second-born, part-Celtic son of an Englishman of the same name who had an eye for Irish lasses and whose pharmacy in Mill Street, Ancoats, was something of an institution in working-class Manchester. A product of the first of several broken marriages, John William Brown, raised in the heart of 'scuttling' country, was in constant trouble with the law as a teenager. A close confidant and one of John McLoughlin's earliest criminal collaborators back in Ancoats and again, later, on the Witwatersrand, Brown made his entrance on the highveld stage in the mid-1880s, at the height of the mineral revolution. He had little intention of working, however. In his mind's eye, he too was simply a man of the times; a composite figure, part English highwayman from the literature of his youth, part Californian via Bret Harte.[22]

In 1888, Brown and two others, Howard Hicks and John Wiggans, all in their late twenties or early thirties and given to being well 'not to say flashily' dressed, were working the roads leading north and east out of Kimberley.[23] Shortly after 6.30 a.m. on Wednesday 14 March, the mounted brigands were positioned near the farm Welgevonden in the Boshof district of the Orange Free State, only five miles from the Griqualand West border. They spotted a party of thirteen Africans, who had recently completed their contracts at the Central Mining Company, making their way back to Basotholand. Brown, captain of the bandits, dressed in a 'woolly hat' with 'a handkerchief on his face covering his mouth and chin' right 'up to his eyes', remained on his horse. Hicks and Wiggans dismounted and, with Brown firing his pistol into the air at random, they approached the migrants.

Hicks and Wiggans told the workers that they were going to be searched for diamonds. The leader of the party, Tojane, and four others were instructed to remove their money-belts and were systematically fleeced of sovereigns, which were handed to Brown. Tojane forfeited £20 in gold, and the four other workers presumably lost similar amounts. The brigands left the morning's labour and, on the way back to Kimberley, called in at Thomas Whittock's trading store. Fifteen minutes later, Tojane and his companions appeared at the establishment and informed the proprietor of what had transpired. The storekeeper suggested that they return to Kimberley to notify the police, which they did. The brigands were tracked, arrested, subjected to a careful preliminary examination and extradited to the Orange Free State for trial.[24]

Predatory activities across the interior's corridors of migratory labour severely disrupted the flow of cheap black labour to the highveld's mining capitals, something that magistrates and judges on both the diamond and goldfields were at pains to impress upon transgressors when sentencing members of the Turpin fraternity to lengthy periods in prison.[25] It is within this context that we need to return to Cooper and the McKeones to develop a fuller understanding of the magnitude of the challenge that the Irish Brigade and its loosely linked affiliates mounted against the Kruger state in the years leading up to the Jameson Raid.

Having lost Jack McKeone, the leader, the oldest and probably the most circumspect member of their tiny band of brigands, to the republican police on the eastern Free State plains in April 1890, nineteen-year-old Hugh and the demented William Cooper were left on their own, without a place of refuge in Basotholand. Although lacking the panache of Butch Cassidy and the Sundance Kid, the pair set out on a criminal odyssey that was to take them across the face of southern Africa and end, literally, in the shadow of the gallows. Unfortunately, only the barest outline of the earliest parts of their journey has survived.

Slipping in and out of the hem-folds of the Maluti Mountains, the brigands worked their way round and out of the Orange Free State before riding into Natal for purposes that are subject now only to conjecture. It may have been an intention to raise funds, make their way to an east-coast port such as Lourenço Marques and then secure a passage for Cooper to some unknown Indian Ocean destination. Whatever the objective, it was never achieved. By the time the pair reached Newcastle, the decision had been taken to wheel round and push back into the interior.[26]

McKeone, who had once been a photographer's assistant in Kimberley, and Cooper, who had picked up some experience as an artisan while working in various capacities on the Cape railways, both saw themselves as journeymen capable of working, when necessary, with chemicals, glass, metals or wood. On their way back into the Orange Free State, at Harrismith, they cut and polished fragments of glass with sufficient skill to pass them off successfully as diamonds.[27] With the cash raised from 'diamond' sales they retraced the steps of their outward journey, hugging the foothills of the Malutis. But by the time they reached Ladybrand, nemesis-ville for the McKeones, their funds were exhausted. Forgoing the planning and restraint that defined Jack McKeone and Dick Turpin's operation as bank robbers, the two highwaymen – as 'Patrick McKeone' and 'John Williams' – were overcome by the brutality and impulse that characterised the many less noble members of their profession. They moved in on a trading store, severely assaulted the owner and, having helped themselves to his modest cash takings, fled.[28]

It was a vicious attack and the police, accustomed to tracing cross-border raiders from Basotholand, responded with alacrity. The bandits were tracked and arrested, all seemingly without resistance. But they had already crossed some vital psychological threshold and, in a pattern found in brigand careers known to have flared briefly and then died, were manifesting increasingly violent tendencies. In mid-May, while being held in the police cells pending their trial in the Circuit Court, Hugh McKeone attempted to escape. When thwarted by a constable, the young bandit beat him so savagely that he was prosecuted. Most unusually for a white man, he was sentenced to fifteen lashes.[29]

Closer acquaintance still with the whip was swiftly forthcoming. At Ladybrand on 19 July, Judge Gregerowski sentenced Cooper and McKeone to five years' imprisonment and fifty lashes apiece as punishment for the trading-store robbery.[30] Considerations of health presumably dictated the need for the whippings to be administered in separate tranches of twenty-five lashes each. In the customary display of contempt for justice by 'hard men', the two brigands were escorted to their cells singing the ditty 'For we are two roving Irishmen'.[31]

But Ladybrand was just another small town in an agrarian republic that, in the midst of industrial revolution and economic depression, was spewing out marginals faster than the prisons could accommodate them. Its holding facilities, like those in rural areas of the neighbouring ZAR, were wholly unsuited to the detention of desperadoes. After McKeone and Cooper had each received their first twenty-five lashes, they were transferred to the Orange Free State's most secure prison in the capital city of Bloemfontein.[32] But even the Republic's finest was no match for the brigands. McKeone escaped, but was recaptured by a posse of civilians – only to escape for a second time, accompanied by seasoned Irish Brigader Charles Harding. McKeone lingered in the district before he was joined by Cooper, who had escaped in the company of another prisoner named Belmore. The two bandits had served just five months of their five-year sentence and had received only twenty-five of their fifty lashes when they were once again on the move. This time they struck out north and east, as if heading for the oldest of prisoners' friends in the region, Mozambique.[33]

But the pair was not quite ready for Lourenço Marques. Instead, they holed up in the gold-rich De Kaap Valley, one of Cooper's favourite hunting grounds. There they were also likely to encounter the absent father of the McKeone clan, John, who was following his calling as a prospector. Cooper set them up by stealing a set of fresh mounts, and they continued to go about their business with relish. Soon, however, the pair faced new problems when Cooper was imprisoned for the theft of two horses and highway robbery.[34] How and when he was freed, in Barberton, remains a mystery, but no sooner was he out of jail than the roving Irishmen set off overland on what was to be the most profitable, but near-fatal, next leg of their wanderings over the southern interior.

Cruising midstream, with eyes peering from masked faces like crocodiles waiting for approaching antelope, the brigands moved along the channels in which they were most likely to encounter black workers returning from the diamond and goldfields. By their own accounts, they gorged themselves. It was later claimed – quite plausibly – that while on this extended looting spree the pair accumulated £2 000. It was an extraordinary, perhaps even fanciful, sum, but it was in line with other large hauls made by the elite safe-cracking division of the Irish Brigade at about the same time. Even today, estimated conservatively, it would approximate to more than two hundred thousand pounds sterling. The spoils remained hidden somewhere along the roads linking lowveld gold mines to the distant Kimberley diamond fields.[35]

By autumn 1891, the two had worked their way across the breadth of the South African Republic and, some distance north of the diamond fields, found themselves at Vryburg and in need of fresh mounts. With a highwayman's unerring eye for good steeds, they stole a pair of horses said to belong to the High Commissioner, Sir Henry Loch, but were once again almost immediately tracked and trapped by a ZARP, Constable P.S. du Plessis.[36] The Vryburg cells, however, were no more secure than any of the others, and it was not long before they were once again free.

The escape and flight from Vryburg marked a turning point. The pair of bandits already possessed significant sums in cash, which were either stashed along the roads leading back to the lowveld or being held in trust for them at Barberton, possibly by John McKeone. With the funds for their departure secure, they turned east, back into the mainstream of migrants pouring out of Kimberley. There they planned to stage a last raid before making their way to the coast. In Lourenço Marques they could at last board the ship of dreams that would transport them to Australia, to Jack McKeone and to freedom.[37]

In little more than a year – in actual travelling time, probably closer to nine months – the two young highwaymen had covered more than a thousand miles on horseback, criss-crossed four states, held up storekeepers, defrauded credulous diamond buyers, stolen any number of horses and robbed black migrant labourers of thousands of pounds. It was a colonial epic driven in unequal parts by inspiration and insanity, one that, amidst an extraordinary act of collective white amnesia, was also about to be subsumed in a whirlpool of imperial and nationalist politics.

The appeal of the thinly populated Klerksdorp district had less to do with its poorly developed gold mines than with the fact that it lay on the route of the north-bound journey of African workers returning from their labours in Griqualand West. For two saddle-weary Irishmen operating in midwinter, it held an added attraction in the shape of a comfortable farmhouse owned by Jack O'Reilly, who, when not staging coach robberies on the busy Johannesburg-Kimberley run, did some farming.[38] It seemed like the ideal base from which to operate – warm, hospitable and secure.

Their decision to move back into the main channel appeared to be vindicated when, one morning in the second week of June 1891, the heavily armed highwaymen spotted a party of twelve black travellers heading north on the road between Bloemhof and Klerksdorp.[39] They intercepted the migrants and presented themselves as policemen in search of illegally acquired gemstones. The workers were divested of over £400 in cash, a sum equivalent to the earnings of about a decade or more of black hard labour in the diamond mines. Satisfied that they were safe with O'Reilly, they felt it unnecessary to hide the stash. By late afternoon, the bandits were back at the farmhouse, where the money was secreted. With the winter darkness plummeting down, they settled in for the night.

But long-distance migrants left destitute unexpectedly were, almost by definition, more desperate than workers drawn from local communities, who could look around closer to home for succour and support. They were also – unless extremely ill-fated – unlikely to encounter the same highwaymen for a second time, or to run into them subsequently as farmers. Labourers drawn from far-off places were therefore sometimes more willing to report armed attacks to the police than were local blacks. Before the sun had set, the workers had reported the robbery to the ZARPs at Klerksdorp, where, by chance, they found the same Constable Du Plessis who had been instrumental in arresting Cooper and McKeone back at Vryburg weeks earlier. From the descriptions offered by the workers, Du Plessis must have had an idea of the attackers' identity and, if he did not, the local police would have been familiar with the location of the robbery and aware of Jack O'Reilly's part-time profession.

In the early hours of the morning, Constable Du Plessis and two ZARPs – P.J. du Toit and J.C. Schultz – set out for O'Reilly's hoping to roust the suspects before daybreak. The police entered the house without triggering resistance from the sleepy occupants and proceeded to search the premises. A large revolver was recovered from beneath McKeone's pillow, but there was no sign of the stolen money. Cooper and McKeone were arrested and it was decided to separate the prisoners, who would remain mounted for the trek back to Klerksdorp. Young McKeone would be accompanied by Du Toit, and the pair would ride slightly ahead of Constables Du Plessis and Schultz, who would bring up the rear with the more dangerous Cooper. Approaching a small rise a few miles from the farmhouse, and in full view of the rest of the police and his partner in crime, McKeone feigned illness. Du Toit instructed him to pull up so as to allow him to be sick. McKeone dismounted gingerly but sprang into life as soon as his feet touched ground. He dragged the startled constable from his horse and, whipping out a hitherto concealed weapon, pressed the revolver against the officer's head. When Du Toit resisted vigorously, McKeone twice pulled the trigger, but each time the pistol jammed.

Du Plessis, observing what was happening ahead of him, spurred his horse into action. By the time he reached the crest and the still-wrestling couple, McKeone's revolver was once again functional. He spun round and fired a shot at the constable, but missed his target. When Schultz and Cooper reached the scene, not an instant later Cooper, too, suddenly produced a revolver from nowhere. Taking more deliberate aim, he sent a second shot in Du Plessis' direction. But the God of the ZARPs was not about to desert his people; the bullet was deflected by a decorative five-shilling coin that Du Plessis had attached to his watch chain. The police, regrouping, managed to regain control of the situation.[40]

Twelve weeks later, after a protracted preliminary examination in Klerksdorp and yet another attempt at escape, Cooper and McKeone were moved to the central state prison in Pretoria to await trial in the High Court before the Chief Justice.[41] The country was reeling beneath an epidemic of armed robbery and safe-lifting. Much of the blame for this, along with the crisis in the penal system, could be laid at the door of the Irish Brigade.

In Pretoria, Cooper was said to be utterly 'indifferent' and 'nonchalant' in spite of the extremely serious charges he and his partner faced. But his actions belied his attitude. He announced his arrival at the prison – the same prison that he had once infiltrated as a warder to facilitate the disappearance of Jack McKeone – by making repeated attempts at escape, each more desperate than the last. He sought to dig his way out of the cell, tried to saw off the bars of the cell window and, most alarmingly of all, somehow acquired the ingredients for an explosive cocktail of nitroglycerine that was confiscated before he could use it.[42]

Hugh McKeone, on the verge of his twentieth birthday, was said to be 'dejected' and full of 'remorse', and made no further attempts at escape.[43] But whatever the brigands' moods, there was no want of company during their brief excursions into the prison yard. By the time the highwaymen arrived at Pretoria there was already a significant build-up in the number of prisoners linked to the Irish Brigade. These included Charles Harding, who had been with Cooper when he escaped from the Bloemfontein prison, and, more importantly, the trio of Brown, Sutherland and Todd. The threesome, whose fates we shall learn in due course, were set to appear before the Chief Justice at the same sessions as Cooper and McKeone on charges relating to a spate of coach and safe-robberies. The thefts, which had targeted state property, had taken place earlier in the State President's backyard, in the troubled Rustenburg district.[44]

Cooper and McKeone appeared before Chief Justice J.G. Kotze on 21 October 1891, charged with attempted murder and highway robbery. The judge, sensing that the state was facing a serious challenge from organised crime that threatened to envelop town and countryside alike, was in no mood for leniency. Visibly annoyed, his conduct and pronouncements throughout the Criminal Sessions were open to criticism and question. To the amazement of many if not all whites, he sentenced Cooper and McKeone to death for their attempts on the lives of the policemen. It was an unprecedented sentence: prior to that, the state had seen fewer than half a dozen white men hanged for far more serious offences. Kotze's judgment was, in effect, overturned when on 6 November the State President and his Executive Council granted the condemned men clemency.[45]

The outcome of the Cooper-McKeone trial occasioned mass political mobilisation among English-speakers throughout the region for reasons that had little to do with ethnicity and organised crime and a good deal to do with expanding imperial ambitions. This is a fascinating tale, one that we shall explore, separately, later. For the moment, however, our focus will remain on the response of the Irish Brigade to the plight of Cooper, McKeone and its other members in the weeks leading up to the reprieve of the highwaymen and the sentencing of the three Rustenburg coach robbers and safe-lifters. Was the Brigade really a threat to the pressurised Kruger administration and, if so, how did the state respond to this new challenge?

At this juncture it may also be worth recalling that, little more than twelve months earlier, in mid-1890, Jack McKeone had staged a second successful escape from the Pretoria prison. It had been achieved with the assistance of outside help, which had provided him with a change of clothing once he and others had scaled the perimeter wall. That act of solidarity, presumably the work of the same Irish Brigade elements who had been party to the original bank robbery in Krugersdorp, was no doubt prompted partly out of loyalty. The fact that McKeone was in possession of a tidy sum in cash would, no doubt, have encouraged collaborators to consider the opportunities it presented.

By the time that Hugh McKeone and William Cooper were captured and imprisoned they, too, had indirect access to a far larger sum in cash than their bank-robbing brother and comrade had had at the time of his escape a year earlier. The 'two roving Irishmen' were also more willing to parade their Catholic and ethnic affiliations than Jack McKeone had been. Cooper's very public claim to have access to over £2 000 hidden along country roads – a statement later endorsed by Hugh McKeone – might well have been intended to signal to Irish Brigade members that it would be worth their while to come to the assistance of yet another of the men in the McKeone family.

The call did not go unheeded by Irish Brigaders, nor was it unheard by agents of the state. The Kruger government had only one full-time, professional military wing to call on in peacetime – the State Artillery. Immediately after Kotze's controversial imposition of the death penalty on 21 October, two Artillery detachments comprising eight men each were deployed in shifts to guard the prison walls around the clock. On 30 October, information was received that an attempt would be made by 'McKeone's friends from Johannesburg' to storm the jail and release the inmates. The guards were placed on alert, the prison was linked to the

Artillery barracks by telephone and the police were instructed to monitor passengers on all inward-bound stagecoaches.[46] The state's central prison was, in effect, under siege.

That night at about eleven, a shower of stones – directed from the grounds of the neighbouring convent – descended on the prison roof. The intention was to lure the warders, who would want to investigate the source of the disturbance, into opening the gates and linking up with the guards outside. The opportunity would then be used to invade the prison and free a half-dozen or so Brigade members. But all that happened was that the full detachment of the State Artillery was roused to encircle the facility while armed warders took up defensive positions along the top of the prison walls.[47]

The cascade of stones on the rooftop continued unabated and, when a patrol of State Artillery guards ventured beyond the convent, they saw the outline of two figures lurking beneath the trees. They advanced and called out the traditional challenge, but the men took flight, darting into a neighbouring timber yard. Bullseye lanterns were handed out and the area searched, but without success. The assault ended.[48]

The following morning the State Artillery contingent was doubled and placed directly under the command of the unit's lieutenant. Two of the new arrivals were assigned to occupy the copse opposite the jail entrance by night. The streets around the prison were barricaded and eighty burghers called up by the *veldkornet* to be on standby should their services be required.[49] It was all intended as a show of force. The prison administration, already the laughing stock of the country, was determined not to be humiliated by the escape of yet more notorious convicts. But the attempt at mobilising state power had unfortunate – and, of course, unintended – consequences. While it succeeded in warding off further efforts at rescue by the Irish Brigade, it also showed Kruger's growing number of critics in the mining industry just how thinly stretched the South African Republic's defensive capacity was. In that moment, an idea of criminal recklessness might have been born. It was, however, an inherently flawed idea, one that failed to appreciate the commitment and depth of the back-up Boer commando system – a mistake the Jameson raiders and British government alike were to regret first in 1895 and again in the war of 1899–1902.[50]

A frontal attack by the Irish Brigade had been averted, although, for reasons we shall examine later, not a single English-medium press report openly acknowledged the continued existence of an ethnicised organisation of that name, and only one – an organ close to government – pointed to the existence of a large criminal organisation. Significantly, it was the Pretoria-based *Press* that suggested Cooper and McKeone were part of a much larger gang. In an aggressive leader it argued that the death sentence was not only appropriate for the highwaymen, but necessary, because '[i]t was, in fact, becoming more apparent that we were on the point of being confronted with an organised campaign against the forces of law and order, and that, unless severe steps were speedily undertaken to crush it, life and property could no longer be even tolerably secure'.[51]

Even newspapers moved to appeal for a reprieve, however, were forced to concede the extent of the crime wave that had engulfed the Republic. The *Star*, which led the political drive to advance the imperial cause in the region, granted that 'highway robbery with violence has been rampant' but pleaded that the men be flogged rather than hanged.[52] And the *Natal Witness* – equally hostile to the idea of the highwaymen being strung up – was under no illusions about the magnitude of the criminal activity that had overwhelmed the country. It compared the situation to that in Australia during 'the early years of gold-mining' when one was 'filled with the horror of bushrangers, of the waylaying of gold escorts, of the sticking up of lonely homesteads and infant townships', and then acknowledged that 'circumstances were very greatly responsible for similar crimes in the Transvaal'.[53]

And, if one read between the lines of the editorials carefully enough, the ethnic identity of the perpetrators, too, could be detected. F.R. Statham, Lancashire-born editor of Kimberley's *Independent*, was willing to grant that there was probably an 'organised gang' at work but put its membership at only a dozen or so. More pertinently, however, he warned the authorities about the dangers of hanging Cooper and McKeone by reminding them of how potent a symbol the 'Manchester Martyrs' had become for those wishing to advance the cause of Irish nationalism. His choice of example of martyrdom could hardly be ascribed to chance; his readers *knew* that 'the gang' he had in mind was Irish, and that the condemned men were 'Irish'.[54]

The Brigade's half-baked attempt to rescue its affiliates might have signified the final external threat to the security of the Pretoria prison but, as the day of Cooper and McKeone's hanging drew closer, the imagination of the public and state alike became slowly inflamed. Kruger and senior members of his administration were distressed to learn that a fair number of ghoulish visitors from Johannesburg had slipped into the capital to view the hanging. Like the forerunners of an eighteenth-century mob at Tyburn, they hoped to witness the thrill of the ultimate horror – seeing a man killed. It was an unpleasant development and the State President and his political allies resolved to avoid any such occurrence in the future.

As the excitement mounted and the would-be onlookers waited, they began to hear things. All the screws from the hinges of Cooper's door, it was rumoured, fell out when the door to his cell was opened one morning. The old iron-file-in-the-pie story was dusted down and trotted out: it was claimed that Mary McKeone had smuggled a revolver into the prison in 'a pudding'. More interesting for those interested in classic bandit tales was the suggestion that the big fellow, Jack McKeone himself, had been spotted in town and was preparing to liberate his brother and one-time companion Cooper.[55]

The appointment of a hangman, the night siege, an orchestrated press campaign and the build-up of rumours all made for unbearable tension, not only for the condemned men, but also for the prison staff and a few long-term Irish Brigade inmates. When a reprieve was eventually granted at the metaphorical eleventh hour, it triggered a challenge among Cooper and McKeone's fellow inmates that bore testimony to their own anxieties, frustrations and – perhaps – even relief. Twenty-five white prisoners, including a significant minority of Irishmen, 'mutinied', refusing to go to work until the quality of prison food improved. The strike resulted in an armed stand-off and culminated in seventeen of the offending prisoners being flogged.[56]

The siege of the Pretoria prison and mutiny was not, however, the only resistance that the Kruger administration encountered from members of the Irish Brigade in the early 1890s. To understand the full extent of the Irish challenge to the state's prisons and property and to the mining industry on the Witwatersrand, we need to turn to another important sphere of Brigade activity: safe-cracking.

# 5

# Safe-Robbers and Blasters of the Witwatersrand

> The coward has too much fear and too little courage,
> the rash man too much courage and too little fear.
>
> – Aristotle, *Nichomachean Ethics*

John Hutchings – 'Captain Moonlight' – may have been first to command the Irish Brigade but his leadership was confined to the months spent in the eastern Transvaal lowveld and Mozambique, between late 1886 and 1888. A man of the countryside, as his rural-resistance *nom de guerre* suggested, Hutchings failed to join other Irish renegades on the highveld when they made their dramatic entrance into Johannesburg in February 1888. Instead, he lingered for some time in the lowveld and, after crossing the Lebombo Mountains, contracted a bout of fever. He was nursed back to health by a Swazi woman whom he eventually married and who bore him several children. His descendants are said to be found, to this day, in the modern Mpumalanga and adjacent Eswatini (Swaziland).[1]

Hutchings' successor in Johannesburg, John McLoughlin, proved to be an extraordinarily adaptable and robust leader of the Brigade for more than half a decade, from 1888 to 1894. It will be recalled that McLoughlin was raised in working-class Manchester, where he served a criminal apprenticeship that was rounded off in Australia at the time when Ned Kelly's name was on everyone's lips. He then went on to join the army in Pietermaritzburg. McLoughlin was at home in both town and country, a man capable of drawing together the skills of disaffected urban and rural Irishmen alike. A by-product of the 'scuttling' subculture that enveloped the streets in which he grew up, McLoughlin went on to embrace fully some of the central tenets of nineteenth-century 'masculinity': he had an admiration for 'hard men' – young males who, largely disregarding of women, had a penchant for heavy drinking and gambling and were bound through oaths of loyalty to common purpose in alienated lifestyles.

As with so many notorious 'criminal heroes', however, these adamantine external features were tempered by more yielding qualities that, viewed in isolation, made McLoughlin seem more appealing, if not charismatic. Aggressive, brave and said to be 'impudent' to the point of madness, his qualities of leadership in various social settings and in quasi-military, safe-lifting and safe-cracking operations were indisputable. Moreover, working in an age and in a place where ethnic alliances and Friendly Societies were prominent – including some, such as the Oddfellows, that had their origins in Manchester – he presided over a loosely bound underworld association that frequently came to the assistance of gang members or collaborators experiencing lean times in periods of economic volatility.[2]

Like McKeone the bank robber, McLoughlin benefited from choosing targets that would have received a silent nod of approval from many small-scale independent entrepreneurs, who were living through a recession that was turning most of the town's diggers, prospectors and small-syndicate owners into working-class fodder for mining houses that would, by 1895, dominate the industry. As a nineteen-year-old back in Ancoats, McLoughlin's first recorded criminal targets were pawnshops – working-class institutions that played banker to the urban poor. Along the Witwatersrand, spilling over into the western Transvaal, McLoughlin's favoured victims included bookmakers, government offices, large retail and wholesale stores, liquor outlets, mining commissioners' offices and the premises of mining companies where free-standing safes were not built into the masonry.

Although known to be *the* leading safe-cracker on the Rand during the early 1890s, McLoughlin was only once arrested, and was never prosecuted successfully on charges of safe-robbing. This spoke not only of careful planning and arrogant opportunism, but of his ability to silence would-be informers or witnesses through his command of a deadly combination of loyalty and terror. Ironically, it was his insistence on oath-bound secrecy that was to prove his undoing in the end. By the same token, although we have a good idea of the breadth and scope of the Irish Brigade's operations while under McLoughlin's command, it is extremely difficult to pin with precision individual safe-robberies on him or his accomplices. Given this, we are often forced to track his progress indirectly, by taking cognisance of what his closest colleagues were doing.

In the months leading up to the recession of 1890, McLoughlin remained closest to Irish deserters – graduates of the College of Banditry – whom he knew and trusted, including Jack McCann, William Kelly and John O'Brien. McCann, like McLoughlin, Kelly and several others in the Brigade, had picked up some rudimentary mining experience while in Barberton. When not working as a barman at Connolly's Sportsman's Arms, McCann used this knowledge to obtain short-term positions on various West Rand mines, where he occasionally worked as a winding-engine driver. His real purpose, however, was to determine how the company was dealing with the gold amalgam that emerged from the refining process, and when, where and how the product and the mine payroll was stored. In this he was often assisted by another Mancunian, Tommy Whelan.

In March 1888, McCann was unsuccessfully prosecuted for the theft of a revolver and, only weeks later, was acquitted on a charge of stealing amalgam. Five months later, in mid-September 1888, with mercury in increasingly short supply in the industry, McCann and compatriots based at Langlaagte stole twelve jars of mercury containing residual amounts of amalgam from storerooms at various mines. Chief Detective Bob Ferguson investigated the case, arrested the accused and then attempted, without success, to persuade one of the gang to accept immunity from prosecution in exchange for turning state's evidence.[3] It was a tactic that most Irishmen loathed, born as they were with an almost innate hatred of the Dublin Metropolitan Police, Royal Ulster Constabulary and informers. Ferguson became a marked man. In this respect – and probably only in this respect – Bob Ferguson stood in relation to Irish criminals on the Rand as famous Irish detective John Mallon did to the revolutionary Fenians in nineteenth-century Dublin.[4]

In mid-October 1888, before the case could be brought to a conclusion, McCann escaped from jail in Johannesburg and, in the company of a man named Burns, made his way to Komatipoort via Steynsdorp. There he abandoned the idea of fleeing the subcontinent and instead stole a horse, riding across the country to Durban. In March 1889 McCann was extradited from Natal and made to stand trial in the ZAR. He was found guilty in July of that year of having stolen amalgam from the Croesus and George Goch Mines, and was sentenced to two years' imprisonment with hard labour. He was released from jail in August 1891.[5]

McCann, McLoughlin's eyes and ears through most of 1892–94, was also his closest confidant and most trusted lieutenant. But it was yet another trusted former Mancunian and deserter, wild William Kelly, who provided the robbers with a basic tool of their trade – dynamite. At one time Kelly served briefly as manager of the small Royal Mining Company, but after he lost the position he returned and stole four cases of dynamite from his former employers. Even before he was tried he attempted to escape from custody but, in January 1892, he was found guilty of theft and sentenced to four years in prison with hard labour.

Thereafter Kelly made increasingly desperate but always unsuccessful attempts at escaping from prison, once deliberately infecting himself with smallpox in order to be moved to the lazaretto. Over a period of thirty-six months, he was confined in chains, administered forty-five lashes and sentenced to many months of additional imprisonment. His enforced absence did not interrupt the gang's activities. It remained well supplied with dynamite throughout 1892–94 – either by Brigade members taking up temporary employment on the mines or via sympathetic white workers.[6]

John O'Brien, despite his penchant for small-time confidence tricks and petty theft from priests, met most of the Brigade membership requirements. Another Mancunian and a Fort Napier deserter with fierce Irish nationalist sympathies, he was courageous to the point of stupidity, impetuous and loyal. When the seriousness of the economic downturn became apparent in the early autumn of 1890, O'Brien was one of the members that McLoughlin, already based in Krugersdorp, told of his plan to extend the Brigade's core operations beyond Johannesburg and reef towns and into the nearby western Transvaal.[7]

In the twenty-four months before that, however, McLoughlin, employing different combinations of manpower that drew on a central reservoir of between twenty and fifty Irish-Catholic Brigaders, slowly perfected a *modus operandi* that was to characterise an extremely successful criminal enterprise. It was a project that, under McLoughlin's leadership, dominated the Witwatersrand underworld from 1888 right up to 1894–95, when it was eventually supplanted by Eastern European, New York-trained Jewish gangsters led by Joseph Silver, men who specialised in crimes against people – including prostitution and white slavery – rather than property. The former, highwaymen and safe-crackers, thrived in the absence of national rail links while the latter, pimps and traffickers, depended largely on its presence.[8]

The basic plan, although varied occasionally to deal with local idiosyncrasies, seldom altered over the half-decade that McLoughlin commanded the Irish safe-lifting detachment. Once a target had been identified, a hand-picked crew that worked best on moonless, heavily overcast or wet nights would wait for the darkness to be punctuated by sounds, man-made or natural, that helped mask the noise of dynamite exploding. The mines themselves were a great help. All along the reef, day and night, the gnashing and grinding of battery-stamp teeth provided background noise banishing stillness to a bygone bucolic age. Festivities with fireworks, including New Year's Eve, provided added cover, as did unpredictable events such as store or house fires occasioning noisy diversions. But nature herself was the safe-cracker's best friend. Fierce highveld summer storms accompanied by almost tropical downpours sent people scurrying for cover amidst vivid lightning strikes and waves of rolling thunder that threatened to burst the vaults of heaven.

Depending on the size of the safe in question, a team of three to twelve men would take up positions around the premises holding the safe and then set to work with military precision. The latches on windows, glass panels above doors or locks would be broken to gain access to the premises. Using ropes and blankets, the stand-alone safe would be manoeuvred onto a waiting handcart, covered by blankets and pushed swiftly to the nearest and noisiest perimeter of the town, its handlers attempting to avoid unnecessary attention or recognition.

Once on site, a few Irishmen who had been exposed to a bit of tinkering or working with heavier metals in Manchester's many foundries regrouped and assumed their new identities as self-taught engineers. Some holes would be drilled into the edges or hinges of the safe's door and charges set using locally manufactured dynamite that was notoriously unstable and unpredictable. Additional muffling would be provided by yet more blankets, and the safe blown open. In the first few months of operation the gang tended to ignore negotiable instruments such as cheques or scrip, concentrating on amalgam, gold or specie, but they soon learnt the value of paper money.

Despite necessary precautions, a significant number of the earliest safe-robberies went wrong as Brigade members struggled to perfect their craft. Some operations had to be abandoned because sloppy reconnaissance work underestimated the size of the safe in question. On other occasions the gang members were interrupted mid-event, or the dynamite was detonated too close to town, attracting unwanted attention.

In mid-1889, a unit of unknown men, estimated to be two- to three-strong, removed safes from three different retailers, including one belonging to Payne & Trull. Later, an even larger safe was taken from the International Wine & Spirit Co. but abandoned on the Pretoria road when it could not be opened. On a Monday morning in December that year, a large, locked safe was discovered standing on the pavement outside Barberton Chambers. The premises of the Permanent Mutual Building and Investment Society in Rissik Street were breached in February 1890, but the safe proved too heavy to remove. In August the same year, Thomas Cahill and John Michell, spotted drinking earlier at the popular Oddfellows' Arms, botched a job undertaken at Dunton Bros. They carried the safe only as far as a vacant stand near the law courts and the sound of the explosion attracted James Watt, a detective with whom they were on suspiciously friendly terms. They were nevertheless arrested.[9]

Although largely self-inflicted, some small part of Cahill and Michell's misfortune could be attributed to the fact that they were stragglers who had become detached from the hard core of the Brigade, which had by then repositioned itself around Krugersdorp to be better able to plunder adjacent country targets and, when necessary, push on to the more economically buoyant diamond fields beyond. Signs of the sharp downturn in Johannesburg, including the drying up of casual employment and a falling-off in trade – things that affected safe-robbers negatively – had been apparent to all for some time. In February 1890 the *Standard & Diggers' News* noted how white miners were boarding mule trains bound for Kimberley in worryingly large numbers. And, at the far end of the highveld highway, the *Diamond Fields' Advertiser* braced itself for more than a mere influx of respectable men seeking work, warning of 'a serious invasion of loafers and other dangerous characters from the Transvaal'.[10]

McLoughlin and his most trusted Manchester-Irish lieutenants led from the front. In late April 1890, they set out from their West Rand stronghold on horseback, traversing the Magaliesberg to explore the Rustenburg, Potchefstroom and Klerksdorp districts. Rustenburg, a small market town set amidst a prosperous agricultural district, served as the regional centre despite the fact that it lacked a commercial bank. Paradoxically, it was the *absence* of a bank that appealed most to the brigands. Wherever banks were scarce, cash accumulated in larger amounts and safes tended to proliferate. Large retail stores, in effect, became small local banks; mail coaches were forced to transport larger than usual quantities of notes and specie; and it took significantly more time to clear the magistrate's office of accumulated state revenue.

Over twenty months, between April 1890 and December 1891, by which time signs of prosperity were slowly returning to the heartland of the Witwatersrand, Krugersdorp, Roodepoort and Rustenburg were subjected to repeated raids by Irish Brigade highwaymen and safe-lifters. In essence the raiders, displaying great flexibility, took a rural sabbatical from the urban recession, once again switching between urban gangsterism and rural brigandage. Seen from this perspective, Irish Brigade members were quite unlike Hobsbawm's classic 'social bandits', who were quintessentially rural creatures. They were far more akin to the American criminal heroes of the same epoch who operated in and around areas where there was no indigenous peasantry to provide fugitives with sympathetic social cover.[11]

This time not even hostile Johannesburg journalists could refrain from expressing grudging admiration. Although the scribes once again did not refer explicitly to the 'Irish Brigade', they knew that the Boers as well as aspiring citizens were being confronted by a single, integrated outfit and wrote tellingly about 'The Gang in the Country'. It was 'generally supposed', they suggested, that 'the burglaring-dynamitards are from Johannesburg' and that they were 'able, business-like and talented members of their profession', men who had achieved 'high rank in the Old Country before trying a new field'.[12]

On Friday 16 May 1890, John McLoughlin and two companions checked into Brink's Hotel in Rustenburg. The following morning they appeared at Messrs Somers & Co.'s store and attempted, without success, to persuade an alert assistant to cash a cheque bearing an indistinct signature. On Sunday evening the trio was seen drinking at a local bar until about eight o'clock. Somewhere between eleven o'clock that night and two o'clock the following morning they broke into the store, tipped the safe onto a blanket, hauled it onto a barrow and then pushed it two miles beyond town, where dynamite was used to blast open its belly.

Three hundred pounds in cash, over a thousand pounds' worth of negotiable instruments and policies, and a few gold and diamond rings spilt out. The proceeds were divided between the brigands. One of them set off for Mafeking and the Bechuanaland border and successfully eluded a constable sent to intercept him. The other two were traced 'to within an hour of Krugersdorp', where the trail was lost, but there was no doubt that McLoughlin was one of them. Indeed, the description of him was so accurate that the report might as well have gone on to name him directly rather than refer to him and his companion merely as 'well known desperate characters'. He was 'below medium height, being about five feet four inches, dark complexioned, with a black moustache', 'stout and well built'. In fact, so perfect a picture of him was it that McLoughlin did not return to Krugersdorp, turning instead towards Potchefstroom. It was a decision that was to change his already remarkable life.[13]

The Brigade remained active throughout what later transpired to be the enforced, albeit brief, absence of its leader. Shortly after the robbery at Somers' store, the post cart between Rustenburg and Pretoria was held up by unknown men, resulting in a loss of £400. On a particularly dark and stormy Saturday night, 9 August 1890, the landdrost's offices in Rustenburg were entered by a party – estimated to have been ten-, perhaps twelve-men strong – using skeleton keys. A huge safe was carried away and then blasted open with dynamite. The intruders collected over £3 800 in cash. It was an enormous – no, a staggering – haul worth approximately half a million pounds in today's currency. The following night, the safe of the Roodepoort Central Hotel, containing £100, was carried off in seven blankets and blown up beneath the din of explosions coming from nearby mining works.[14]

Tolerating such brazen attacks on government assets, in the very constituency where the State President farmed and lived when he was not in attendance at the capital, was unthinkable. Within hours of the break-in at the landdrost's office, the Pretoria administration responded, sending two detectives and six mounted men from its only military unit, the State Artillery, to Rustenburg. The officers made good progress insofar as they were soon on the tail of some of the leading suspects, although they never managed to apprehend the majority of the contingent.

Charles Brown – antecedents unknown, but seemingly unrelated to William Brown the highwayman – along with two other Manchester-Irish, James Sutherland and William Todd, a seasoned Lancastrian offender, were arrested, in different places, within days. The three all had large sums of cash on their persons. Todd, apprehended near Krugersdorp, was carrying his loot in a rolled blanket strapped to his back in the style of an Australian or New Zealand 'swagman', and the coins were found to be bearing the striations characteristic of a dynamite explosion.[15]

The state was determined but largely unsuccessful and very slow in its attempts to find all those responsible for the safe-robbery at the Rustenburg landdrost's offices. In the end it took until October 1891, close on a year, to bring the three accused before the Chief Justice at the Criminal Sessions in Pretoria. Judge J.G. Kotze, already facing a storm of discontent for having sentenced Hugh McKeone and William Cooper to death, sentenced each of the accused to twenty years' imprisonment with hard labour. In addition to that, for reasons that we shall examine in greater depth later, Sutherland was sentenced to an additional five years in prison for contempt of court.[16]

McLoughlin, lying low after the Somers job, missed out on most of the Rustenburg campaign, although, always an avid newspaper reader, he no doubt followed the fate of the Brigade members and the siege of the Pretoria prison with considerable interest. In Potchefstroom, having already consumed his share of the proceeds from the safe-robbery, McLoughlin linked up with John O'Brien and hired a room in a public house. O'Brien, pleading destitution, had long since talked himself into a position as general factotum to Father Trabaud, a priest serving with the Oblates of Mary Immaculate, a Catholic order with Irish and French roots. It may have been the anti-clerical O'Brien who suggested to McLoughlin that he, too, approach Father Trabaud, then overseeing the construction of a convent, for employment. The priest, mindful of the depression on the Witwatersrand, took him on as an 'act of charity', thereby doubling his vulnerability.

Shortly before pay day, in the last week of June 1890, O'Brien and McLoughlin were overcome by the thirst that water could not quench.

O'Brien pointed out some boxes in the priest's room that he knew to contain cash, including one holding about £20 destined for book purchases for a library. But Trabaud returned unexpectedly and, when he saw O'Brien with the box already under his arm, the priest avoided a potentially ugly physical confrontation by suggesting that he leave to buy some beer so that they could talk the matter over. The priest somehow managed to alert the police but, by the time they got there, men and money were gone. Father Trabaud, however, had a good idea of their habits and haunts and, within a few days, both the Mancunians were apprehended.[17]

The Potchefstroom jail, designed to hold cattle rustlers and pig stealers, suddenly found itself unwitting host to two founding members of the Irish Brigade – men hardened in the furnaces of the Industrial Revolution; graduates of the College of Banditry; one, allegedly, a brother of a 'Manchester Martyr' no less, the other an Australian bushranger with experience acquired in Ned Kelly's backyard. O'Brien and McLoughlin were equally unsuited to incarceration in a small provincial jail guarded by sons of the soil. This at a time when it had become *de rigueur* for anyone of Irish descent to attempt to escape from ZAR prisons. It was a situation ripe for death or glory; compulsive gamblers, they found the choice irresistible.

Shortly after midnight on Saturday 26 July 1890, the warders heard the noise of digging coming from cell walls and, they said, the sound of bricks and mortar being removed. Fearing that they might be overwhelmed and uncertain of what to do, the turnkeys took up their rifles, retreated behind the prison walls and positioned themselves opposite the main gate. At around 4.00 a.m. they saw three convicts rushing towards them – O'Brien, McLoughlin and a prisoner named James Reid. The warders shouted a warning but failed to halt the men, who, although unarmed, were trained to storm enemy positions. But the Boers, as the world was to discover, were equal to the challenge. The guards opened fire, picking off the prisoners one by one. O'Brien died on the spot, the first fatality in the mounting crisis in the ZAR's archaic prison system. Reid was seriously wounded; McLoughlin fell with a bullet through his wrist.[18]

The injured men spent several months in the prison sickbay. Reid, considered at first to be the more seriously wounded of the two, made slow but steady progress, but McLoughlin, in considerable pain, languished. The wrist joint of his working hand – the right hand – had been shattered, leaving him with an appendage of desiccating flesh dangling from the lower forearm. It had to come off. In September, he was transferred to the hospital in Johannesburg, where the withered hand, the wrist and part of the lower arm up to a point midway beneath the elbow were amputated. He was nursed back to health by an order of Catholic nuns whose awareness of the events at the convent with Father Trabaud apparently left him extremely uncomfortable in their company. He later did his best to avoid them, refusing to enter the hospital itself to visit his sickly brother, opting instead to meet him in the adjacent gardens.[19]

McLoughlin, who weeks earlier had helped to lift a heavy safe into a barrow and then pushed it several miles, had been reduced to the use of one – untutored – arm and hand. Simple actions, like lighting a fuse or counting banknotes, things best done with two hands, were beyond him. He now struggled to pull his trousers on and off. A man who took pride in appearance and dress, and who revelled in his independence and physical mobility, had been cut down to the sort of war veteran Victorian commuters encountered selling matches outside railway stations. Always a serious drinker, possibly even an alcoholic, he drank even more heavily than before – not only to draw a veil over his newfound misery, but to mask the pains emanating steadily from his missing hand, something attributable to his 'phantom limb'.[20]

The ensuing months were disastrous. While ordinary men and women on the Rand soaked up tales about Jack McKeone as working-class hero or later took an admiring interest in the Brigade's coach- and safe-robbing exploits in the Rustenburg district, McLoughlin's disintegration and uselessness remained palpable. For the better part of a year he was just another drunk in the pub, a recipient of charity and an object of pity. On the last day of March 1891, possibly amidst yet more drinking, he was put in prison for seven days for the destruction of property.

A week or so later, with the recession showing no sign of lifting in ways that could benefit ordinary working people, a few long-standing Irish friends and fellow Brigade members, including two of Jack McCann's amalgam-stealing pals, George Fisher and Tommy Whelan, took the matter in hand. Acting like members of Friendly Societies who dedicated the proceeds of their beanos to ailing, disabled or unemployed brothers, they agreed to pull a large job. They would use some of the loot to provide

McLoughlin with a little cash to tide him over the short term, and the capital that would, over the longer term, allow him to buy a barrow from which he could sell vegetables. It could have been a project that harked back to Manchester days, when McLoughlin may have picked up some experience while working in one of the many markets around Ancoats.[21]

It is impossible to know now who exactly the Irishmen targeted, but April and early May 1891 saw a good number of important robberies. On 7 April, several unnamed men were discharged from the Jumpers Mine; a search of their rooms revealed gold amalgam to the value of £2 000. Less than ten days later, on 16 April, 700 ounces of gold belonging to the Robinson Mine was stolen from the trendsetting Gold Recovery Syndicate employing the newly introduced MacArthur-Forrest process. The latter was a mysterious business but, as we shall see shortly, not wholly unlike another major safe-robbery involving Irish Brigade members. The gold was reported missing, but the police soon received information that led to its speedy recovery. (This resulted in a £120 reward being paid to a certain Brown, who may well have been McLoughlin's old Mancunian friend J.W. Brown, the highwayman.) In the first days of May 1891, two weeks after the Robinson Mine robbery, a battery manager at the City & Suburban Mine was charged with being in unlawful possession of 280 ounces of gold. Shortly after that, when a fire broke out in the inner part of the town on 5 May, two safes were removed and the contents never recovered.[22]

The Brigade's more immediate project – to assist their stricken leader – an initiative born out of fraternal hope and overseen almost entirely by Manchester-Irish very close to McLoughlin and McCann (who was still doing time), ended in near-tragedy. Tommy Whelan, George Fisher and others pulled off the job successfully enough but then handed the loot, including McLoughlin's share, to yet another Mancunian crook, Henry Higgins, for safe keeping and eventual distribution. Higgins, proprietor of a low drinking den boasting a name that hinted at Munster origins – the 'Queenstown Hotel' – drew in the experience of a small-time fence and thief, Morry Hollander.[23]

But nothing happened. Each time Whelan and company asked for the dividend to be declared and the money shared, Higgins and Hollander offered some limp excuse. The delays became so embarrassing and the proposed beneficiary so desperate that eventually Whelan and others simply took up a cash collection among themselves and handed the proceeds to McLoughlin, who, for a brief moment, was indeed reduced to selling vegetables.[24] Frustrated and humiliated, McLoughlin returned frequently to the Queenstown Hotel to drink and find a bed for the night, but he never failed to ask for his share of the robbery.

Matters came to a head over the first weekend of May 1891. After yet another round of heavy drinking, a payout of sorts was made, but when McLoughlin awoke from his makeshift bed in the stable, he found his share missing. Higgins and Hollander claimed later that the money had been removed as part of a practical joke that went wrong. McLoughlin, incensed, stormed into the pub, hauled them aside and demanded the return of his 'swag'. An argument quickly ensued, and Higgins ran out to summon the police, who, upon entering, found Hollander struggling with McLoughlin. But before they could overpower McLoughlin, he whipped out a revolver and fired a shot that grazed Higgins's head. Higgins was less than half an inch from death.[25]

The preliminary examination commenced the following morning and a charge of 'attempted murder' was set down for hearing at the next session of the Circuit Court. While awaiting trial, McLoughlin shared a cell with one J.S. Mead, a forger. Within six weeks, using empty fish tins as tools, they set about excavating a hole through the floor of their cell, eventually reaching the foundation of the prison's outer wall. Poor housekeeping, however, proved their undoing when one morning the warders detected telltale traces of dirt and fresh soil in the cell. In late June, they were each sentenced to three months' imprisonment with hard labour for having attempted to escape. In McLoughlin's case the venture had been a measure of desperation.[26]

The sentence of nine months with hard labour for attempted murder that followed, handed down in August 1891, was a blessing in disguise. By the time he was released, in winter 1892, the worst of the depression had passed and McLoughlin had come to terms with some of his demons. The pains in his missing hand had eased and, having been denied alcohol for several months, he was capable of more measured responses.

He decided that he needed a prosthetic limb, hardly a novelty in a mining town where inferior-quality dynamite had added significantly to workers' woes. The largest pharmacy in town, on the Market Square, had a range of prostheses of the kind developed by American suppliers during the Civil War. For the equivalent of a white worker's monthly wage, McLoughlin acquired a prosthetic hand with movable fingers. The artificial hand – rumoured later to be so sophisticated that it could be used to plunge a stiletto into a man as readily as it could be used to eat a meal – added significantly to the air of mystery surrounding the bandit. It became an indispensable aid until, many years later, on another continent, he got a blacksmith to replace it with a large metal hook. However, the prosthesis also singled him out in ways unhelpful to a professional criminal. His brisk soldierly gait, a by-product of time in the army, became further exaggerated when he took to tucking the hand firmly into his side when walking. And he drew yet more attention to it when he developed the habit of unexpectedly putting the hand on, or taking it off, in public places.[27]

Originally right-handed, McLoughlin had already taken a pot-shot at Higgins with his left that could, quite easily, have killed the publican. He set about further training with a revolver until he became as proficient at shooting with his left hand as he had once been with his right. Abandoned mineshafts, some used by black bandits owing their allegiance to Nongoloza, probably served as shooting ranges, as well as offering excellent places in which to stash loot. And, even though the southern railway crept closer to the Rand with each passing month, McLoughlin taught himself to mount a horse single-handedly so that, if necessary, he could resume a life of rural brigandage. These adaptations were undertaken at the age of thirty-four, an age at which lesser men might have considered abandoning banditry as a career altogether. By mid-1892 and still drinking, McLoughlin was ready to resume active service and a prominent role in the underworld.

In the absence of arrests and almost no successful prosecutions – in itself a measure of Irish Brigade professionalism – it is unwise to see *all* safe-robberies on the Rand at the time as being the work of McLoughlin and his Lancastrian friends. There certainly were other, often amateurish, safe-robbers at work in the town and on the surrounding goldfields, but they tended to work on a smaller scale, avoiding large operations requiring a half-dozen or more men. That said, it seems reasonable to assume that McLoughlin, who had lost a hand, and other veterans who had lived through the Rustenburg campaign were probably more poorly disposed towards the Kruger state after 1891 than they had been before that year. If that is accepted, then there are a few other robberies that occurred in the latter half of 1892 worth noting.

The Johannesburg Turf Club, a place of enduring interest for the Manchester-Irish, was visited twice, the safe removed and blown open on each occasion, and the contents looted. The amounts stolen were unrecorded but they are likely to have been substantial. In mid-June, the mining commissioner's office in Boksburg on the East Rand was entered and, when removal of the heavy safe proved too difficult, an attempt was made to burn down the place. It was a target and an aspiration in keeping with the wishes of disaffected diggers and prospectors. In late August of the same year, the government offices in Florida, a township bordering Krugersdorp, were entered, the safe's door dynamited on the premises and £1 000, along with other lesser valuables, taken. It was yet another very large haul and, once again, the target was unlikely to have induced widespread tears in the ranks of white workers.[28]

In many of these cases there were two factors at work in favour of the raiders. First, there was often an unusual build-up in cash on the premises at certain moments when it was difficult, if not impossible, to deposit money in commercial banks. The Turf Club, which held its meetings over weekends and was located on the outskirts of town, presented an obvious target, as did government offices that operated beyond banking hours from less commercial sites. Second, a significant number of those who relied on large safes were often either too stingy or too smug to build safes into the buildings' masonry. Stand-alone safes, unsecured by bricks and mortar, no matter how large, remained vulnerable to lifting by determined brigands.

William Grey Rattray, who operated the totalisator at the Turf Club, knew all about the problem. Said to be a 'speculator' at a time when the term was often used to cover legal as well as illegal dealings, Rattray was a well-known member of both the Johannesburg and the Kimberley communities, where, aside from his interest in horses, he dealt in jewellery and scrip. His business may, however, also have extended to dealing in stolen amalgam, diamonds and share certificates. Whatever the truth of the matter, Rattray's activities were a predictable source of interest to members of the Irish Brigade, who, in addition to being avid punters, had interests of their own when it came to valuables.

After the last day of the summer race meetings on Saturday 31 December 1892, Rattray and his brother returned to their offices in town and placed the day's taking into the safe. By the time they left the premises, it contained cash as well as gold, rings and diamonds worth, in total, more than £4 000. It was, and for many people would still constitute, a small fortune.

That night, with the noisy New Year celebrations providing excellent cover, McLoughlin and a hand-picked detail took up positions around the premises. The offices were entered via a latched window, and a safe weighing 600 pounds (it took ten men to haul it back onto the premises) was positioned on a 'truck' and dragged to nearby Wemmer Pan, where dynamite was used to split the door. Everything of value was removed.

Within hours Bob Ferguson arrested five men and was reportedly searching for eight or nine others. In retrospect, the presence of so many Mancunians was a sign that membership of the Brigade was changing, and that an ageing leadership was reaching out to recruit younger, less experienced men, some of whom may not have been Irish. Unusually, McLoughlin himself landed in the police net along with his boyhood friend J.W. Brown. The rest consisted of Hart Bucklow (an unknown alias or a newcomer), Thomas Stewart (better known as 'Deaf Peter' Jones, the town's most notorious pickpocket) and Mike Hart, one of Chief Detective Ferguson's long-standing gambling buddies. 'The arrest of Hart,' it was rightly noted in the local press, 'caused considerable surprise.'[29]

Surprises were the order of the day. When the five accused appeared for preliminary examination on 9 January – six days after their arrest – the Public Prosecutor asked for the release of Bucklow and Hart for reasons that were not recorded. The request was granted, the examination scheduled for hearing in the Police Court a week later and collective bail set at £1 000. When the three remaining accused next appeared, on 16 January, they were suddenly represented by counsel, who asked for the bail to be lowered. The magistrate refused to do so but then recused himself on the grounds that, having signed the original warrants for their arrest, he was not eligible to hear the case. It mattered little, since most of the developments in the case were by then taking place well beyond the view of a bemused public.

Next, the Public Prosecutor had second thoughts. When the examination resumed, on 19 January, he asked for McLoughlin to be released for want of evidence, leaving just two to face the music. But the music was fast fading. 'Deaf Peter' – who probably would not have heard it anyway – was the next to go and, just three days later, the curtain finally came down when 'John Brown, the last of the accused to be discharged, had the diamonds found in his possession returned to Mr. Rattray'.[30]

It was, and still is, all most peculiar. A major safe-robbery, one among scores of others over a period of several years, simply disappeared from official view. What is to be made of this is difficult to know. Perhaps all that can be concluded is utterly banal – that, once organised crime has successfully inserted itself into the fabric of a society, it can draw the police, perpetrators, victims and members of the judiciary together in ways that mitigate against notions of accountability and public interest. Be that as it may, the Rattray case appears not to have dented the confidence of the Irish Brigade or its leader unduly.

It was at about this time – early 1893 – that McLoughlin renewed his acquaintance with twenty-five-year-old George Stevenson from Stoke-on-Trent in Staffordshire. Ten years younger than him, 'Stevo' was another troubled by-product of the Industrial Revolution, a lad from the potteries whose background any Mancunian would have understood. The son of an agricultural labourer who had married a much younger woman, Stevenson may have been an illegitimate child who, before he was four, was sent to be brought up by relatives in town. It did not work out. The boy kept poor company and, by age ten, had been committed to the Industrial School at Werrington, where he was to remain until 1885, when, at the age of seventeen, he was sent to labour in the clay pits under his father's supervision. He fled the pits to enlist with the 64th Regiment, the First North Staffordshires, and, by 1887, found himself in Natal's College of Banditry, from which he soon deserted.[31]

Boisterous, risk-taking and seemingly vigorously heterosexual amidst all the usual Victorian focus on manly activities and sport, Stevenson became the alter ego of the ageing, marginally more measured McLoughlin, who had always manifested a strong preference for male company and friendship. Stevenson's earliest Johannesburg exploits showed great promise; he was that rare being, an Englishman worthy of Irish support. In late 1889 – as befitted an aspiring highwayman – he had stolen a horse but had been caught, sentenced to six months' imprisonment and bound in chains. He found prison life unbearable, escaped and remained on the run for nearly two years. By then he was also wanted for the theft of a watch and chain and, foolishly, managed to get himself arrested for creating a disturbance and assaulting a policeman. By the time he linked up with McLoughlin in early 1893, Stevo was ready for the step up into more professional organised crime.[32]

He and McLoughlin were soon frequenting all the normal haunts of hard-drinking, gambling and whoring gangsters. They spent their days in pubs with Irish connections, at the horse races and ratting contests, or in shops poring over lottery tickets. Over weekend evenings they attended 'dances' in seedy canteens or hotels where unattached males sought out young 'coloured' prostitutes who had abandoned the increasingly well-policed diamond fields for the less controlled Witwatersrand. It was this latter dimension to twenty-five-year-old Stevenson's life – an increasingly intimate association with Sarah Fredericks, a part-time prostitute with links to the police – that came to shape, and later dominate, his relationship with McLoughlin and the Brigade.[33]

McLoughlin, who had known Fredericks for several months, introduced her to Stevenson. By then, however, Fredericks, who had a habit of falling in love with some of her clients, had for some weeks been living with a burly mason named Harry Lobb, yet another of McLoughlin's male admirers. Fredericks' favours were soon being contested. Matters came to a head when Lobb and Stevenson became embroiled in an argument over her, and a drunken rough-and-tumble ensued outside a pub. The longer-term solution to the conflict, drawn directly from English working-class culture, was obvious. Ever since the world-title fight between Bendoff and Cooper in Johannesburg a few months earlier, the town's testosterone-driven males had been caught up in a boxing frenzy. 'A fight to the finish with skin gloves', held at a private venue so as to avoid the attention of the disapproving police, was won by Stevenson, who was backed only by McLoughlin. After Stevo's boxing triumph, he and McLoughlin moved into a set of rooms, which they shared with Sarah Fredericks and another 'coloured' prostitute, Ali ('Lizzie') Ahmed.[34]

These arrangements worked tolerably well through most of the cold winter months of 1893, but tensions emerged when Stevenson and Fredericks became increasingly emotionally intimate. McLoughlin, who appears to have been infatuated with the young Englishman, saw less of his Manchester-Irish cohort, who were, in any case, cautious after the Rattray debacle. Jack McCann, too, sensed that his friend was moving closer to Stevenson. McLoughlin, for his part, was hostile towards and suspicious of Fredericks, whose long-standing informal relations with the police may have been less sinister than he thought. Fredericks resented McLoughlin's closeness to her latest conquest and that, in turn, spilt over into tensions between her and Lizzie Ahmed. The potential for conflict escalated exponentially.

Perhaps inevitably, messy developments on the domestic front led to ugly professional consequences. Without easy access to his Mancunian mate, Tommy Whelan, as a source of information about gold amalgam, or William Kelly, the dynamite supplier, who was still behind bars, McLoughlin had to find them a temporary source of income as they undertook more of their own longer-term reconnaissance work. With most semi-skilled positions on Witwatersrand mines dominated by pockets of ethnicised workers drawn from the wider anglophone-British world, McLoughlin fell back on his own Celtic network. Under the management of C.R. O'Flaherty, the Langlaagte Mine was, throughout the 1890s, known as an Irish-friendly employer – a reputation that extended in the latter half of the decade to its hosting at least one Fenian of advanced-nationalist persuasion. By April 1893, with the economy at last showing signs of sustained improvement, McLoughlin had managed to find them positions as 'riveters' on the mine despite the fact that he, once an 'Irish' navvy on the Komatipoort-Lourenço Marques line, had only one arm.[35]

In the absence of official records of arrests, prosecutions or suspects, it is impossible to know with certainty which, if any, of the safe-robberies that followed could be attributed to McLoughlin. In May 1893, the safe at the nearby Champ D'Or Mine – a property close to Jack McCann's heart – was removed and dynamited but yielded a disappointing £21 and a few useless documents. Safe-lifting without first-class reconnaissance work became just another lottery, another form of Irish gambling. It was an error that the Brigade, when fully functional, avoided. In July, there was a more successful operation of the sort that could have put McCann's excellent house-breaking skills to good use. The room of the manager at the New Black Reef Mine was entered, the keys to the safe taken and

700 ounces of amalgam as well as £200 in cash removed. And, in September, a box containing scrip and other documents of significant value was stolen from the May Deep Level Mine. If McLoughlin and Stevenson were indeed involved in one or more of the heists, it would have provided Stevo with a considerable amount of information and leverage over his Irish partner.[36]

For reasons that can only be speculated upon, no successful safe-blastings of the type associated with the Irish Brigade were reported in the Johannesburg press during the final quarter of 1893 or the first few weeks of the new year. It would seem that Christmas came and went without incident. But, by late January 1894, with cash in shorter supply after the festive season, tensions ran higher than usual in the small McLoughlin-Stevenson camp. Lizzie Ahmed complained to McLoughlin about uncalled-for remarks directed at her by Fredericks and when he, in turn, berated Stevenson, there was a breakdown in the relationship between the men. It was placed back on a rickety footing only when a part-time butcher and shadowy underworld figure, Tommy Howard, acted as intermediary.[37]

With a rapprochement barely in place, McLoughlin put together a team of four for a robbery at an undisclosed venue in Pretoria. On 30 January 1894, he, Stevenson, Howard and that jack of all trades with a penchant for arson, Charlie Harding, set out for the capital via the recently completed rail link. But the iron road to Pretoria led to disaster just as surely as had the dust track to Potchefstroom only a few years earlier. Both cities linked death and spontaneity, the difference being that whereas the road to one had been short and led almost directly to the death of John O'Brien, the other wound its way with infinite patience through most of the southern hemisphere and culminated – with fifteen years between them – in the deaths of two men.

The short expedition north, bearing a superficial similarity to the Brigade's earlier Rustenburg campaign, was a failure almost from the moment of conception. Members of a small Anglo-Irish unit never trusted one another fully and, when the party reached Pretoria, it ran into unknown difficulties that caused it to abandon the original objective. Lacking sufficient funds to cover a retreat to Johannesburg, the commanding officer, McLoughlin, was forced to innovate, increasing risk. The railway station, like the offices of mining commissioners, was a state-owned target that might have held an unsecured safe holding cash accumulated from ticket sales. While one of them stood guard, three others forced the door and removed a small safe, which, when opened and the contents shared, left them with barely £13 each. They hired a horse-drawn cab but, unwilling to stump up the amount quoted by the driver for the return journey, disembarked instead at the first station on the outskirts of the capital to catch the train back to Johannesburg.

Still squabbling about overhead expenses, they boarded the train at Irene without paying, which attracted the attention of the conductor, H.E. Gill. Gill, who hailed from Krugersdorp, had heard about the robbery at the station and recognised McLoughlin, a well-known figure on the West Rand. Sensing that they were being watched, Stevenson got off at the first stop and walked back to Johannesburg. On the train itself things spun out of control when Gill suddenly sealed the coach in which the three remaining robbers were travelling. McLoughlin, undaunted, waited for the train to slow down. Near the serendipitously named Jumpers Mine, he leapt from the window, dusted himself off and walked the better part of twenty miles or more to McCann's rooms at Luipaardsvlei.[38]

Howard and Harding were arrested when the train entered Park Station, Stevenson shortly thereafter. The epidemic of unsolved safe-lifting and blasting cases all along the reef dating back half a decade, coupled with the mysterious outcome in the Rattray case, prompted a convergence of interests emanating from very different quarters. The Chief Detective, never keen on going head to head with the Irish Brigade, and more especially its one-armed leader, saw in the Pretoria job a chance of bringing McLoughlin to book without too much personal risk. Ferguson sensed that the young Englishman, Stevenson, was the weakest link among the suspects and, as with McCann years earlier, sought to 'turn' him.

Stevenson, in truth, was ready for turning. Increasingly enamoured with the soft-hearted Fredericks – and she with him – the young man was distressed by the thought of another lengthy period in prison. Fredericks, a low-level informer on reasonable terms with the local police, knew that her lover's best bet was to cooperate with the Rand detectives. Stevenson, however, remained extremely wary of his oath-taking Irish co-conspirators.

For ten days McLoughlin monitored developments from afar, from a lair somewhere around Krugersdorp. Stevenson had sufficient information to implicate him not only in the Pretoria robbery but in several others too. If Stevo *did* decide to help Ferguson, then it would be in his interest to have McLoughlin put away for as long as possible. When the fugitive learnt that Stevenson had agreed to turn state's evidence, he knew that his lengthy stay on the Rand was drawing to a conclusion. At the age of thirty-six, after ten years of brigandage on two southern continents, he had been slowly coming to terms with a more settled existence and with living with a woman for the first time. But there was nothing for it. He and Jack McCann acquired some horses and set out across the veld for Mafeking. From there, they travelled upcountry to one of the least settled frontiers in the region, Matabeleland.

In April 1894, the station case was heard before the Criminal Sessions in Pretoria. Stevenson provided the prosecution with all the evidence it needed. Tommy Howard was sent down for five years with hard labour, but Charlie Harding got off on a technicality. Stevenson left the court a physically free man, but one sentenced to a lifetime of psychological imprisonment.

Irish hatred of paid informers dated back to the turbulent post-Famine era of politics. In late 1858 and early 1859, Karl Marx had pointed out how the actions of the Lord Lieutenant in Dublin had placed 'Ireland, so to say, in a state of siege' by 'turning, through the means of £100 and £50 rewards, the trade of the spy, the informer, the perjurer and the *agent provocateur* into the most profitable trade in Green Erin'.[39] It was a dismal development that was to have fatal consequences not only in Ireland but, on more than one occasion, in southern Africa as well.[40]

Ferguson *knew* how the Irish dealt with informers. When James Carey, an 'Invincible' – a radical Fenian offshoot – gave evidence against those who had assassinated British officials in Phoenix Park, Dublin, in 1882, it was only a matter of months before he was executed. A Donegal man, Patrick O'Donnell, shot Carey while he was aboard the *Melrose Castle* off Port Elizabeth on his way to establishing a new home for himself in Natal under an assumed identity.[41] The Irish Brigade was never an overtly 'political' organisation, but there was no mistaking the republican sympathies of many of its members, or their dislike of most Englishmen. The police gave Stevenson permission to carry a revolver and, for some weeks after the trial, he and Fredericks tucked themselves away in a small room in Pretoria, living off her meagre earnings as a laundress. A few months later they returned to Johannesburg, where Stevenson resumed a career of small-time crime. But he was *persona non grata*, loathed by the Irish and, as it was later claimed by McLoughlin, 'despised by all' in the underworld.

McLoughlin, whose apprenticeship as Australian bushranger came shortly after the Kelly gang itself had executed a police informer, was outraged by Stevenson's treachery and upset by Howard's lengthy sentence. He felt responsible for Howard insofar as it had been he, McLoughlin, who had introduced Stevenson to the group. Ned Kelly's transformation into folk hero, a man in pursuit of fairness in an unjust world, could not have failed to register in McLoughlin's mind, and may have struck an even deeper, far more personal chord. His first conviction, for a break-in at a Manchester pawnshop in 1879, had come as a result of a gang member turning against him and others to give evidence for the Crown. And, if Ned Kelly's iconic status had eluded him, there was another, recent example of 'Irish' nobility of spirit to draw on. Jack McKeone, wronged by a mining commissioner, had won the sympathy of every right-minded working man when he had robbed the bank at Krugersdorp and turned on his police persecutors. Somewhere amidst these swirling influences McLoughlin may have glimpsed the spectre of social justice and public approval beckoning.

It may have gone better for McLoughlin had he responded instantly to that inner call to kill. Judges understood, even if they did not approve of, an element of spontaneity in revenge killings. And, were the Irish not widely thought of as a temperamental people given to mindless violence? But he was no longer as young and impetuous as he had been in his Eureka City days. Age, and the time that had elapsed between the station robbery, the trial, and any subsequent action, would only compound his problems should he decide to murder Stevenson. So he turned his back on the demons and, with McCann at his side, instead pushed towards Bulawayo. Almost at once, a safe and its contents went missing and, a few weeks later, unknown highwaymen were reported to be active on the outskirts of the mining town.[42] McLoughlin felt vulnerable to the possibility of extradition from Matabeleland and so, like Jack McKeone before him, looked around for an autonomous African state in which he might seek refuge and perhaps sell his military skills.

The north-eastern part of the South African Republic, covering an area significantly larger than many a European Low Country, was home to several powerful black chieftaincies all bent on resisting the increasing demands of a state that sought to fold cheap African labour into the burgeoning agricultural and mining sectors of its economy. The 1890s were marked by escalating tensions followed by outright resistance from Mojaji (1890–94), Malaboch's Hanwana (1893–94), Makgoba (1895) and then Makhato's Venda (1898). McLoughlin, constantly on the move and not wanting to be snared in any ongoing military campaigns, avoided the kingdoms of Malaboch and Mojaji, looking instead towards the Bavenda.

Makhato, realising that it was a matter of time before he, too, was at war with republican forces, had – or so it was rumoured – already found himself an arms supplier and military instructor. A former naval officer, Keith dressed in flamboyant chamois-leather outfits rounded off with a broad-brimmed hat and jackboots, and commanded half a dozen other deserters. He was an obvious port of entry into cautious Venda society.[43]

McLoughlin's exact location during this period of his strange life is impossible to determine, but it is significant that, when the police searched for him more actively only months later, their attention was focused on the Venda and the Zoutpansberg. One contemporary who had more reason than most for charting McLoughlin's exploits at the time was Louis Cohen. The son of a Cockney Jew and an Irish mother, Cohen was an occasional contributor to the *Standard & Diggers' News* and in this capacity he would collect information on underworld characters, intent on working them into reminiscences about life in Kimberley and Johannesburg. Here again, the detail might be open to dispute, but the drift of Cohen's observation seems to be right on the mark: that, during the time he spent in the northern Transvaal, John McLoughlin was living with 'Kaffirs, freebooters and horse-thieves'.[44]

For most of 1894 McLoughlin used his base among the Venda as a platform from which to stage low-level raids into, or undertake short-term stays in, the tiny Rhodesian gold-mining townships developing to the south and east of Bulawayo. It was an existence on the road that spoke well of his stamina and versatility as an ageing brigand but offered only a pale imitation of the life once led by members of the Irish Brigade in Barberton or Lourenço Marques, not to mention Johannesburg. And, no matter how much drinking, carousing or moving about he and McCann indulged in, he never quite shook off those demons reminding him that his rightful inheritance – the chance of leading a reasonably comfortable life as an urban safe-lifter – had been snatched from him by men like Gill, Higgins, Hollander and Stevenson.

Fleeing, McLoughlin reasoned, had caused him to lose face and caste; he would never be able to reinsert himself into the Witwatersrand underworld. A man of honour, an Irishman – let alone a British officer – would kill anyone who had succeeded in infatuating him only to go on to betray and humiliate him. The one concession he was willing to make – and it was a measure of the affection he had once had for Stevenson – was that Stevo would not have thrown him to the wolves had it not been for another Irishman-turned-policeman, Bob Ferguson. The question no longer concerned whether or not he would return to the south, but under what circumstances, when and to what end. They were serious matters that had to be settled by real men, among real men.

This view reflected part of a pattern of thinking that was widespread in the nineteenth century, including among swathes of the British Empire and the United States. Richard White, the American historian who explored the history of Jesse James and others, noted: 'The portrait of the outlaw as a strong man righting his own wrongs and taking his own revenge had a deep appeal to a society concerned with the place of masculinity and masculine virtues in a newly industrialized and seemingly effete order.'[45]

But was it all just so much male business? Was it really *only* about notions of fidelity and honour embedded in the cult of masculinity dominating the times? Was there not more to it? The Basotho chief, Jonathan Molapo, had betrayed Jack McKeone to the police at Ladybrand for love of a woman when he sensed that her brother was intent on spiriting her away, back into colonial society. Stevenson's treachery was the work of a policeman, it was true, but had Ferguson's path, too, not been cleared for him by a woman? Was Sarah Fredericks, a 'coloured' woman – who McLoughlin was later alleged to have described as 'that little prostitute' – not just as culpable as Bob Ferguson? All these questions, locked into a matrix of ethnicity, gender, poverty, life, love and death, were about to be answered.

In the closing weeks of 1894, McLoughlin undertook a final raid into southern Matabeleland to raise funds for what, in retrospect, might be seen as an odyssey of ritual purification, an attempt to reverse the process of pollution unleashed by the misfortunes of his earlier, ill-fated journey north. He turned and crossed the border back into the Republic, sold his horse and, at Pietersburg, boarded a stagecoach on the regular service south. Like a pilgrim making his way to Rome in the hope of obtaining absolution, he stopped off at shrines along the way to obtain the forgiveness of those he might have wronged and receive their blessing for the quest ahead. In the second week of December, artificial hand and military gait unmistakeable, he was spotted at the Pretoria races, spending money freely. Tommy Howard, locked up in the state prison, was beyond his reach, but Charlie Harding, soon contacted, communicated with Howard easily enough. News of 'One-Armed Jack' McLoughlin's sudden materialisation – information that somehow eluded Ferguson and the rest of the police force – was transmitted instantly to Johannesburg via the usual spidery underworld networks.

There was nothing ghost-like about the man. By early January 1895, he and McCann were back in their old haunts in Johannesburg doing some drinking, a bit of gambling and making casual enquiries about the whereabouts of old friends and acquaintances, including Tommy Whelan. As in days of yore, they appeared to be collecting information about amalgam, payrolls, refineries and safes as a prelude to putting together a group of Irish 'reliables' for a job on one of the West Rand's larger mines. McLoughlin, seemingly intent on recreating the world as he knew it before the Pretoria Station robbery, even moved back in briefly with his old girlfriend, Lizzie Ahmed.

Sensing that there was more afoot than simply another round of safe-robberies, Ahmed sought out Sarah Fredericks and told her that Ole Mack was back in town and asking around about her and Stevo. Ahmed's actions contributed to the growing sense of foreboding among the ranks of McLoughlin's enemies. For the moment, however, McLoughlin was wrestling with another half-English, half-Irish demon. Although neither an officer nor a gentleman – men who epitomised the highest values to which Victorian males could aspire – McLoughlin shared some of their notions of honour, including a hatred of cowardice. He had no desire to lie in wait for Ferguson or Stevenson, to sneak up on them from behind. Like any good soldier, he wanted to see the whites of their eyes when he rounded on them and, if that gave them the opportunity to defend themselves against a one-armed man, then so much the better; he *wanted* them to know he was going to kill them and that they should ready themselves for what was coming.

But there was a hidden asymmetry to his reasoning. Ferguson, a policeman by choice, bore responsibility for his own well-being but could, if necessary, choose to become aggressive, with or without the help of his officers. Stevenson, on the other hand, caught up in a caring – nay, a loving – relationship, was responsible for *two* people and would assume a defensive posture. As soon as Ahmed told the couple that McLoughlin was out looking for Stevo, they changed their accommodation. Thereafter they moved frequently, letting only trusted friends and relatives know where they were staying. But downtown Johannesburg was too small to conceal them effectively. McLoughlin, bearing the mark of Cain and well known to the police, walked the streets openly and soon discovered the quarter where the two lovers were living. He remained focused, allowing a few days more to slip by, waiting for the month's end so as not to compromise his line of retreat. His was a plan on a global scale, one befitting the age of empire and of a Mancunian raised to scan the world's horizons for the most distant markets.

On Saturday morning, 26 January 1895, Fredericks said goodbye to Stevenson in a room behind the Red Lion Beer Hall, off Commissioner Street, and set off to work as a char in the cottages in nearby Kerk Street, which were run by 'coloured' prostitutes. But it had been a good Friday night and Sarah O'Reilly, a woman with her own links to the Irish underworld, was not ready for Fredericks, so she went instead to scrub Rosie Pietersen's kitchen. She returned only much later to O'Reilly's, the kitchen cleaning having taken the entire morning.

In nearby Sauer Street, McLoughlin's day started late. Round about midday he popped into the Silver King Bar for a drink, where he either happened to bump into or had a pre-arranged meeting with Stevenson's one-time rival for Sarah Fredericks' favours, Harry Lobb. Both men had reasons for disliking the couple – McLoughlin because Stevenson had betrayed the safe-lifters to the police and Fredericks had robbed him of Stevenson's undivided companionship; Lobb because Fredericks had abandoned him for Stevenson. Both men had, in effect, lost lovers – one to a man and the other to a woman. The overlapping triangles, differentiated only imperfectly as a result of gender, reinforced one another. Lobb confirmed that Stevenson was 'in town', close by and living with Fredericks.

If McLoughlin was dynamite, Lobb was a detonator. The priming continued over lunch at the fashionable Café Weiner. Suitably fortified, McLoughlin eventually left for the cottages in Kerk Street to warn Fredericks of a sunset showdown with Stevenson. For a time, it seemed as if the gods would deny him the chance to set up something resembling an old-fashioned duel with pistols: he could not find Fredericks. Almost comically, they twice bypassed each other. When McLoughlin put in an appearance at Rosie Pietersen's, she was across at O'Reilly's, and by the time she got back to Pietersen's he had already moved back across to O'Reilly's.

Frustrated, McLoughlin told Pietersen that, should she happen to come across Fredericks before him, she should tell her 'to go home and tell Stevo that he will be a dead man tonight'.[46] He returned to O'Reilly's, where he was sitting sharing a bottle of stout with the Madame when Fredericks entered the cottage for the second time that day. McLoughlin accused her of being a police informer, a charge she chose not to deny. He told her, in the most vulgar language imaginable, what he thought of Stevenson and again vowed to get even, failing only to specify where and when the fatal encounter would take place. Fredericks, suitably alarmed, retreated to Pietersen's to collect her wages, only to be informed of the exact day, time and, possibly, place of her lover's execution.

It was late afternoon by the time Fredericks got back to the Red Lion. She relayed to Stevenson the recent events of her day, telling him that she had been tracked, that McLoughlin knew where they were staying and that he had told Pietersen that he – Stevenson – would die that night. McLoughlin, who had been drinking for most of the day, went from O'Reilly's to the Mancunian hangout at the Oddfellows' Arms, where he downed yet more beer while waiting for the sun to set. While there, so it was first claimed and then hurriedly denied, he told companions that he intended killing George Stevenson, Henry Higgins, H.E. Gill and Robert Ferguson. It was a comprehensive, entirely plausible list of enemies with three of the four intended victims 'Irish' and Stevenson English.[47]

Back at the Red Lion Beer Hall, Stevenson attempted to assuage Fredericks' fears, agreeing that they should wait for her sister to call, as arranged, before moving across to her aunt's for the night; perhaps even for the weekend. It would be their fifth move in as many weeks, but he was taking no chances. Stevenson pulled out his police-issue revolver, loaded it and slipped it into his pocket. Then, seeking to busy himself as the last rays of the day's summer sun disappeared, he used Fredericks' sewing machine to fashion a makeshift holster from a cotton tobacco pouch. That done, Stevenson slumped into a chair in the corner of the room. Staring up at the small curtained square concealing the glass-panelled door to their room, he prepared for whomever and whatever was to come.[48]

The light was neither of this world nor of the next when there was a rap on the door that led off a passage. Expecting her sister, Fredericks chirped, 'Who's there?' but there was no response. The modesty curtain made it difficult to identify who was at the door. There was a second, single rap followed by a pause, and then more insistent knocking. Stevenson got up and unbolted the door. It was too late. As it levered open someone shouted, 'It's you, you fucker!'

'Look out, it's Jack McLoughlin,' Fredericks yelled.

The terror of the town filled the doorway, the Colt in his left hand. From close range he fired a bullet into Stevenson's chest. His victim fell backwards onto the bed, shouting out that he had been shot. Fredericks screamed, mortified by the sight of her lover lying wounded on their bed. Turning on her, McLoughlin growled, 'Shut up, you cow, or you will get one too.' When her screaming persisted, he fired a second shot in her direction. It missed.[49]

Remarkably composed, McLoughlin turned on his heel and strode towards the exit. In the passageway, revolver in hand, he encountered some men who had been attracted by the commotion. 'All right boys, I will not harm you,' he reassured them before making his way through the beer hall and out onto the street, all the while followed by a small but growing posse of customers shouting, 'Stop him!'[50] McLoughlin seemed to be heading towards the Bricklayer's Arms, once the 'Prince Bismarck' but, by then, run by another *bête noire*, Henry Higgins. The pursuing mob forced him to abandon that plan. Walking briskly, he pushed on south, towards Main Street. Near the Princess Bar, he fired a third shot to warn off men closing in on him. It sent a bullet, so the terrified proprietor Max Goldberg claimed, that grazed his head.[51]

In Main Street, striding towards the closest mine property, McLoughlin spotted a few 'coloured' Muslims – 'Cape Malays' – standing on a corner chatting, having just left the mosque. Composed of cab drivers, shopkeepers and tailors he knew, he cautioned them, 'If you come near me I will shoot you.' Hearing the howl of the approaching mob, Hadji Mohammed Yussuf shifted the weight from his one foot to the other and McLoughlin, mistaking it for a lunge towards him, put a bullet in his head. The pilgrim, just back from Mecca, fell dead. McLoughlin ran off, followed by one of Yussuf's party, but, on reaching the fence of the Robinson Mine, again chose not to fire at the one remaining pursuer, warning him instead, 'Stand back.' He then disappeared into the property and its abandoned shafts.[52]

Back at the Red Lion, Stevenson, bleeding profusely, had hauled himself out through a blood-smeared window and collapsed in an alley. From there he had been carried to another room and placed on a bed to await the arrival of a doctor and the police. He knew he was dying, as did those who attended him. While the doctor attempted to make him comfortable, the state's newly appointed Acting Chief Detective Andrew Trimble, an Irishman, assisted by the *veldkornet*, appeared to take a 'dying deposition' in which Stevenson identified his assailant and the motive for the attack. Of Ferguson, lead detective in the Pretoria Station robbery case, the man who had persuaded Stevenson to turn state's evidence and the officer in charge of the Rand Detective Department, there was no sign. Stevenson was taken to the hospital, where, with his lover in attendance, he died in the early hours of the morning. His body lay in her room and, in keeping with Islamic practice, he and Hadji were laid to rest the following day.

In the meantime McLoughlin, in whose mind notions of courage, honour and masculinity floated about in uncertain swirling patterns, embarked on the next stage of his exit strategy. With mounted police deployed along the town's outskirts, he abandoned his redoubt on the Robinson property and, taking his cue from Hermes the Trickster, doubled back, making his way directly into the town centre. It was the act of a bandit-hero or a psychopath, of a man intent on coaxing out Bob Ferguson if not to kill him then to excise any residual vestige of his manhood.

It was Saturday night. The weekend after month end and pay day. The place was alive with people and wild stories circulated about a sensational downtown shooting. But one short, stout man with an artificial limb tucked into his ribs bestrode lower Commissioner Street like a colossus, unperturbed, unchallenged by mere mortals. It was Bret Harte all over; an outlaw dressed in a broad-brimmed hat casually making his way down a town's dusty main street with all of humanity averting its eyes.

He found McCann and Lobb near the Central Hotel just before 11.00 p.m. and, with much to talk about, they entered Rosenthal's restaurant for a celebratory drink and meal.[53] No effort was made at hiding. Indeed, it was as if McLoughlin *wished* to be seen, as if he hoped that someone would send for Ferguson or the police. A rumour did the rounds that he had vowed to shoot any man who attempted to arrest him. One person who *did* get a glimpse of him was Higgins's sidekick, Morry Hollander, who entered the restaurant, caught sight of his adversary and fled.[54] By the time the three left Rosenthal's an hour or so later, Ferguson's reputation as man, Irishman and detective lay bleeding in the gutters of Commissioner Street.

The Monday press, recovering from weekend sloth, bent double beneath the weight of heavily inked headlines devoted to the shootings: 'A Sensational Saturday Night', 'Shocking Double Murder', 'The Arresting Asiatic', 'Mr. Goldberg's Narrow Escape' and, of course, 'The Man with One Arm'. McLoughlin, following the stories from within walking distance, noted that early accounts failed to report his first name accurately or spell his surname correctly. Even narcissism, however, has a context. Beyond self-interest, he may have been probing the press for underlying signs of approval or an understanding of the codes of manly behaviour that informed Stevenson's murder. It was an exercise that was not entirely fruitless.[55]

'The Chum that Split' and 'Terrible Revenge' linked loyalty and death in ways Victorian schoolboys would have understood. 'An Informer's Fate' and 'The Carey-Tragedy Repeated' hinted at an Irish dimension nobody seemed eager to explore. The closest McLoughlin got to sympathetic understanding in respectable – as opposed to criminal – circles came in a marginally more reflective piece in the *Star*, which acknowledged that the perpetrator 'was not without excuse' since, while he had been exposed to the hard life of a fugitive, 'Stevenson [had been] living on the fat of the land, and apparently on the best possible terms with the police'.[56] More intriguingly, an evening paper noted that just hours after the shooting there had been a safe-robbery at the Durban-Roodepoort Mine on the West Rand, and that it was suggested in some circles that this pointed to McLoughlin's retreat. It was indeed a straw in the wind.[57]

These subtleties eluded underworld figures who, like Bob Ferguson, knew – or imagined – their names to be on McLoughlin's list. The audacity of the late-night dinner at Rosenthal's had captured the imagination of the press and public. Among those dreading a chance encounter with or visit from McLoughlin was a small-time crook who had just missed taking a bullet from the one-armed man once before. Morry Hollander – whom the murderer had already spotted entering Rosenthal's – panicked when a Brigade member informed him that McLoughlin was going to 'blow his head off his shoulders' – a variant on the threat that Higgins had heard in the Queenstown Hotel just before the bullet had parted his hair some years earlier.

The police, according to Hollander, told him to go to hell when he pushed his demands for protection too far. Still in search of a shield, this time more ideological than material, he went to the offices of the *Star* and, after confessing anonymously to having played a pioneering role in crime in Johannesburg, lodged a complaint about the treatment he had received at the hands of the ZARPs. This prompted the editor to assert, more in hope than anticipation, 'The truth is that a good many members of the fraternity which he apparently adorns will be as heartily glad to hear of McLoughlin's capture as the police themselves.'[58]

Harry Lobb, having been identified as the man who had directed the killer to the rooms behind the Red Lion, also lost his nerve. Not wanting to be named as an accomplice, he too called in at the *Star* to deny any complicity in the two shootings.[59]

McLoughlin had disappeared. With detectives making no progress in tracking a one-armed man capable of disguising himself only with difficulty, the press rounded on the police. Ferguson's nose was out of joint, it was said, because of Trimble's appointment as the state's most senior detective. The result was a split in house loyalties between Pretoria and Johannesburg. Amidst headlines such as 'The Desperado at Large', 'Whose Fault is it?' and 'Where are the Police?', journalists picked up on the story that, on the night of the shootings, Ferguson had been told that McLoughlin was dining in Commissioner Street, but that because of the treatment he had received from the government he had 'no desire to distinguish himself' or 'poach on Mr. Trimble's preserve'.[60]

With the stick in the hornet's nest just three days after the shootings, editors stirred away, ensuring that Ferguson was stung mercilessly. If the reports were true, one leader-writer argued, then Ferguson was a 'coward' or a 'rascal' and, if not, he would sue the newspaper that had carried the first accounts for libel. Ferguson replied two days later, denying that he had known about the Commissioner Street dinner. But it was a lie. Everybody knew it was a falsehood, and a week later he announced his intention to retire: he was planning to establish a private detective agency that would focus on the theft of gold amalgam – a field of endeavour in which McLoughlin's gang had specialised, and one in which Ferguson had enjoyed no conspicuous success for more than half a decade.[61] There may, of course, have been other, hidden reasons for Ferguson's reluctance to confront his Mancunian nemesis directly and for the fugitive's extreme hatred of the detective. Could McLoughlin have been in possession of other unknown but explosive information about the Irish detective?

Ferguson, it will be recalled, had failed to bring McLoughlin's gang to book for the Rattray safe-robbery. At the time, an embarrassing and puzzling public failure that appeared to spring largely from unexpected legal problems and inadequate police work. In retrospect, however, it seems possible that he and McLoughlin may have been in league when it came to gold or other thefts, and that their deep-seated differences may have sprung from joint criminal exploits that had gone wrong. How else is one to account for Ferguson's not going on to resign his position as promised, for his continued, self-proclaimed interest in amalgam theft, or the fact that he was dismissed from his position in 1898 by State Attorney J.C. Smuts for trafficking in illegally acquired gold? Ferguson was a bent copper, one whose interests, like those of the one-armed murderer, ran to gold.[62]

McLoughlin may or may not have planned to shoot Ferguson, but he nevertheless succeeded in bringing him down even before he left Johannesburg. Ferguson was to be humiliated by McLoughlin on two further occasions over the next fourteen years before their unfinished business arising from the Stevenson betrayal was settled. It was a rout, but where *was* McLoughlin immediately after the murder? He may well, as speculated at the time, have been hiding in an abandoned mineshaft on one of the nearby mining properties. From his own testimony years later it is known that he stayed in Johannesburg for five days after the shootings.[63] It is also clear that, on one of those nights, in yet another display of blind courage or narcissistic madness, he walked into town to inspect the notice board outside the police charge office, where he learnt that he was 'wanted dead or alive'.[64] Knowing that, like Ned Kelly, he was beyond the law and liable to be shot on sight may have triggered his next move.

The attempted safe-lifting at the Durban Deep Mine the night after Stevenson's death may have been the work of the Irish Brigade. The robbery that followed, undertaken by a small team of professionals, certainly was. It was unusual in that it was marked by excessive violence, bearing the imprimatur of a man desperate to raise funds enough to carry him half a world away from the Witwatersrand. In the early hours of Saturday 2 February – exactly a week after the murder at the Red Lion and the slaying of Hadji Yussuf – McLoughlin, McCann, Harding and Whelan broke into the premises of the Champ D'Or Mine in Krugersdorp. Roused by noises emanating from the office, the secretary, Simpson, went to investigate and was battered so severely that, months later, he remained unable to testify. The safe was removed, dynamited and relieved of £2 000 – a king's ransom. The haul would have been bigger if, as planned at Durban Deep, the operation had coincided more precisely with the month's end.[65]

Lieutenant De Wit Tossel of McKeone fame was soon on to the suspects, most of whom had been in and out of town ever since the Irish Brigade had launched its campaign into the Rustenburg district five years earlier. Within forty-eight hours he had the dog by the tail. He found Tommy Whelan still in Krugersdorp; Charlie Harding was discovered with 'lots of gold and silver', and brought back from Pretoria. But of a real Irish terrier and his foxy companion, Jack McCann, there was no sign.[66]

McLoughlin and McCann – one with no arm and the other with a shortened arm; masters of the switch from urban gangsters to rural bandits; flush with cash; and heads filled with the experience of living off veld and vlei – were off on their last epic ride across the face of southern Africa. But where to? With one riding literally for his life and the other seeking to avoid a life sentence for his part in armed robbery, it was inevitable that they would swap ideas about how to negotiate the unknown terrain ahead.

McLoughlin, once of Manchester and the South Lancashires, endorsed the Rhodesian goldfields to the north, where some spoke hopefully of discovering a second Rand, living along the banks of the Limpopo and moving among the Venda in the Zoutpansberg. It offered the frontier experience he craved and was worth a try. McCann was sufficiently persuaded to ride on west to Mashonaland and Salisbury, where they ultimately parted. (There, several months later, he was picked up by the police and extradited to the ZAR to face charges for the attack on the secretary and the robbery at the Champ D'Or. But Simpson remained so feeble in body and traumatised in mind that his assailants were never arraigned. Years later, McCann was said to have died of fever somewhere out in the northern bush.[67])

McCann, once of County Tyrone, the Inniskillings and the Straits Settlements before being posted to Natal, spoke of the allure of the East, of the magic of India and the possibilities opened up by dynamite on the Mysore goldfields. The idea of Asia resonated with McLoughlin, who, as a boy, had worked with Indian cotton in the Lancashire mills. But the pair had a more immediate problem: they were being pursued by Sergeant J.S. Hamilton, formerly of the Bechuanaland Border Patrol, who assumed that they were heading for McLoughlin's old redoubts deep in Makhato's kingdom. But if they did pass through Vendaland, it was but part of a feint since, having avoided the Barberton corridor, where the agents of the state no doubt lay in wait for them, the fugitives drove on north. When McCann eventually peeled off west to Mashonaland, McLoughlin turned east towards Mozambique so that he might approach Lourenço Marques from the north. It was a skilfully executed set of manoeuvres, a retreat that would make a general proud.

Hamilton had been outmanoeuvred and outstripped. Yussuf and Stevenson were barely fourteen days cold when McLoughlin was back in Lourenço Marques drinking beer in old haunts last visited as an Irish Brigade navvy. He made some enquiries and booked himself a passage aboard a steamer that was Madras-bound. Days before embarking, however, in a sign of things to come, the Kruger government alerted him that it was intent on pursuing him. Bob Ferguson, acting on information supplied by Hamilton and still struggling to save face, appeared in the port city, ostensibly to persuade the Portuguese authorities to have McLoughlin extradited. But the one-armed fugitive, who encountered the detective and his underworld sidekick G.H. 'Chinaman' Woolf flitting among dockside pubs, sensed that Ferguson was not serious about the mission. In effect, he once again stared down the detective.[68]

Days later, McLoughlin set sail for Madras. It was the first leg of an epic flight across oceans that would take him halfway around the world – through India, down through the Straits Settlement, on to New Zealand and then right across the width of the Australian Outback – before he was to return to southern African waters. It was a journey of fourteen years over three continents, during which every month, every week – no, every day – was a battle to conceal a troubled past. An expanding network of imperial police intelligence, powered by the telegraph and its parasite, the provincial press, draped the southern hemisphere, the tentacles of the times. The South African War disrupted the hunt for half a decade as governors in far-off colonies waited for empire to digest the enormous chunk of wealth that a ravenous Britain had bitten off the southern part of Africa.

In 1909, amidst coincidences coordinated by mischievous gods who had tired of playing with him, McLoughlin was recognised on the Brisbane dockside by a policeman, arrested and extradited to the Transvaal, which was about to be folded into the Union of South Africa. His subsequent trial, for the murder of Stevenson at the Red Lion but not for Hadji Mohammed Yussuf, was a triumph for the prosecution. Fourteen years after the shootings, the state assembled virtually every witness of importance to the events on a night that had seen two men lose their lives and a third his reputation. John McLoughlin was hanged on 10 January 1910, in the same Pretoria prison in which Hugh McKeone had once faced the prospect of the gallows and to which the Irish Brigade had laid siege two decades earlier.

But the search for justice is never fully extended when decontextualised, when the events in question and the trial are excised from their more proximate historical, ideological, personal and social moments. McLoughlin, pleading 'not guilty' before Chief Justice James Rose-Innes, denied any involvement in the shootings, suggesting a case of mistaken identity – a singularly unpersuasive line given his unmistakeable appearance. He was defended *pro Deo* by an inexperienced young advocate of Irish-Australian descent, F.A.W. Lucas. Lucas, a specialist in criminal procedure, was direct and focused in defence but totally unimaginative in his approach. He also failed to mount a plea in mitigation that might have spared the ageing Mancunian his premature meeting with the hangman.

Not a single direct or indirect reference was made to the fifty-year-old accused's ethnic background and socialisation, to the complexities of Anglo-Irish political relations in the late nineteenth century, to his military training, to codes of honour and duelling, to notions of masculinity and sexuality, or to the bonds of Victorian male friendships. Nor was the significance of McLoughlin's meetings with Lobb and McCann before or after the execution of Stevenson probed. Both of these men would, albeit for different reasons, have approved of, if not encouraged, the decision to kill the informer. In the absence of such a defence there was little point in dissecting the nature of McLoughlin and Stevenson's prior relationship, or of exploring ways in which love and betrayal might speak to one another. Nor was there any attempt to explore why McLoughlin seemed so intent on warning his victim – a man who was himself armed and ready to defend himself – of his execution. It is possible that members of the jury, who recommended 'mercy on account of the time which has elapsed between the crime and the trial', sensed but failed to articulate these pertinent complications. If they did, then so, too, did the Chief Justice and, later, the State Executive.

In his time, in mining towns on the frontiers of empire and industrialisation, John McLoughlin was capable of eliciting loyalty from Irish Brigade members as well as fear, if not respect, from many working men on the Witwatersrand. Like the bank robber Jack McKeone, who pre-dated him, McLoughlin's standing in the lower echelons of white society in the 1890s approximated that of a 'criminal hero' or an 'outlaw legend'. It was a status achieved in an era when independent but beleaguered diggers, prospectors and syndicates were being surpassed by capitalists and the emerging mining houses. By the time that he was laid to rest, in 1910, John McLoughlin was just another murderer. Time corrodes memory and judgement alike.

# 6

# The Parameters of Popular Support: Criminal Heroes, Outlaw Legends and Social Bandits

Show me a hero, and I will write you a tragedy.
– F. Scott Fitzgerald, *The Notebooks*

Single men and small bands of criminals operating on the margins of agricultural economies – those exploiting popular notions of 'justice' in culturally homogenous settings undergoing the turbulent transition to industrial capitalism – have never lent themselves to easy definition.[1] 'Criminal heroes', 'outlaw legends' and 'social bandits' are unlike the one-dimensional characters portrayed in the chapbooks of yesteryear. Yet, for reasons that are difficult to understand, simple-minded Robin Hood notions of them persist. Given this, it is perhaps best to start by placing our 'social bandits' in their broad context, reminding ourselves what they 'achieved' and which groupings took ownership of them and their actions.

First, it should be kept in mind that the 'Irish' brigands chosen for in-depth examination here – John McLoughlin and the brothers McKeone – were not Irish, but of Irish origin. Their fathers and mothers were Irish men and women, but the children were born in England or South Africa and were merely of Irish descent. Although the offspring identified closely with many things Irish, they are more accurately described as 'Lancashire-Irish', 'Irish-South African' or, as a South African newspaper with nationalist sympathies once termed Hugh McKeone, an 'Irish-Afrikander' – meaning that he was born on home (that is, African) rather than 'foreign' soil.[2]

This observation forms the backdrop to a puzzling silence about the Irish ancestry of the three bandits in most subsequent reports and contemporary accounts of their activities. At a time when England was struggling to find a political solution to the 'Irish Question' and the anglophone press in South Africa was seeking to advance the imperial cause in the face of growing Afrikaner resistance, there was a reluctance in press circles to draw attention to the real or self-proclaimed 'Irishness' of the bandits. It was as if the protagonists of imperialism, filled with misgivings about the wrongdoings of the 'Irish' brigands, wanted a sense of 'Englishness' to override any differences they may have had with other anglophone elements amidst a hostile Afrikaner presence. The editors of English-medium newspapers, often extremely sensitive to supposed ethnic slurs by outsiders, were content to see McLoughlin and the McKeone brothers routinely described as 'English'. So, too, of course, for very different reasons, were most Afrikaner editors.

Born of parents who survived the Great Famine and lived to see the dream of Irish independence thwarted, McLoughlin and the McKeones identified themselves, in differing measures, with Irish causes. McLoughlin, seemingly apolitical and laconic in everyday speech, deserted the British Army to join the pointedly named 'Irish Brigade', whose actions, on one occasion, embarrassed the imperial power when members overran a Portuguese gunboat in Delagoa Bay. One of his close associates, John O'Brien, claimed to be the brother of a 'Manchester Martyr' and may have enjoyed Fenian connections, while McLoughlin himself certainly acted in quintessentially Irish-nationalist mode when he took it upon himself to execute English police informer George Stevenson.

It would be a mistake to see McLoughlin as a man devoid of nationalist sympathies, even though his choice of targets for criminal activities seems to be founded more on eclectic, class-based considerations than on political antipathies. The most careful observer of the South African-Irish notes that, in the 1890s, 'several gangs of Irish brigands roamed the Transvaal robbing *English* mine managers'.[3] There are reasons to debate that expansive formulation but, to the extent that McLoughlin and his Irish safe-lifters preferred robbing mines along the central West Rand, it clearly tugs in the right direction. To leave it there, however, would also be misleading, for, as already noted, the Brigade was equally willing to ransack state-owned premises. This was especially true during the depression of 1890–92, when the offices of Rand mining commissioners attracted resentment from independent, small-scale white mining entrepreneurs unable to compete with emerging larger companies.

It is within this context, the demise of small-scale diggers, prospectors and syndicates, that bouts of brigandage mounted against the rich and powerful by disaffected 'Irishmen' have to be assessed as acts of 'social banditry'. The criminal hero, as one influential analyst reminds us, 'expresses the discontent of a wide spectrum of people. Of course, he appeals to many people for reasons that have nothing to do with politics, but the political nature of the Robin Hood criminal is the *fundamental* reason why a criminal becomes fashioned into a social hero.'[4]

Perhaps it is necessary to warn again against any simplistic 'Robin Hood' test. Neither McLoughlin nor the McKeone brothers, let alone lesser members of the Irish Brigade, were known to have handed all or even parts of their proceeds to the deserving poor in town or countryside. If we insist on applying that test alone, the Irish were no more than ordinary criminals. Even that, however, should be enough to evoke some caution since, as the great Hobsbawm warns us, 'in practice social banditry cannot always be separated clearly from other kinds of banditry'.[5]

But if the ethnic and class affinities of the bandits are conceded and an only slightly less stringent test imposed, the status of the brigands becomes clearer. The consideration that McLoughlin received from his comrades after the loss of his hand is instructive. Not only did the brigands support him through a period of readjustment and enforced professional inactivity, but they actually clubbed together – in the fashion of a Friendly Society – to provide him with funds that would allow him to set himself up in business as a hawker.

It should be granted, however, that even the lesser test should not, in the first instance, be applied to beneficiaries drawn from *within* the ranks of the bandits, but to those who lay *beyond* the leadership. McLoughlin and most of his close associates spent the greatest part of their ill-gotten gains on themselves and on lifestyles characterised by conspicuous consumption. McLoughlin was known as a snappy dresser, drank very heavily, dined out continually, gambled seriously and often bought the sexual services of 'coloured' live-in lovers or prostitutes.

As leader of the Irish Brigade, McLoughlin was expected to spread some of his largesse, if not directly by way of cash obtained from robberies or winnings from gambling, then indirectly, in kind. 'Treating' others to drinks and meals or making available bridging loans in cash were actions extended regularly to other gangsters, as well as to a significant number of mine workers who supplied the bandits with information about gold amalgam or payrolls. In the same way, informants who were hard up or unemployed could expect to benefit from Irish Brigade assistance. Not surprisingly, then, when one of McLoughlin's 'pals' was interviewed by the press after the shootings at the Red Lion Beer Hall he said, 'I may tell you that he has any number of friends all over the Rand who act as loyal spies and would risk their lives to save his neck.'[6]

Those sceptical about claims of McLoughlin as a 'criminal hero' or 'social bandit' will probe the basis of such loyalty. It is a line of questioning that, for the most part, derives from those in search of ideal types of historical figures, figures capable of eliciting affection to the exclusion of fear and terror. But, as battered wives know, it is an inappropriate test because it is founded on a false dichotomy. Turkish author Yashar Kemal perhaps puts it best: 'Brigands live by love *and* fear. When they inspire only love it's a weakness. When they inspire only fear, they are hated and have no supporters.'[7] That said, it would be a foolish man who did not concede that, in McLoughlin's case, love and fear were seldom in equipoise. He probably inspired far more fear than he did love; otherwise why the long silence about his strange career?

Yet Jack McCann could attest to McLoughlin's ability to engender affection and trust. So, too – ironically – could George Stevenson. Indeed, it was, in part, the betrayal of McLoughlin's love that did most to prompt the Mancunian's revenge. Throughout his trial in 1909, McLoughlin resorted to language that, albeit unintentionally, revealed the affection he once had for Stevo, and Stevo for him: 'I could not say that *I was in love with him* after that naturally'; 'if I would only make friends again, *he [Stevenson] would not care for anyone [else] in Johannesburg*'; 'there was a row between us' [classic Victorian formulation of disagreement among spouses]; and '*I knew he did not care* when he turned state's evidence against me'.[8] On the other hand, Bob Ferguson and Morry Hollander could both testify to McLoughlin's ability to instil naked terror.

Although the proportion of charm and coercion that McLoughlin employed to evoke loyalty from his many followers is impossible to determine with any precision, it succeeded in providing him with a blanket of secrecy and security that his enemies and the state found impenetrable. For six weeks before the slayings in and around the Red Lion, he – a conspicuously one-armed man – moved freely in and out of the town. After the murder of Stevenson he dined openly in the heart of Commissioner

Street and for a week thereafter was up and down the West Rand, where he was something of an institution. McLoughlin twice crossed the length of the republican highveld on horseback, undetected, an achievement that may also have owed something to a thin network of Irishmen spread across the far northern and eastern Transvaal. And, for the better part of a year, he was based among the Venda in the Zoutpansberg. Not once was his presence betrayed to the authorities by black, Boer or Brit in a region that also boasted a shopkeeper and *veldkornet* by the name of Kelly.

An elusive bandit whom police found impossible to track, he soon assumed mythical proportions. Paradoxically, he was often glimpsed by ordinary citizens. 'The man is now some sort of pimpernel – being seen and sought everywhere,' reported one newspaper. In Johannesburg, insistent questions were put to the authorities about how 'such a notorious and easily recognised criminal could slip through their fingers'. McLoughlin was once even said to have been spotted in Bloemfontein, making his way to Cape Town.[9] And, as accurate data and memories of the one-armed man dimmed with the passage of time, so the pimpernel myth assumed ever larger dimensions for dreamier scribes: 'For months afterwards he was some sort of bogeyman in the Transvaal. He went into bars and restaurants as large as life, and nobody interfered with him. Policemen slipped around corners on urgent business at a rumour of his approach.'[10] It is fair to say that much of this working-class reluctance to reveal his presence to law-enforcement agencies could as easily be attributed to the qualities of a 'criminal hero' as to those of Hobsbawm's classic 'social bandit'; to the uneasy mix between affection and fear. But that, surely, is precisely the point at issue. Why does it have to be one or the other and not some of both? Surely elements of both the criminal hero and the social bandit could have been present in John McLoughlin. Who is now to say – with great conviction – where the characteristics of a 'criminal hero' give way to those of an archetypal 'social bandit'?

Predictably, McLoughlin's artificial hand, replete with fingers – a prosthesis he preferred to use for cosmetic rather than utilitarian purposes – became the subject of macabre speculation. For the most part, it was without foundation. The press, which was the poor and working man's cheapest approximation to theatre, churned out the first such myth within just thirty-six hours of the shootings. 'This revengeful Corsican-like individual's wooden arm,' it was suggested at a time when knife crimes were supposed to be an 'Italian' speciality, 'is so arranged that, when he opens his hand, a mechanical dagger leaps out.'[11]

Louis Cohen later took such unsubstantiated nonsense further. McLoughlin, he claimed, possessed a mechanical paw that could wield a 'stiletto', 'and when a man was found in Commissioner Street, stabbed through the heart, the crime was undoubtedly committed by him'.[12] Later, yet another chronicler saw McLoughlin as brandishing a 'polished steel hook' at a time when he had no such thing.[13]

Green shoots of fabrication, early signs of an 'outlaw legend' putting down tentative roots, sprouted almost as rapidly as Bob Ferguson's reputation withered.[14] Within days of the slaying at the Red Lion, one enterprising stationer took to advertising 'Ken Donaldson's Time-Table and Diary' in the morning paper. 'McLachlan the Murderer,' the blurb suggested, 'always carries a little book in his waistcoat pocket, and having completely mastered the contents has hitherto been able to avoid detection.'[15] A few of McLoughlin's drinking mates and working-class admirers went further, writing letters to the press in mock-proletarian prose purporting to emanate from the will-o'-the-wisp himself. One, copying a letter supposedly sent by 'Jack the Ripper' and 'written in blood', warned readers: 'Just yer let the 'tecs do their own dirty work, I ain't afeerd of them. I know ten where they are, and that ain't where I am you bet.' A second, from 'Johannesburg Subburbs', explained, 'I left my home at an early age [but] I am still an Irishman in my ways', and 'only an Irishman knows what revenge is'.[16]

Most of this mythmaking, it should be remembered, occurred without McLoughlin having been identified publicly as a former Australian bushranger and Mancunian, as the Witwatersrand's chief safe-lifter, or as a founding member of the Irish Brigade with links to bank robbers and highwaymen dating back to Barberton days. Indeed, had his early career been better explored and recorded at the time, McLoughlin's life might have approximated that of Scotty Smith, South Africa's most famous 'social bandit'. Smith, however, was cut from different cloth. He grew up in a reasonably well-off rural Scottish family rather than in an urban Irish slum in industrial England. Although no stranger to the army, Australia or robbery of many types, the Scot preferred to work on his own as a horse

The approach to Eureka City, a mining camp near Barberton that was invaded and occupied by the Irish Brigade during a week of mayhem in February 1887
National Archives of South Africa

Elephant's Creek, site of numerous ambushes by members of the Irish Brigade and other highwaymen during the late 1880s
National Archives of South Africa

Thomas M. Menton, Irish deserter and, as poacher-turned-gamekeeper, later a jailer at Barberton and Johannesburg
National Archives of South Africa

Dr W.J. Leyds, State Secretary to the Executive Council of the ZAR and the official responsible for dealing with requests for remission of sentences and extradition of bandits from neighbouring territories in the 1890s
National Archives of South Africa

Advocate J.W. Leonard QC, who, in 1891, together with H.B. Sauer (brother of Hans Sauer), argued for the right of appeal against the death sentence imposed on highwaymen Hugh McKeone and William Cooper
National Archives of South Africa

Chief Justice J.G. Kotze of the ZAR, who the pro-British press felt was in need of the 'complete change of air and scene' that would restore him to 'mental and bodily health' after sentencing an Irish Brigade coach robber to five years' imprisonment for contempt of court in 1891
National Archives of South Africa

Rimer's Creek mining camp, Barberton, late 1880s
National Archives of South Africa

Postal coaches in the Rustenburg district were a favoured target of Irish highwaymen who had temporarily abandoned the Witwatersrand for the countryside during the economic depression of 1890–92
Museum Afrika, Johannesburg

Departure of the goldfields coach from Potchefstroom for Johannesburg, circa 1890
Museum Afrika, Johannesburg

The Government Buildings in State President S.J.P. Kruger's prosperous
Rustenburg constituency, targeted by Irish Brigade safe-robbers in 1890
Museum Afrika, Johannesburg

Johannesburg Law Courts, circa 1895, an occasional port of call for members of the Irish Brigade
Museum Afrika, Johannesburg

Johannesburg Prison, circa 1895, which saw repeated attempts at escape – some successful – by bank robbers, highwaymen and safe-robbers during the early to mid-1890s
Museum Afrika, Johannesburg

Luipaardsvlei Estate Gold Mine, Krugersdorp, a favourite haunt of Irish safe-robbers Jack McCann, Tommy Whelan and Jack McLoughlin in the early 1890s
National Archives of South Africa

Krugersdorp Railway Station, base of H.E. Gill, the conductor who in 1894 attempted to seal off a train compartment of Witwatersrand safe-robbers led by 'One-Armed Jack' McLoughlin
Museum Afrika, Johannesburg

Cecil John Rhodes, opportunistic bandit-prince who, at crucial junctures in the 1890s and much earlier, hired brigands and mercenaries to advance either his own corporate or British political interests throughout southern Africa
National Archives of South Africa

Hans Sauer, Rhodes's 'genial ruffian' who recruited 'Sauer's Irish Brigade' to protect the partners' valuable West Rand mining claims in the late 1880s
National Archives of South Africa

Charles Leonard (brother of J.W. Leonard), who in 1890 formed the Political Reform Association which fed off some of the popular discontent of white workers who were beginning to show signs of support for 'criminal heroes' and 'outlaw legends' during the depression of 1890–92
National Archives of South Africa

Dr L.S. Jameson, contemptuous brigand-captain of the ill-fated capitalist-backed raid of 1895 that was defeated by Boer forces around Krugersdorp
National Archives of South Africa

Irish Republican Brotherhood members and unlikely refinery workers John MacBride (far left) and Arthur Griffith (third from left) photographed outside the single quarters of an unknown West Rand mine at the height of the upsurge in gold-amalgam theft in 1898. MacBride went on to lead an Irish commando into the South African War on the Boer side, while Griffith became the first President of the Irish Free State
Courtesy of the late Brian Mooney, Mrs M. Doyle and D.P. McCracken

The smelting room at the Langlaagte Deep Mine. John MacBride – who, like Griffith, was an 'advanced nationalist' – was employed at the mine in 1899 on the eve of the South African War
Museum Afrika, Johannesburg

thief on the remote highveld, and was singularly uncomfortable in the city. Indeed, it was probably *because* Smith operated primarily among the semi-literate of the countryside, where oral traditions can sometimes survive for longer than the written records of urban gangsters, that his name is still associated with 'social banditry' while McLoughlin's is largely lost to latter-day history.

McLoughlin's speedy exit and escape into the wider southern hemisphere, where he remained concealed for fourteen years, did at least as much to ensure that his actions and image alike were obliterated from public memory. By the time he returned to Johannesburg in 1909 to stand trial, his life and the two shootings had been so effectively decontextualised by the passing of time that the defence mounted on his behalf by a well-meaning young lawyer was wholly inadequate, and the trial remarkably one-sided. McLoughlin, who paid for these stark deficiencies with his life, probably deserved a lesser sentence. His life certainly remains worthy of a much fuller account.

Jack McKeone, who roamed the kingdom of the imagination almost as readily as he did the southern highveld, is yet another 'social bandit' poorly served by historians. As a child, 'with a strong stream of Irish blood running through his veins', he may well have been raised on the mother's milk of primitive radicalism.[17] His father, John, would have been full of tales of Alfred Aylward, the Fenian who, while on the diamond fields in 1870, was a champion of the idea of a diggers' republic. Aylward later went on to support the Boer republican cause and edit the *Natal Witness* at Pietermaritzburg shortly before Fort Napier bloomed as the College of Banditry.[18] As a failed prospector, Jack McKeone would also have known about the Black Flag Rebellion of 1875, when diamond diggers on the Kimberley fields challenged the legitimacy of British authority.[19]

McKeone claimed that grievances stemming from his bruising experiences in the mining commissioner's office prompted him to rob a bank of funds belonging to an unsympathetic government that raised its revenue from ordinary working folk on the goldfields. Like his younger brother Hugh, Jack McKeone entertained romantic notions of fairness that fed into ideas about social justice in frontier societies. In the mid-thirties the story was repeated of how, as an adolescent, he had stolen sheep and distributed them among friends who were said to be 'hard up'. When challenged about his stock-raiding proclivities McKeone argued that 'the farmer from whom he had taken the sheep was a very rich man, and that he could not miss these few animals'. In a similar, romantic vein it was asserted that the robbery at the Standard Bank was beyond ethical reproach because 'the money was lying idle in the bank, and there were poor families he knew in Basutoland who could make much better use of it'.[20]

In his 1890 letter to the Kruger administration in which he belatedly sought a pardon for his crimes, McKeone drew on a sense of righteous indignation at injustice – something of an Irish speciality – as well as Victorian codes of masculinity to justify his deviant behaviour. 'I comitted myself from a spirit of revenge,' he confessed, but 'I also ask you to see the manner my crime was done in. Was there any want of manliness?'[21] It was the plaintive call of a young man who had been thrust prematurely into the role of father in an utterly dysfunctional family, in difficult times.

When McKeone's younger brothers Hugh and Bernard lost their employment as a result of his having robbed the bank, the stage was set for the family to be seen as victims of an administration paving the way for the emergence of a full-scale industrial capitalist system of production. Diggers, prospectors and syndicate owners, having already witnessed the De Beers Company consume the Kimberley diamond fields during their lifetime, sensed that mining houses and banks bent on exploiting the depression and gaining control of the Witwatersrand goldfields were in the throes of swallowing small-scale mining operations. Neither the banks nor the mining companies were friends of the ordinary man or woman. The economic climate was tailor-made for the appearance of 'criminal heroes' or 'social bandits'.

Even the Transvaal-based English press, for the most part overwhelmingly willing to advance the cause of British imperialism and the interests of big business, could not but admire Jack McKeone's 'boldness', his 'daring' and 'pluck' – English public school-speak for courage. By manifesting quintessentially British virtues amidst perceived Afrikaner intransigence, he became an honorary Englishman, resulting in the deafening silence about any self-proclaimed sense of Irishness. The fact that he later wrote to his brother Bernard to tell him, 'I hate the Dutch dogs as much as I hate hell' no doubt facilitated his transformation.[22] But this process of ethnic appropriation occurred largely unintentionally and, as we shall see, later helped give birth to great political tensions when the death sentence of his highwayman brother Hugh was confirmed by a politically besieged Kruger government. At the time, however, Jack McKeone loved the public parading of his exploits and supposed virtues. He could not get enough of it. Like McLoughlin, he wanted to see it in print. 'Send me papers of my escape,' he wrote, '*every* paper that has accounts of me.'[23]

McKeone had other merits that were difficult to deny, and the anglophone press worked hard at either appropriating or reshaping them. Unlike the priest-hating McLoughlin, McKeone was a devoted Catholic and, despite his readiness with the revolver, a God-fearing man. His concern for his siblings and the plight of their mother was palpable; it made him 'a family man', albeit one without the benefit of a caring or involved father.[24] Nor did his affection for horses go amiss among the equine-loving anglophones, who celebrated his self-sacrifice in the name of his horse: McKeone famously gave himself up rather than see Brian Boru shot – a courtesy he was unwilling to extend to other horsemen. But since his imposing stallion had been inconveniently named after an all-conquering Irish king, it, too, had to be reinvented. Brian Boru was consistently likened to the more famous Black Bess; with the retelling of the tale over time, the name had, by the mid-thirties, mutated into the almost unrecognisable composite of 'Black Brian'.[25] McKeone himself was referred to as a 'South African Dick Turpin' rather than any Irish highwayman of note – despite the fact that it was his partner in crime, Stevens, who had consciously chosen to cast himself as Dick Turpin in their wild highveld adventures.[26]

The son of a diamond and gold prospector who had witnessed the frailties of fortune-seekers in the face of big money, first in Beaconsfield and then Barberton, and as a failed digger himself, Jack McKeone became the darling of working men as the Witwatersrand economy slid deeper into depression. The *Standard & Diggers' News*, which aspired to being – simultaneously – a conduit to the Kruger government and the voice of the common man, was bewildered by the depth of feeling McKeone evoked among its readers and in the pubs. 'Whether right or wrong,' one hack observed, 'the general feeling in town is sorrow at hearing of McKeone's capture, hope that it is not true, and if true, that he will escape again.'[27]

As in the case of McLoughlin, five years later, several street champions sought to defend McKeone with the pen, protecting him against any allegations of antisocial behaviour that might have been at variance with the emerging myth of him as 'noble robber'. A 'Letter from the Veld', supposedly emanating from the quill of McKeone himself, denied that he had ever been involved in a robbery and assault at the Central Diamond Mining Company.[28] And when the chant of praise continued to echo through the pubs, even the *Standard & Diggers' News* was forced to respond with a forlorn, 'Why is McKeone set up as a hero, a second Dick Turpin or Robin Hood?'[29]

Invisible to the Kruger state and its law enforcement agencies, Jack McKeone allegedly moved about freely among working men, always safe from detection. After his escape from prison, the Irish brigand, forging 'one of the mysteries of the period', simply walked from Pretoria to Johannesburg, where he 'was seen by quite a number of people but the detectives and police could not lay hands upon him'. Myths spewed forth faster than banknotes from a counterfeiter's press and journalists were hard-pushed to keep up: 'Many queer stories have been current as to his impudence, but they are probably greatly exaggerated.'[30]

Probably. But then again, how can one be certain? Numerous bandits had quasi-magical powers and the Irish, it was often claimed, were a strange and superstitious people. After his first escape from prison, near Kroonstad, the mounted men pursuing Cooper and McKeone caught sight of their quarry 'some miles ahead of them galloping for dear life'. Undeterred, the police 'urged on their horses, and after six hours' hard chase across the veldt one of them fired his carbine at the fugitives'. The result was startling. When the bandits 'saw the smoke of the gun they drew apart and the bullet passed between them'.[31] Indeed. Faster than a speeding bullet.

It is worth remembering that, amidst all this English-Irish magic and mystery playing itself out in the minds of working-class men along the urban Witwatersrand, Jack McKeone had another attribute. It was one that enabled him to penetrate parts of indigenous society on the highveld in ways that made him a more authentic 'South African' outlaw hero than almost all of his contemporaries. McKeone was '[a] master of Basuto [Sesotho]' who 'even in his sleep rambled off in long soliloquies in Basuto'.[32] He cultivated friendships among Africans not only in the prison from which he escaped (with their help), but 'all along the route' back to Basotholand and beyond, when he eventually staged his second, ultimately successful escape from the country to, so it was rumoured, the bushrangers' Valhalla of Australia. It was a neat exit, one worthy of someone who, casting himself as an 'American' bank robber in a setting that could have come from the Wild West, fashioned himself into a self-styled bandit-hero.

Hugh McKeone and William Cooper, on the other hand, were neither 'heroic criminals' nor 'social bandits'. They were armed, deeply disturbed young men who, following their calling as highwaymen, confronted, terrorised and robbed ordinary citizens and black migrant workers on the public roads leading to and from the diamond and goldfields. Their violence, barely controlled during a spree of robberies and store-breakings enacted across the highveld during the depression, erupted into physical assaults and shootings when they were arrested by policemen or confined by prison warders.

Many men and women found the deeds of McKeone and Cooper abhorrent. It is significant that, among all the brigands identified here, they alone were once chased and captured by a posse of armed citizens.[33] If invited, black South Africans would no doubt have joined the pursuit readily. Yet it is equally instructive to note that, when the pair were sentenced to death for having robbed a party of migrant African labourers of their wages and attempting to murder the two white policemen who had taken them into custody, it provoked so profound a public outcry among white South Africans that their sentences were commuted to life imprisonment. In a racially divided setting where independent republicanism was being contested by imperial power, even instances of 'Irish' brigandage could be rendered subservient to the political persuasions of anglophone 'public opinion'.

When Hugh McKeone and William Cooper appeared before Chief Justice J.G. Kotze at the Criminal Sessions in Pretoria in late October 1891, they were not the only members of the Irish Brigade to stand before the judge that month. The day after having donned the black cap to pass the death sentence on the highwaymen, Kotze called back James Sutherland, who, along with Todd and Brown, had been convicted of the safe-robbing at Rustenburg. The judge sentenced him to an additional five years in prison for contempt of court. Sutherland, displaying the customary contempt for non-Irish justice, had jokingly offered to play the judge 'double or quits' for his original twenty-year sentence. The extra five years, handed down to a first offender, caused outrage in press and public circles. The fact that the sentence came in the wake of the death penalty for two other young whites – also English-Irish – added to concerns, and the cases were soon conflated in the public mind.

Chief Justice Kotze was an unusual man. The son of a Cape politician who had been Mayor of Cape Town and later a leading member of the Legislative Assembly, Kotze was something of a cultural hybrid: a man with a profound interest in both the law and politics. Christened 'Johannes Gysbert', he went through life preferring to be known as John Gilbert Kotze. Although educated at the University of London, a member of the Inner Temple at the Inns of Court and married to a woman from Clapham, he nevertheless retained a profound curiosity about the principles of Roman-Dutch law, and translated Simon van Leeuwen's *Het Rooms-Hollands Recht* (1644) into English. In 1878, aged twenty-seven, Kotze was made Chief Justice in the ZAR. He was certainly a figure to conjure with. The young Rider Haggard once served as his clerk, while another novelist, Anthony Trollope, saw him as 'a boy judge'.[34]

A lifelong Anglophile, Kotze was well regarded in mining circles. He was generally sympathetically disposed to the needs of the industry, which throughout the 1890s battled to bend the Pretoria administration's will to ever-changing demands as it struggled to make the transition from outcrop to deep-level mining. The Chief Justice's desire to protect the industry's supply of cheap black labour by coming down hard on the activities of white highwaymen would have met with widespread, albeit silent, approval in the inner circles of the Witwatersrand. But by the time that McKeone and Cooper appeared before him, Kotze had fallen into disfavour in some of the same quarters for having earlier inflicted a heavy fine for contempt of court on the voice of the mining industry, the *Star*.

Moreover, Kotze had also had a serious dispute with the State President in 1886, when Kruger pardoned A.H. Nellmapius, an economic advisor and close friend of Kruger's who had been convicted of theft. That clash was a straw in the wind. Kotze went on to oppose Kruger in the presidential election of 1893 without first resigning from his position. In 1898, Kruger dismissed Kotze from office when the judge precipitated a political crisis by calling into question the procedures followed by the Volksraad when amending the constitution. In retrospect, Kotze heightened his vulnerability when he sentenced McKeone and Cooper to death on 22 October 1891 and then decided – rashly – to increase Sutherland's sentence by an additional five years for contempt of court.

Within hours of the session ending in Pretoria, there were ominous rumblings of protest in Johannesburg's English newspapers. Taken at face value the manoeuvre was simple enough: a public questioning of the Chief Justice's decision to hand down the death sentence to two young men who, although guilty of armed robbery, had not actually taken anyone's life and who had appeared in court without the benefit of counsel for their defence. But, as the press campaign spread and took root throughout southern Africa, producing a full-scale political convulsion, it soon became clear that there was more at stake than the lives of a pair of highwaymen and a gang of contemptuous, nondescript Irish safe-blasters.

The Chief Justice was subjected to merciless *ad hominem* attack for having imposed the death sentence. The criticism was compounded by his ill-considered response to Sutherland's courtroom buffoonery, which might have amazed the judge but would have been something many English-speakers would have expected of an Irishman, a Mancunian and possibly even a scuttler. The judge was said to be out of touch with the modern world and its general sentiment against the death penalty. He was thought, not to put too fine a point on it, to be quite mad. He had an 'inherent unfitness for the office' and should apply for extended leave so as to seek the 'complete change of air and scene' that would restore him to 'mental and bodily health'.[35] The highwaymen had evoked 'a barbarous sentence' from a man 'unfitted for the bench' who was an embarrassment to the Inns of Court. Indeed, it was hoped that the benchers back in London would take 'immediate steps to purge their Inn and the Bar of England of one who does them such dishonour'.[36]

But if the judge was insane then the law, too, it was suggested, was an ass. The burghers of the South African Republic had embraced principles of Roman-Dutch law that stemmed from the seventeenth-century settlement at the Cape. When imposing the death penalty the Chief Justice had drawn on an antiquated corpus of law unsuited to the needs of a modern, industrialising state. The McKeone-Cooper case – it was claimed without specifying who the 'our' was in the argument that followed – 'demonstrates the faultiness of our criminal law'.[37] Even if the sentence had sprung from the 'Roman-Dutch recesses of the Judge's brain', however, 'there was not a shadow of doubt but that the law had been allowed to fall into desuetude both in Holland and South Africa'. The whole sad business pointed to the need for 'a conference of the best jurists whom the country can produce to amend and consolidate a criminal code for the whole of South Africa'.[38] The attack on Kotze was swiftly extended from a critique of Roman-Dutch law and the McKeone-Cooper case to a suggestion that the time had come for a united 'South Africa' governed by a single British legal system.

Afrikaners and the burgher press in the two Boer republics saw these arguments and the political developments that accompanied them for what they were – opportunistic attempts by new imperialists to divide the Chief Justice and the State President and undermine Roman-Dutch legal systems for the benefit of jingoes. But grasping the underlying forces of a campaign was one thing; stopping it another. Amidst escalating tensions of the kind experienced four years later, after the Jameson Raid, Afrikaners were pitted against English, the anglophone press against the Dutch, British-educated lawyers against Continentally trained jurists, English clergymen against Dutch ministers and imperialists against nationalists. That much of this could be traced indirectly to the actions of a few 'Irishmen' who had metamorphosed into Englishmen without any direct mention of the Irish Brigade was deeply ironic.[39]

All eyes were now on Pretoria to see how, between them, the executive and the judiciary might absorb or deflect such unprecedented pressure without doing lasting damage to the machinery of state. It was a severe test that played itself out during the first week of November in 1891. The Chief Justice looked, in the first instance, to the State President and members of the Executive Council to approve his decision to impose the death penalty. Kruger, anxious to present a united front in the face of imperialist enemies, had to work extremely hard to get all the members of the Council to underwrite the death sentence. On Monday 2 November the first hurdle was successfully negotiated when, after three full days of deliberation, the Executive Council confirmed – unanimously – that the highwaymen would be hanged on Saturday 7 November.[40]

But Kruger's decision to back the Chief Justice served merely to heighten the clamour for the sentences to be commuted. Calls for petitions and public meetings to plead the case of the condemned men were encouraged by the English press, which focused on the anglophone working-class strongholds where the McKeones were best known. In Johannesburg a request for a public meeting by leading member of the Irish community J.W. Quinn fell on deaf ears, but workers readily joined those in Krugersdorp and elsewhere, including Pretoria itself, to sign petitions calling for a lesser sentence. But the loudest cry of all was from the diamond fields. In Kimberley a 'monster petition' backed by a mass meeting in the City Hall, which was addressed by the Acting Mayor and the mining baron Barney Barnato, Kimberley's member of the Legislative Assembly, concluded with a spirited rendition of 'God Save the Queen'.[41]

Where sparrows flock, hawks take to the air. As citizens and working men and women in the principal mining centres mobilised to produce petitions bearing the names of signatories numbering more than 10 000, consuls, Commissioners and even a member of royalty suddenly soared into view. The American consul addressed an appeal to the Kruger government, as did the British High Commissioner.[42] More impressively, some unknown political strategist conjured up the idea of obtaining the support of the Portuguese government, whom the South African Republic continued to court in order to realise its dream of gaining independent rail access to the east coast. It may, originally, have been through the good offices of the church that support for a plea of commutation was received first from the Portuguese consul and then from the King of Portugal himself. It was an extensive, sophisticated campaign.[43]

In Pretoria itself, ordinary Catholics were equally active. Almost immediately after the death sentence became known, the cause of the condemned men was embraced by Father L.J. Vigneron.[44] He, along with many others on the Rand who were involved in circulating the petitions to obtain signatures, made no overt mention of Cooper or McKeone's ethnic roots, even though the links between the church, Ireland and the condemned men were there for all to see when the petitions from Johannesburg were eventually handed to the authorities by Fathers De Lacey, Kelly and yet another Irish notable, St John Carr.[45] Important segments of the Afrikaans-Dutch press, deeply embroiled in their ongoing fight against jingoes, simply dismissed them all as 'English ministers'. Ideological battles, as in war, bury the need for finer distinctions.[46]

With the State President and Executive Council increasingly boxed in by external political interventions that were proving difficult to deflect on the one hand, and by mounting local public opinion in favour of commutation on the other, members of the Johannesburg legal fraternity with imperialist sympathies turned up the heat on the Chief Justice. Twelve months earlier, sensing that the depression had heightened disaffection among unenfranchised diggers and prospectors, creating the possibility of a mass political base among labouring men, Cape-born Queen's Counsel J.W. Leonard had launched the Political Reform Association. The Reform Association was a forerunner of the National Union, which was headed by his brother, Charles Leonard, a leading member of the Reform Committee that was to guide the Jameson Raid. By stepping up to advocate the cause of McKeone and Cooper *pro Deo* before a full bench in Pretoria, J.W. Leonard would be serving the high cause of justice in a way that would do him no harm in white working-class circles.[47]

The Chief Justice, a man known to have presidential ambitions, must have realised that he was about to be trapped in a legal-political pincer movement from which escape was nigh impossible. On Wednesday afternoon, 4 November, he had fulfilled his duty when, accompanied by the State Attorney and the Pretoria landdrost, he had made his way to the prison to inform the highwaymen that the death sentence had been confirmed by the Executive Council. A sterner test of character came within hours, on Thursday afternoon, when J.W. Leonard QC, assisted by Advocate H.B. Sauer (brother of Hans Sauer, another member of the Reform Committee and later implicated in the Jameson Raid), rose in the High Court before Judges Ameshoff, De Korte and Morice to plead that McKeone and Cooper be allowed to present an appeal before a full bench. The judges heard arguments from the defence and state before adjourning to prepare judgments for the following morning.[48]

Vulnerable on several fronts, the Chief Justice's political instincts did not desert him. Even before Leonard's appeal to the High Court, Kotze had made it known that he was strongly opposed to a lesser sentence in his report to the Executive Council, in which he argued that the imposition of the death penalty was 'indispensable to the interests of the country and justice'.[49] Now, as his brother judges busied themselves deciding on whether or not to allow the condemned men the right of appeal, it was rumoured that the Chief Justice would resign if the death sentence were commuted – a suggestion that, if true, would have added significantly to the pressure not only on the most senior judges in the land, but also on the State President and a beleaguered Executive Council.[50]

But Kruger's own political instincts were second to none. Even before the High Court could deliver its judgment on Friday 6 November, the President had persuaded the Executive to agree to the commutation of the sentence from death to life imprisonment. When the three wise men of the High Court announced that McKeone and Cooper were to be denied the right to appeal, something only the President and Executive Council were empowered to do, J.W. Leonard was disappointed but the Chief Justice was congratulated by his supporters. Leonard, Sauer and the Catholic clergymen hastily re-formed themselves into a deputation to appeal to the State President but, by the time they reached Kruger's offices, it was known that the highwaymen had been granted a reprieve.[51]

In the face of strong external opposition and the weight of public opinion, the State President and Executive Council had, with great reluctance, decided to sacrifice the Chief Justice, who, so his opponents claimed, had been humiliated.[52] Kotze had certainly been badly mauled, and the outcome of the McKeone-Cooper case contributed to his growing disillusionment with the Kruger administration. He staged a retreat as best he could. Within days of the commutation, he was the recipient of a letter signed by fifty-six supporters in the Klerksdorp district expressing appreciation for his willingness to impose the death penalty on highwaymen with 'fiendish propensities'. This prompted a self-indulgent reply in which Kotze was at pains to point out that he had always 'understood that fearless courage [was] one of the first essentials pertaining to the office of Judge'.[53]

William Cooper, informed of the reprieve, lost his chance to address the world from the scaffold like the dapper highwaymen of yesteryear at Tyburn. He contented himself with cursing and ranting, vowing to kill the Chief Justice and to return to the Johannesburg-Kimberley road as a highwayman just as soon as he could escape.[54] Hugh McKeone, who like his brother Jack entertained quasi-socialist ideas about the causes of injustice, was relieved and wise enough to keep his own counsel.[55]

If the two highwaymen entertained residual notions of themselves as criminal heroes or social bandits, few others did. Even at the height of the campaign to commute their sentences, correspondents and leader-writers had viewed their crimes with abhorrence. It was chance that had dictated their appearance – with Brown, Todd and Sutherland, core members of the Irish Brigade – before an angry Chief Justice at the Criminal Sessions in Pretoria at the height of an economic depression. The fact that the downturn had exacerbated political tensions in a region where the struggle for dominance was being ever more closely contested by British imperialists and Afrikaner nationalists only added to their misfortune.

From the moment that questions were raised publicly about the appropriateness of the sentences handed down in the McKeone-Cooper and Sutherland cases, the fate of the highwaymen was intertwined with issues of imperialism and nationalism, as well as the manner in which those forces played themselves out in terms of race, class and colour. As one analyst noted at the time, 'If we were to deal with Cooper and McKeone's case on mere principles of abstract justice, we should say that the world would be well rid of such desperadoes.' He then quickly conceded, however, 'In every noted crime we cannot escape from discussions on the race or nationality of the murderer[s].'[56] McKeone and Cooper became a *cause célèbre* not only because they were highwaymen who might end up on the gallows, but because they were *white* highwaymen in a deeply racialised setting.

The Irish Brigade was not merely a band of renegades fighting displaced proto-political battles around issues of social justice against Afrikaner nationalists, British imperialists or anybody else it happened to encounter in the remote colonial settings in which it operated. Its highwaymen in particular were more of a gang of dangerous criminals of European descent who preyed on black peasants and migrant workers – men who, if anything, were even more vulnerable than the Irish themselves. The discredited Chief Justice may have had more insight into both this phenomenon and the 'mere principles of abstract justice' than his critics gave him credit for. Directly after sentencing the highwaymen, '[t]he Chief Justice had the Kaffirs who were robbed by Cooper and McKeone called into Court', where he informed them that their assailants would be hanged. 'They could see,' he said, 'that they were protected by justice on coming to work in the Transvaal.'[57]

Perhaps the Afrikaner nationalists, too, were slightly – albeit not hugely – more exercised by notions of 'abstract justice' than their anglophone adversaries were willing to admit. Thus, those imperialists who saw in the McKeone-Cooper case an illustration of the 'unconscious drift towards a unity of interests' in the region were quick to trumpet the reprieve as a triumph for 'the people' who were 'sovereign' without bothering to explain which 'people' they had in mind. Nor did it help for jingoes – who had suddenly embraced the cause of men whom they refused to acknowledge as Irish – to attribute the salvation of McKeone and Cooper to 'the inherent sense of fair play which distinguishes South Africans' at a time when it was the British above all others who considered themselves to be the pre-eminent repositories and practitioners of 'fair play'.[58] As in all contested political systems, there was a marked divergence between the exercise of power and the mouthing of propaganda.

A week after McKeone and Cooper were reprieved, the State President and the Executive Council met again to consider the case of two black men convicted of murder in Johannesburg but recommended for mercy by a jury composed of burghers. Their sentences were commuted to life imprisonment and twenty-five years in prison.[59] Interestingly enough, only a few months later, in June 1892, the Volksraad, with the backing of Kruger, resolved to abolish public hangings. Such executions would henceforth take place within the confines of the central prison.[60] It would seem that the Irish Brigade had, unwittingly, contributed to a wider search for justice and a more modern approach to the problem of capital punishment in the South African Republic.

# 7

# The Birth and Death of 'Outlaw Legends': Social Banditry in a Racially Divided Setting

Myths which are believed in tend to become true.
– George Orwell, *The English People*

In racially contested environments, where the collective memory of the sufferings of ethnic nationalists has to be kept fresh for contemporary political struggles, arguments about 'the blood of the martyrs' will always take precedence over those depicting historic class struggles. In semi-literate societies personalities from the past are more effective for purposes of political mobilisation than are anodyne, impersonal processes. The competition for racial dominance can cloud and distort the understanding of history. In South Africa, marked by a divisive past and an uncertain future, this phenomenon poses difficulties for historians drawn from various 'schools' of interpretation, be they liberal, radical or nationalist.

Unlike the diamond fields of Griqualand West, where the emergence of a giant mining corporation, the consequent dispossession of the diggers and the Black Flag Rebellion of 1875 have all attracted some scrutiny, the early history of the Witwatersrand goldfields has been comparatively neglected by those interested in the social history of class struggle. Whereas the rise of the great finance houses and the rapid development of the gold-mining industry have both been fairly well documented, the resulting decline in the fortunes of the diggers, prospectors and small syndicates – unflagged by anything as dramatic as full-scale 'rebellion' – has been largely ignored.

The historiography of the Witwatersrand reads as if, after the stumblings of a few prospectors in the late 1880s, only the change in 1890 to the gold-recovery process stood between the discovery of the mineral and the advent of the modern world in 1895, which was signified by the staging of an attempted coup by a few mine owners. Accordingly, aside from the introduction of the MacArthur-Forrest process, little of consequence happened between the uncovering of the reef and the bungled attempt by some leading mine owners to capture the machinery of government. It is a narrowly geographical, state-bound perspective that suggests that for almost a full decade, from 1886 to 1895, there is little more for a social historian to do than concentrate on the rise of the deep-level owners of note or chart the careers of the self-styled 'Rand pioneers'.

This Genesis-like view of social change – in the beginning there was darkness and then came Rhodes and the Raid – is extremely limiting. It is precisely *because* the Jameson Raid offers us such an easy, well-signposted route into the issues of race, nationalism and imperialism – problems that attained their apogee four years later with the outbreak of the South African War in 1899 – that our understanding of the highveld's regionally integrated social history has become both badly foreshortened and unnecessarily fragmented. Allowing the Raid to become *the* dominant marker of change on the way to the 'Anglo-Boer War' has allowed it to overshadow the late 1880s and early 1890s, denying us fuller understanding in both length and depth.

With the historical focus fixated on 1895, we are disinclined to ask questions about the supposedly murky decade that preceded it. Thus we have largely failed to explore how thousands of whites in the mining industry, who, to a greater or lesser extent, were self-employed between 1886 and 1889, negotiated the path down into the ranks of wage-earning miners, the unemployed or the criminal outcasts of 1890–95. And, because we have not charted *that* process, we have also not grasped fully the degree to which the newly formed underclasses perceived the region as having a large integrated mining economy that enabled them to move relatively easily between labour markets for the semi-skilled and criminal enterprises in Kimberley, Barberton and Johannesburg.

The principal point of departure for an exploration of this 'dark age' in early highveld social history has to be the sharp downturn in the Witwatersrand economy in 1890, which matured into a full-scale depression lasting more than twenty-four months. The gravity of the 1890–92 depression has long been badly underestimated, as have its social consequences. On the Rand, the early weeks of 1890 were characterised, as we have already noted, by the mass departure of men who, to varying degrees, had been self-employed or working for companies in the mining industry. This exodus was sustained for several months while, at the far end of the highveld, observers on the diamond fields nervously monitored an influx of unemployed white workers and criminal elements. By late September it was estimated that, in inner Johannesburg alone, the European population had shrunk by up to a quarter, falling from around 20 000 to 15 000.[1] It follows that the figure for the decline in population of the Witwatersrand as a whole was significantly higher.

Johannesburg and adjacent towns had experienced a steady increase in crimes against property by the European underclasses ever since the opening of the fields. This increase was broadly commensurate with the growth in population, which, in turn, had been driven partly by the decline of the Barberton mines in the mid-1880s. The depression of 1890–92, however, precipitated a major outbreak in organised crime by whites along the length of the reef. At its western extremities, this spilt over into rural centres including Potchefstroom and Rustenburg and, beyond that, Klerksdorp and Bloemhof. Burglars made up the rank and file of the criminal fraternity in built-up areas, while the senior officers – bank robbers, highwaymen and safe-lifters – frequently extended their activities to peri-urban areas and outlying mining properties, profiting from the railways' slowness in arriving on the Rand. Again, it is impossible to know the exact numbers involved, but in August 1891 it was estimated by the local press that there were about 300 full-time 'professional' burglars at work in Johannesburg and that 'not a few' of them had travelled to the goldfields 'as deserters from the British regiments stationed at Maritzburg and from elsewhere throughout the Colony'.[2]

The ZAR government, just months earlier ministering to the needs of a slow-moving agricultural economy focused on farms worked by cheap black labour, found itself suddenly having to cope with the demands of a modern mining industry served by a large population of urbanised immigrants from the northern hemisphere. The modest judicial and penal system, accustomed to dealing with the crimes of a few miscreants in remote rural settings, was overwhelmed. The depression unleashed a white crime wave powering hundreds of professional criminals, many of them former soldiers drawn from the great industrial cities of the world, through an antiquated legal system based on Roman-Dutch law and served by outdated Continental prison practices. The resulting crisis, manifest between 1890 and 1895 but never fully resolved, was seized upon as an issue by both domestic and foreign critics of Kruger.[3] It was a challenge administrations elsewhere, confronted with similar problems, would have found extremely difficult if not impossible to overcome.

The ZAR government's ability to combat antisocial activities and punish wrongdoers during and after the depression was complicated by the fact that, beneath a seemingly amorphous mass of disorganised English-speaking criminals, there were often cohesive, well-trained criminal units with sufficient ethnic and organisational muscle to render them well disciplined and highly effective. Leading officials in the Kruger administration must have sensed who the principal enemy was. It was presumably not by chance that both the positions of Chief Detective and head jailer in Johannesburg were, at different times during the 1890s, occupied by Irishmen, one of whom – Thomas Menton – was himself a deserter from the British Army. But not even fighting fire with fire could halt a crime wave radiating from an economic depression. Nor could it prevent the country's leading prison from having to be guarded by the State Artillery, or stave off an embarrassing conflict between the State President and the Chief Justice. The years from 1890 to 1892 were, albeit in very different ways, no less challenging for the hard-pressed Kruger government to manage than was the better documented post-Raid era of 1895–99.

The root cause of the Boer state's immediate problems could be traced back to the Irish Brigade – a loosely coordinated, ethnicised, secretive, premodern organisation of indeterminate size devoted to crimes against property on the highveld and dominated by, but not confined to, deserters from the British Army and other expatriate renegades. The Brigade, membership of which was never restricted to the Irish-born, may have taken (or been given) its name from those Fenian sympathisers termed 'Irish brigands', who in the 1860s infiltrated the Liverpool-based 64th Rifle Volunteers as a prelude to becoming members of the Irish Republican Brotherhood in Lancashire. The original 'brigands' were thus largely motivated by an underlying love of Ireland, their anti-imperialist sympathies cultivated in the shadows of industrialising Britain's cotton mills.

The 'Irish Brigade' – an idea, as we have explored, incubated in the barracks of the British Army at Pietermaritzburg's Fort Napier and born out on the Barberton goldfields in the mid-1880s – was never entirely composed of 'Irish', nor was it strictly a 'brigade'. It was thus no local perversion; it was true to the original source of inspiration. Like its Lancastrian forerunner, whose members were more political than criminal, the Irish Brigade in South Africa – more criminal than political – was open to all who identified or sympathised with Ireland, be they Irish-, English- or 'colonial'-born. And as in Lancashire, the men of the Irish Brigade in southern Africa found themselves stranded amidst an incoming tide of industrialisation, giving rise to particularist political sentiments that often brought them into conflict with the demands of British imperialism. As 'social bandits' these Irishmen operated in closer proximity to proletarians – miners – than peasants. This, too, should not surprise us unduly for, as Hobsbawm once pointed out, 'miners are a peculiarly archaic body of workers' and 'the *Mafia* had some of its strongest roots among the sulphur-miners in Sicily before they turned Socialist'.[4] But even in Johannesburg, which the Irish found reasonably congenial, the Irish on the mines were hopelessly outnumbered by English miners from Cumbria, Cornwall, Lancashire and elsewhere. The Irish, nominally Catholic, remained a minority within a white minority on the Rand and, unlike the English or the Scots, were never represented – let alone well represented – in the leadership of the Witwatersrand Mine Employees' and Mechanics' Union.

Although locked into a mining economy, leading members of the Irish Brigade were adaptable and moved freely between the towns and countryside of southern Africa. Seen through the cold lens of geography, most members of the Brigade were closer to urban Englishmen than rural Irishmen. But when their actions and behaviour are scrutinised more carefully for signs of political consciousness, it soon becomes apparent that, although Brigade men were hardly country bumpkins, they nevertheless were the sons of men and women who were products of those Irish peasants who had either lived through or fled from the Great Famine. Even those members of the Brigade who were Lancashire-born were, albeit in unequal parts, 'men of two worlds' – peasants as well as proletarians – insofar as facets of the culture and traditions of rural Ireland had been passed down directly to them by their parents and reworked in the settings of industrial England. Codes of manly honour, including duelling, faction fighting and stick-wielding, elements seen as constituting the hard backbone of the Irish subculture manifesting itself in 'scuttling', went side by side with the softer tissue of folklore, language and music. Given this, the capacity of Brigade members to present at times as urban gangsters and then as rural brigands is hardly surprising. There may, however, have been other factors underscoring this noted 'Irish' adaptability.

In southern Africa, two leaders of the Irish Brigade – possibly reflecting the fact that although they were neither English-speaking or 'English' nor Afrikaner-Dutch intent on preserving an imagined racial purity – developed intimate relationships with 'African' or 'coloured' women and, when in retreat from mainstream society, took cover in disaffected black peasant communities resisting white control. Irish-Catholic marginals, men with a yearning for independence, were for reasons of class and culture already on the fringes of 'respectable' English society that was bent on the imperial project and the Afrikaner community that was set on distancing itself from almost everybody. Could it have been, then, that these men found the prospect of being assimilated into an oppressed African majority more acceptable than did other whites of, say, Protestant backgrounds? Perhaps the Irish Brigade shows us the way by suggesting that, when studying banditry in multicultural and multiracial societies, we need to pay more attention to religion in general, and perhaps Catholicism in particular. We need to understand not only those processes of exclusion leading to marginality but also those of assimilation and inclusion that are born out of greater tolerance of human imperfection.[5]

When probing the actions and behaviour of Brigade members for manifestations of political consciousness in a purely urban environment, other similarly pliable notions emerge. Members of the Irish Brigade were possessed of no easily identifiable, coherent political philosophy. Displaced proto-nationalists commanding an inchoate set of ideas of a low political order, they were, in essence, emigrant Irishmen attempting to come to terms with the twinned ravages of industrialisation and imperialism in a remote African setting. Far from the dreamt-of fields of Ireland and the factories of Lancashire that they had been forced to accommodate as they sought to find a vision of a just social order, they reflected a range of ideas drawn from contemporary ideologies, ideas that were not always easily reconciled. Anti-clerical sentiments, sceptical – if not outrightly misogynistic – ideas about the role of women in modern society and notions of social Darwinism went hand in hand with views deriving from Fenianism, socialism and the Victorian cult of masculinity. The result was an Irish stew of partially formed ideas. When further fuelled by alcohol, these notions often readily degenerated into anarchic behaviour and fed into practices that were more often conservative than progressive in nature.

Most men in the Irish Brigade, which was composed in the largest part from an alienated, feckless, hard-drinking cohort of highly mobile immigrants, had removed themselves from their families. As males drawn from a generation noted for its high incidence of celibacy, they eschewed marriage and steady relationships with white working-class women. This social profile, consistent with that of the classic 'social bandits', exacerbated criminal tendencies and further inhibited the development of an integrated set of ideas compatible with mainstream society.

Thus, while conceding that those members of the Brigade manifesting a degree of political consciousness tended to target the institutions of the rich or powerful, there can be no denying that others often indulged in opportunistic antisocial acts prompted purely by the prospect of self-enrichment or survival rather than the pursuit of social justice. The large phalanx of burglars on the fringe of the Brigade proper preyed as mercilessly on the property of vulnerable white miners as did highwaymen on the wages of black workers. Such men were, on occasion, capable of acting as extra-legal agents or hired hands for some of the very capitalists that the Brigade, taken collectively, despised, including the grand master of imperial opportunism himself, the bandit-prince Cecil Rhodes.[6]

Interestingly, Rhodes's principal mining interests on the Rand were clustered some miles west of downtown Johannesburg. His Kimberley-based agent, Hans Sauer, had arrived relatively late on the fields, forfeiting the chance of acquiring properties on the more centrally located main outcrop close to the main camp.[7] It may therefore have been fortuitous that a few freelance Irish thugs were around to benefit from capitalist largesse. But, from that point on, any links between chance, the Brigade and proto-nationalist Irish politics on the far West Rand have to give way to more rigorous enquiry and plausible explanations. There is a faint yet discernible line that runs through the far West Rand to form an important link between Irish and South African history. It may help to take another look at this neglected connection.

The ridges and white waters that give the Witwatersrand its name make token appearances around Johannesburg itself. It is only when one moves further west that the rugged beauty and peculiarly South African nature of the scenery – best captured by vernacular descriptors like *dal*, *kloof*, *laagte*, *poort*, *rand*, *spruit*, *stroom* and *vlei* – truly becomes evident.[8] It is broken, hilly country punctuated by steep white sandstone ravines and small streams that have had to work hard to carve out space among the thick, low bush that abounds. Twenty to thirty miles west of the big noise and smoke of the Rand's principal town, it presented itself proudly as bandit country: it lent itself to ambushes and hideouts and offered secluded rocky enclaves in which a man might practise shooting or dynamite a safe without attracting attention. It was also the natural gateway to the far north – beyond it lay Rustenburg, Mafeking, the Waterberg and a few fever-free routes leading to Matabeleland and Mozambique. By the same token, the broken terrain around Krugersdorp was ideal country for the frequent incursions by Boer guerrilla forces characterising the closing stages of the South African War.[9]

The West Rand was the favoured haunt and 'home from home' of the McKeone brothers, John McLoughlin and several Irish bad boys. The McKeone lads opted for prospecting around Krugersdorp when wanting to earn an honest living, and, when McLoughlin felt the need to lie low after the aborted Rattray project, he and Stevenson were for a while employed at Langlaagte 'Block B'. It was here, on the West Rand, that Jack McKeone and 'Dick Turpin' staged the robbery of the Standard Bank, the expedition that ended in a furious chase on horseback and a shoot-out near Witpoortjie. It was to his redoubts on the West Rand that McLoughlin retreated after the robbery at Somers' store in Rustenburg, the botched job at Pretoria Station and the shooting of the police informer. It was also from here that he twice fled, successfully, to the far north and east.

The hilly West Rand not only offered protection for bandits in need of a safe retreat, but it sat atop some of the most valuable veins of gold to be found along the length of the reef. Crudely put, the further west one moved along the arc of mines and towns – Robinson Deep, Langlaagte, Florida, Roodepoort, Witpoortjie, Luipaardsvlei, Krugersdorp and Randfontein – the richer were the gold-bearing reefs below them. This geological quirk was of little importance to most Irishmen on the Witwatersrand, who, in any case, were under-represented in the ranks of white miners. It was, however, a matter of considerable interest to assayers and refiners, and more particularly to those of them who supplied information about or worked directly with the amalgam thieves, payroll robbers and safe-lifters of the Brigade.

George Fisher, Charlie Harding, William Kelly, Jack McCann and Tommy Whelan – a refinery worker – were all Brigade members who were either sent to jail for or deeply implicated in the theft of gold amalgam. McCann and Whelan, two of McLoughlin's closest lieutenants, were part of a small but dedicated grouping centred on the West Rand. In 1895, they were both with McLoughlin when, after shooting Stevenson, he removed and dynamited the safe at the Champ D'Or Mine in Krugersdorp in order to help finance his grand flight across the Indian Ocean.

In much the same way, we can note here, in passing, until we explore it in greater depth in the next chapter, that when a half-dozen advanced Irish nationalists – Fenians from Dublin – chose to relocate to the reef in 1896–97 for reasons that appear to have had more of an economic than a political motive, they eschewed work on the lower-grade mines of the eastern Witwatersrand to take up instead employment closer to Johannesburg, on the Central or West Rand. Arthur Griffith, later the founder of Sinn Féin, attended a cyanide vat on the Robinson Mine for some months, as did John MacBride, who worked as an assayer on the same mine until he moved to a better position on the Langlaagte Mine. MacBride subsequently led yet another 'political' as opposed to criminal Irish Brigade into battle on the Boer side during the South African War. And, still within the greater West Rand orbit of expatriate ethnicity and politics, it may be noted that the Boer official most sympathetically disposed to Irish causes on the Witwatersrand in the mid-1890s, a man who later became a general in the South African War, was Ben Viljoen, who hailed from Krugersdorp.[10]

When standing back to take in the bigger picture, it becomes clear that, for different reasons, Barberton, Johannesburg and Kimberley all had relatively short lives as 'frontier towns'. In all three cases the success of thousands of highly entrepreneurial but imperfectly skilled, under-capitalised operators with assured access to public diggings was of fairly short duration. Mining 'camps' attracting 'pioneers' to 'rushes' are, almost by definition, characterised by open, poorly regulated economies. Such scenarios tend to give rise to 'digger democracies' that never last, politics marked by egalitarianism and the celebration of masculinity. The deaths of all frontier towns with socio-economic conditions capable of sustaining brigands and outlaws are announced by the arrival of professional undertakers devoted to ordered capitalist development – financiers, lawyers and policemen.

As 'frontier town' or 'mining camp', Barberton was ruined by failure, Kimberley and Johannesburg by success. Barberton boomed for barely five years in the mid-1880s and then collapsed when it became clear that the prospects for developing large, profitable mines were limited. In Kimberley the entrenchment of monopolistic capitalism on the diamond fields took about a decade – from 1870 to 1880 – while in Johannesburg, which benefited from the financial muscle developed earlier in Kimberley, the 'frontier town' phenomenon was even shorter lived, lasting from roughly 1886 to 1892. Seen against this background, it is easier to understand why the first Irish Brigade – and the 'criminal heroes' to which it gave birth – flourished between the mid-1880s and the end of the depression in 1892.

To the extent that outlaw legends garnered popular support among diggers, prospectors and syndicate owners destined for the labouring classes, they did so at a time when the Rand goldfields were poorly served – other than perhaps through the church – by institutions capable of articulating the aspirations or growing fears of self-employed or working men. Although the Masons were present from Johannesburg's inception, the orders of most other Friendly Societies – such as the Buffaloes, the Druids, the Foresters, the Rechabites and the Oddfellows – became a feature of local communities towards the end of the depression and over the half-decade thereafter. At least two of these societies had particularly close ties with industrial Lancashire. The Johannesburg branch of the Oddfellows, which was active from 1893 if not earlier, formed part of a 'Manchester Unity', while the Independent Order of Rechabites, associated more with temperance issues, was linked to a 'Salford Unity'.[11]

As in Britain, Friendly Societies sought to strike a balance between the need for conviviality and fellowship on the one hand and the demand for financial support in the event of a death, sickness or unemployment on the other.[12] In a similar vein, it will be recalled that the two principal political outlets on the Rand goldfields – the National Union and the Reform Association – dated to 1892. More importantly, so, too, did the formation of the Witwatersrand Mine Employees' and Mechanics' Union.

Given the absence of meaningful social, economic and political shock absorbers for the white unemployed between 1888 and 1892, it is not difficult to see how antisocial elements ranged against the rich and the powerful were able to constitute themselves as an Irish Brigade in Barberton, and then go on to establish themselves on the Rand itself. J.L. McKeone, the bank robber, and John McLoughlin, the safe-lifter, were able to gain a measure of popular support precisely because they acted in ways that gave voice to the otherwise silent dreams and frustrations of working men confronted by the growing power of both the state and mining companies during a period of economic hardship. Conditions for the emergence of criminal heroes were never again as propitious as they were in the late 1880s and early 1890s. The extension of an integrated rail network between 1892 and 1895 certainly eroded patterns of crime associated with a horse economy, but it was the development of a wide range of specialist institutions capable of absorbing and articulating working-class discontent that did more to ensure the eclipse of the frontier town, open economy and heroic criminals.

Even at the height of their fame as outlaw legends, however, McKeone and McLoughlin failed to plant deep roots in the consciousness of white South Africans. Pushed to name notorious criminals or gangsters, most whites will now look back only as far as World War I and point either to the offspring of another Irish, Kimberley-based grouping, the Foster Gang – active on the Rand in 1914 – or to the long-lived Scotty Smith, horse thief extraordinaire and 'social bandit', who died of influenza in 1919. McKeone and McLoughlin, both probably more urban gangsters than rural bandits, have been largely lost to our oral traditions.

As has been mentioned, the mere passage of time may have contributed to this hiatus in memory. But the deeper truth is that while the southern highveld clearly had a Ned Kelly-like moment in its turbulent history – lasting from about 1885 to 1895 – it never produced a criminal hero, let alone a social bandit, of Irish origin capable of winning sufficient affection or empathy from the public to acquire iconic status. J.L. McKeone and Brian Boru, riding on the coat-tails of the romanticised eighteenth-century Dick Turpin and Black Bess, captured the attention and support of a broad swathe of the English-speaking underclasses across the land. With his love of horses and his connection to the countryside and the mountain kingdom of Basotholand, John McKeone was more akin to the classic 'social bandit', a man partly bounded by rural life.

John McLoughlin, on the other hand, although perfectly capable of surviving through rural brigandage, was more at home in the towns and mining villages of the West Rand. With a menacing if not life-threatening artificial limb, McLoughlin's reputation was more akin to that of Spring Heel Jack, a mythological figure of nineteenth-century urban, industrial Britain that sported clawed mechanical hands.[13]

But regardless of whether our two Irish outlaw legends are seen primarily as urban gangsters or rural brigands, neither were around for long enough to develop enduring reputations of the sort enjoyed by that friend of the widows, Scotty Smith. Within months of having committed their most serious crimes, McKeone and McLoughlin, both bachelor boys, were on their way to the greatest repository of all for nineteenth-century Irish bandits: Australia. And, even as their fame or notoriety flared momentarily, their 'Irishness', too, was lost and folded into the emerging category of English-speaking South Africans as imperial Britain prepared to take control of the rapidly industrialising highveld and extend its territorial hegemony.

The Jameson Raid and the South African War of 1889–1902 no doubt also helped disrupt the successful transmission of any historical tradition of 'social banditry' to subsequent generations on the highveld. But, even if these and other great events of global significance had not contributed to the growing amnesia, there are other, more deep-seated reasons at work that, in a country like South Africa, tend to inhibit the development of lasting, vibrant traditions centred on white criminals as heroes.

The very concept of social banditry as employed by historians is inextricably linked to the pursuit of popular notions of justice by those on the margins of mainstream society. It is locked into the analyses of systems that are largely, if not fully, culturally homogenous. Colonial societies, defined by racial domination and its attendant inequalities, represent moral universes that are inherently unjust. In racialised settings marked by deep, underlying moral contestations, the transmission of ideas celebrating the pursuit of 'social justice' by marginals – however defined – is an exercise fraught with danger and runs the risk, albeit unintentionally, of endorsing other, more ambitious and fundamental programmes for political change. In apartheid South Africa crime became politicised just as surely as in the new, more democratic dispensation politics is being steadily criminalised. In racially ordered societies where the light of justice lingers forever above the horizon like the summer sun in polar latitudes, the long moral twilight does not encourage the telling of tales about outlaw heroes that are unproblematic – be they about 'Nongoloza' Mathebula, the brothers McKeone or John McLoughlin.

# 8

# Illicit Gold Buying, the Arrival of the Advanced Irish Nationalists and the Loss of the *Dorothea*

> A 'strange coincidence', to use a phrase
> By which such things are settled nowadays.
>
> – Lord Byron

The 1895 completion of an integrated rail network that served the labour markets and mineral economies of the southern African interior marked important changes in the patterns of organised crime on the highveld. Prostitution and white-slave trafficking, for example, benefited almost immediately from cheaper and more extensive links to America and Europe, which enabled former New York-based gangsters to 'import' white women to supply the commercial sex trade along the Witwatersrand. But the news was not universally well received in the underworld. The steam locomotive made for cheaper, swifter and more secure transport of not only banknotes, bullion, payrolls and specie, but black migrants, white workers and, of course, detectives and police. The arrival of the Iron Horse, which created new pathways as it ate its way through space and time, heralded a decline in the utility of the flesh-and-blood ponies that had served bank robbers, highwaymen and peripatetic safe-lifters in the remote interior.

But even though the horse economy of yesteryear was ailing, there were limits to what the railway could do for Witwatersrand mine owners and their shareholders. The inner temples of the industry, the refineries and smelting houses – the product of their investments if not their labours – remained vulnerable to human predation. Indeed, with coach robbers and highwaymen out on the road having to bend the knee before the Iron Horse and forgo bullion, and safe-lifters experiencing some difficulty in removing heavier and more secure safes built into the masonry of better-constructed mine premises, the theft of amalgam at the source of production assumed a new importance for those set on acquiring gold illegally.

The deep-level mines produced a stream of molten metal that seemed to grow in volume with the passing of each week; the economy gathered pace through 1893–94 and thundered on into the great 'Kaffir Boom' that unwound in September 1895. Amalgam thieves had to content themselves with a share of proceeds in good and bad times alike but, when the Jameson Raid further deepened an already sharp downturn, the mine owners who had attempted to overthrow the government looked to the same despised Boer state to realign their industry with the realities of profit-seeking. The mobility of unskilled black labour was curtailed through long-delayed implementation of pass laws and there was an attempt to curb gold theft, including that by semi-skilled white workers and middlemen, through the passage of yet another Gold Law, Act 21 of 1896.[1] Clauses 145 and 146 of the new legislation shifted the onus of proof onto the accused, deeming it an offence to be found in possession of unwrought gold. This may have slowed the loss of amalgam but it hardly eliminated ongoing theft in the industry.

Although neither he nor anybody else in the trade could quantify it with precision, few were better placed to appreciate the extent and nature of gold theft on the Witwatersrand than Percy FitzPatrick. The son of Irish parents, he had worked as a transport rider between Barberton, Lydenburg and Lourenço Marques in the mid-1880s before going on to become editor of the *Barberton Herald*. In 1892, FitzPatrick was made 'Head of Intelligence' at Hermann Eckstein's, the company that handled many of the most sensitive business interests of the huge Wernher-Beit company. Almost predictably, in 1895 he became Secretary of the mine owners' Reform Committee at the time of the Jameson Raid.

FitzPatrick, who as author, editor and citizen set aside his ethnic origins and was to emerge later as the quintessential English-speaking 'South African', could not have failed to hear of the Irish Brigade's activities in Barberton, or of their later exploits as navvies in Delagoa Bay – not least of all because he was in partnership with two men who had financial interests in the east-coast line. Nor, as intelligence chief at Eckstein's in the early 1890s, could he have failed to notice the considerable representation of the Lancashire and other Irish in the ranks of amalgam thieves and safe-lifters. *Nor*, for that matter, could he possibly have missed the fact that, in Johannesburg, Chief Detective Bob Ferguson was Irish and a man about town with few successes to his name when it came to the theft of amalgam.

Yet FitzPatrick remained the soul of discretion when commenting on the illicit trade and writing about the export route of stolen gold through the eastern Transvaal to Lourenço Marques and, from there, either on to Europe or out into the greater Indian Ocean basin, where the precious metal was always highly prized. When pushed, he noted that, in Johannesburg, 'It is notorious that there are a number of persons nominally engaged in the watch making and jewellery business, but who are doing a much better business than their capital and apparent energy warrants.'[2] But FitzPatrick left it to the correspondent of *The Times*, John Scoble, and a member of the Intelligence Department in the Cape, H.R. Abercrombie, to observe later that it was 'pretty certain that a considerable amount of the stolen gold found its way to agents stationed at Delagoa Bay, where the price of amalgamated and cyanide gold is openly quoted'.[3]

Paradoxically, any uptick in the trade in illegal gold could, in part, be traced back to a provision in the new Act. Officers in the state's Detective Department could, upon request, be issued with 'special permits' enabling them to purchase gold amalgam for purposes of entrapment. The system lent itself to abuse, in effect licensing corrupt officers to become gold-runners in their own right.[4] Scoble and Abercrombie put the value of gold purchased through the issue of 'special permits' at not less than three-quarters of a million pounds in the four years leading up to the South African War, and claimed – almost certainly incorrectly – that 'not a single amalgam thief has been discovered through this agency'.[5] But, whatever the truth of such claims, at least two things seem clear. First, 1893–95 saw a boom in Rand gold production. Second, the period immediately thereafter saw significant trafficking in illegally acquired gold, at least some, if not most, of which passed through Lourenço Marques.

## The Flight of the Wild Geese

The explosion of wealth on the Witwatersrand attracted the attention of the investing public around the globe. In November 1895, Rhodes's Consolidated Gold Fields declared a profit of over two-and-a-half million pounds – the largest return by a limited-liability company in the long history of the city. By 1898, the Witwatersrand was producing 27 per cent of the world's supply of the precious metal.[6] By then, however, tales of an African El Dorado had long been circulating, not only in Ireland itself, but throughout the Irish diaspora in America and Australia and, of course, in the sizeable ethnic enclaves of Glasgow, Liverpool and Manchester.

In Dublin, lacking an indigenous bourgeoisie substantial enough to generate a financial focus for globalising markets and a skilled proletariat on a scale to rival that of nearby Lancashire, it was left largely to disaffected and radicalised middle-class representatives to nurture the political aspirations and economic dreams of Irish nationalists.[7] By the mid-1890s, however, small numbers of Fenians – members of the Irish Republican Brotherhood clustering along the banks of the River Liffey – were finding circumstances to be less than propitious for the advancement of programmes involving strategically directed violence against English targets across the Irish Sea. They struggled to develop other, meaningful political campaigns.

The 1882 assassination of the Chief Secretary, Lord Frederick Cavendish, and an assistant in Phoenix Park, followed by a series of dynamite outrages in London and elsewhere during 1883–85, had alienated a significant number of IRB sympathisers, while the death in 1891 of Charles Parnell, the parliamentary advocate of 'home rule', deepened the vacuum developing in mainstream Irish politics. Seeking to regain the impetus for nationalist politics, Fenians regrouped to concentrate on a 'Gaelic revival' centring on authentically Irish cultural, literary and sporting activities.[8] By the mid-1890s, however, the achievement of the broader goal of obtaining Irish independence was jeopardised by an economic downturn. Despite a steady counterflow of funds for underground activities from the United States, the financial slump left both activists and ideologues short of funding. It was a moment, as one observer of Irish-South African connections has noted, of 'economic hardship' and political 'sterility'.[9] It was, however, also a challenge to the entrepreneurial spirit, one relished by the sons of many Irish artisans and shopkeepers.

In short, there existed a critical conjuncture of countervailing global economic and political trends: a pronounced boom in South Africa and bust in Ireland; an upsurge in anti-imperial sentiments on the post-Raid

Witwatersrand; and comparative stagnation in nationalist politics in Dublin. A seeming paradox, it was a development well in keeping with the classic counter-cyclical role played by gold in the trade cycles of the international capitalist economy. For young members of the Irish Republican Brotherhood, constantly in search of new sources of funding for their multifaceted struggles and well versed in diasporic and transatlantic politics, it was a moment filled with possibilities. This pleasant discovery may have been reinforced by information gleaned from two other sources.

One informant might have been Solomon Gillingham, an opportunistic expatriate Irishman on the make who cultivated close ties with the Afrikaner nationalist elite – including elements in Johannesburg that were shamelessly corrupt. He had been based in Pretoria for several years, where he owned a bakery.[10] Another source for middle-class nationalists might have been talk from within the lower ranks of the Fenians. In Ireland, as in Lancashire, the IRB never excluded interactions with those drawn from the underworld. By the mid-1890s, the criminal exploits of the army deserters constituting the first 'Irish Brigade' in southern Africa would also have been well rehearsed in the pubs of Glasgow, London, Liverpool and, especially, working-class Manchester.

Who precisely it was among the Dubliners who closed the circle of thinking about the possibility of IRB men making their way to southern Africa to achieve political as well as economic objectives will probably remain forever unknown. What is clear is that at some point, possibly just before the Jameson Raid in late 1895 or shortly thereafter, in early 1896, this thought pattern crystallised in the minds of at least five Fenian activists. They were already close friends, distantly related or well acquainted – Briscoe (member of staff at the *Irish Independent*), Andrew Gill (formerly of County Mayo, also of the *Independent*), Arthur Griffith (compositor and journalist, son of a printer, and occasional copy editor at the *Independent*), John MacBride (once a draper's assistant in Castlerea and later of Moore's Chemists, Dublin) and John R. Whelan (a salaried graduate).[11]

Historians of Irish nationalism seem, for reasons easily understood, to have emphasised the political importance of the group's decision to migrate to southern Africa. In so doing, they may have seriously underestimated the possibility – other than at the level of supposed individual hardship (a rather unconvincing argument in the case of most men in this group) – that economic motivations may have been at least as significant an objective for the Fenians.[12] Indeed, with the benefit of hindsight it now seems that it may well be that there were economic *and* political reasons behind the move south of this influential scion of the Irish Republican Brotherhood. While it is certainly true that the post-Raid political climate was for Irish and Afrikaner nationalists an attractive environment for jointly orchestrated anti-imperialist activities, the relatively small number of Irish miners on the Witwatersrand limited the possibility for mass political mobilisation in a setting that was, in any case, dominated by English workers with different sympathies. On the other hand, the very same mines offered significant opportunities for the illicit acquisition of gold amalgam by Irishmen. Whatever the core reasons behind the unexpected departure of the group, though, the preliminary activities of its members – at first glance puzzling – were plainly visible and recorded at the time. As one contemporary historian, suitably suspicious but not fully convinced that some new, multifaceted Fenian campaign embracing an underlying economic dimension was evolving, notes:

> For the adherents of conspiracy theories, a case can be made out that scheming was underway between Gillingham and the revolutionary Irish Republican Brotherhood. Gillingham was in London in 1896 and met Dr [Mark] Ryan; they became 'close friends'. The same year, John MacBride travelled to London, met Ryan, returned, resigned his job as a pharmaceutical chemist ('a fairly good salary'), and – to the surprise of Dublin Castle who expected him to become a paid organiser of the Irish National Association – set out for the Transvaal. A further link existed between the IRB activist Fred Allan and MacBride, as indeed it did between Allan and Griffith, who followed MacBride some eight months later.[13]

Again – with the benefit of hindsight – these prior movements between Dublin and England assume increased significance and, as we shall see shortly, strengthen rather than weaken the case for a well-thought-out 'conspiracy' focused largely, if not exclusively, on the illicit acquisition of gold. While involving other Fenians, this scheme seems to have centred on the two closest friends, MacBride and Griffith. Nor can this suspicion be attributed solely to the overexcited imaginations of latter-day historical sleuths. In Ireland, the man following local Fenian activists more closely than any other officer at the time, Inspector John Mallon of the Dublin Metropolitan Police, was equally convinced that the departure of so many IRB men for the far south was decidedly sinister.

On 14 January 1897, Mallon wrote to the Under-Secretary in Dublin Castle about the departure of John R. Whelan for southern Africa.[14]

> The above named [Whelan] who is a B.A. from the Royal University is a prominent member of the Irish National Association. He had a lucrative appointment here and his departure for South Africa [at] this time is very suspicious.
>
> He is the fifth I.N.A. man who has gone to South Africa within a recent very short period.
>
> McBride – Gill, Briscoe – two members of the *Independent* staff, and now Whelan.[15]

The inspector's reservations about the members of a tight IRB grouping's travels abroad might have been extended to include Arthur Griffith, who had slipped out of the Old Country unnoticed about a fortnight earlier. Indeed, some of Mallon's suspicions, including those aroused by MacBride's departure, may already have found their way into the cortex of British counter-intelligence in London. We know this because, as we will have occasion to note later, when MacBride arrived in Cape Town in mid-1896, his movements were monitored by two plain-clothes policemen even before he disembarked. MacBride, in turn, probably realised that his appearance had aroused concern in official circles and warned Griffith, who, when *he* left only a few months later, took the precaution of entering southern Africa via Lourenço Marques, thereby avoiding ports falling within the immediate sphere of British influence.

The Fenians spent the first months of their stay in the South African Republic familiarising themselves with local politics, becoming personally acquainted with leading members of the Afrikaner nationalist elite as well as some of the agents in Kruger's secret service, and working among small ethnic enclaves in Pretoria and on the mines around Johannesburg. By mid-1897 nationalist agitations of the orthodox kind among the Irish, which were conducted largely, although not exclusively, through Friendly Societies, had progressed to the point where Whelan chaired the John Daly court of the Irish National Foresters in Pretoria, MacBride headed the newly established Wolfe Tone court in Johannesburg, and Griffith, along with others, was active in the Amnesty Association on the Witwatersrand. Between them the Fenians succeeded in undermining the previously dominant local adherence to a 'home rule' option for Ireland, replacing it with more advanced notions of republican nationalism.[16]

Deeper covert political machinations – those that sought to harness and coordinate Afrikaner-Irish nationalist sympathies into joint political endeavours that might promote anti-imperialist notions among anglophone workers, or elicit Irish-American support for ZAR independence in a looming war – appear to have centred on Gillingham's business in Pretoria.[17] But it is possible that Griffith and MacBride's most secret project of all, one that could have concentrated on illicit dealings in gold, may have been launched only some months later, in the privacy of their rooms. Both had been employed on the mines since late 1897.

Most of the early political manoeuvrings by the Dublin Fenians took place, as already noted, against the backdrop of the deep-level mines' accelerated development, a sharp growth in gold output and an increase in theft of amalgam. It was during this same crucial period – after the Jameson Raid and in the months leading up to the outbreak of war – that the mine owners and the state, exploiting provisions in the newly passed Gold Law, attempted with mixed success to stem the haemorrhaging of amalgam from refineries along the Rand.

## Old State Machinery, New Illicit Gold Exporters: 1896–1898

After experiencing the shock of an attempted *coup d'état* in 1895–96, the hard-pressed republican government extended a programme of political reform aimed at thwarting imperialist ambitions. It did so by demonstrating a willingness to accommodate the ever-increasing demands of the mining industry. The most visible sign of this was the Industrial Commission of Enquiry of 1897, which presented mine owners with an opportunity to outline grievances about factors limiting the profitability of their enterprises – the infamous dynamite concession, for example. Other, rather more oblique complaints that impacted on their investments in a real, albeit more tangential, fashion were also made, including those about gold theft, the negative effects of organised prostitution and the administration of the liquor laws for Africans.

The Kruger government's response to the Jameson Raid may have been impressive, even substantial, but it was hardly instantaneous. In terms of administering the law – especially insofar as unauthorised gold buying, prostitution and the illicit trade in liquor were concerned – the tipping point came only in June 1898, with the appointment of J.C. Smuts as State Attorney. Before that, from 1896 to mid-1898, Johannesburg and the mining industry remained mired in corrupt maladministration. This state of mismanagement presented gangsters involved in organised crime, and, it would seem, the Dublin Fenians – Griffith and MacBride in particular – with a window of opportunity that was closing rapidly. While it remained open, however, they moved about relatively freely.

The 1890s saw a succession of State Attorneys pass through the ZAR administration, most of them drawn from the small Dutch cohort known derisively as 'Kruger's Hollanders'. One State Attorney who was not from this group was the 'progressive' Ewald Esselen. In 1894 Esselen resigned because he was unable to persuade the Volksraad to support the appointment, in Johannesburg, of a Chief Detective who, along with a special force of detectives, would be financed jointly by the state and the Chamber of Mines to deal with the theft of gold and gold amalgam.[18] On the Witwatersrand this lack of continuity at the most senior level was compounded by corruption in the Public Prosecutor's office as well as in the ranks of the police.[19] This ramshackle judicial system, presided over at local level by Dr F.E.T. Krause, principal Public Prosecutor, and the long-lived Chief Detective Bob Ferguson, was called upon in 1896 to implement the provisions of the new Gold Law. It was not a spectacular success.

Ferguson, who had a publicly declared interest in amalgam theft that stretched back to the debacle surrounding John McLoughlin after the shootings at the Red Lion in 1895, was the recipient of readily granted 'special permits' that allowed him to purchase gold for purposes of entrapment. It also enabled him to mingle in the dark and dusty interiors of public houses where underworld figures, along with current and former policemen, met workers in charge of reduction processes on nearby mines.

It is ironic that the mining house keenest to provide amalgam for the state's drive against illegal gold dealers appears to have been Consolidated Gold Fields, where Henry Birkenruth, a confidant of Smuts, was the person ultimately responsible for overseeing sales of amalgam to detectives.[20] Mundane aspects governing the day-to-day handling of the gold, together with the keeping of the accounts recording the disbursement of amalgam for 'illicit gold sales', was left to another of Cecil Rhodes's cronies, a veteran of his earlier banditry or 'private war' in Manicaland, Major N.L. Sapte. Extracts from ledgers kept by Sapte and passed on to Smuts show that during the first six months of 1898 Gold Fields alone provided police agents with pure gold, amalgam or 'cyanided lead' worth close on £1 000.[21]

Sapte, working directly with the state's undercover agents, including the shadowy Count De Sarigny and detectives such as R. Crawford and J.W. Treu, was held in the highest regard by Smuts and his superior. He was allowed to communicate freely, in writing, with the State Attorney about developments in the illicit gold trade. The one person whom Sapte did *not* deal with directly, however, was the man most suspected of corruption – the Chief Detective himself.[22] Ferguson preferred to obtain his own supplies of amalgam from a different source, H. Eckstein and Company, which controlled the high-yielding, well-established Robinson Mine and the still-developing Robinson Deep Mine.[23]

The net effect of all this was that once Smuts assumed office as State Attorney in June 1898, he controlled, developed and monitored information running through two parallel lines of communication that led into the illicit gold trade. These suitably isolated conduits did not depend entirely on the good offices of the Johannesburg police or the Chief Public Prosecutor. The first line, secret and made up entirely of 'untouchables' who reported directly and only to Smuts, ran through Birkenruth, Sapte and Treu, and from there down into the underworld. The second channel, official but deeply suspect, ran via Chief Prosecutor F.E.T. Krause and Chief Detective Ferguson, and then into the networks of illicit gold purchases. This was a standard counter-intelligence tactic, one familiar to Smuts. Indeed, it mirrored exactly the method he employed over precisely the same period to rout the immigrant white-slave traffickers who dominated the local trade in 'organised vice'.[24]

Before the arrival of Smuts, between June 1896 and June 1898, Ferguson interacted constantly with members of criminal syndicates engaged in illegal gold buying (IGB). As we have already had occasion to note, his efforts produced few successful prosecutions and he certainly failed to win the confidence of those in the leading mining houses. As the IGB trade boomed, alongside the staggered build-up of a small number of committed Fenians from Dublin, the Chief Detective continued to deal with men from the twilight zone whom he either already knew professionally, as they had once been policemen, or got to know well through his own illicit business dealings.

Carl Johan Friederich Hartung had known Ferguson since 1892; he also knew the Chief Detective to be deeply corrupt. An educated man drawn from a middle-class family that moved in influential Cape circles, he was for a time employed as a ZARP. During the Smuts era he was still capable of producing testimonials from the former head of the Rand police, Commandant D.E. Schutte, and the *veldkornet*, Kretzmar. Hartung was confident enough to write personally to the State Attorney when he once made a minor error in an affidavit, and he made such a favourable impression on mine owner G. Albu and the Assistant Secretary of the Chamber of Mines, Green, that he was allowed to collect his mail via the latter's business address. At Consolidated Gold Fields' head office Hartung was trusted completely by Sapte. He offered to provide the major with names and information about the activities of one of the very largest IGB syndicates operating along the Witwatersrand in 1897–98, one, it was said, with extremely close ties to Bob Ferguson.[25]

But, as Sapte, Albu and Green also knew, Hartung was not without an unblemished past. After leaving the Johannesburg police, Hartung had become a speculator dealing in amalgam. In the months leading up to June 1898, he had made a 'fair amount of money' before he was 'done down' by former friends in the leading IGB syndicate. His financial position, however, remained comfortable enough for him to offer his services to Gold Fields and Smuts without payment. He was content to be rewarded solely by any successful prosecutions that might arise from information he provided to the authorities. Hartung testified to the fact that during the closing four months of 1897, the period when IGB syndicates appear to have been at their most active, he, personally, had sold Bob Ferguson gold amalgam worth more than £2 000.[26]

Although neither the names involved nor the ethnic composition of the large syndicate that Hartung identified for the benefit of Consolidated

Gold Fields were ever recorded and are now lost to historians, he, Sapte and Ferguson would have been aware that there was a thin thread of Irishness running through illegal gold dealings on the Rand dating back to the heyday of the Irish Brigade in the early nineties. At some point between 1896 and 1898, however, there was an important but equally poorly documented development in Irish IGB circles that saw the arrival of two new actors – one undoubtedly Irish-South African and the other, it would appear, probably Irish-American.

Dr Leo P. Keller surfaced suddenly on the Witwatersrand in 1896, presumably from America, where he had fled after finding himself in acute financial distress in late 1898. His arrival coincided with a period of great volatility in ethnic intrigue in the United States, where '[r]umours of plots and counterplots in Irish republican circles and in the cauldron of Irish-American politics abounded in the mid-1890s'.[27] Keller's stay also overlapped with the influx – and departure – of those Dublin Fenians who, like Griffith, were fleeing the 'sterility' of post-Parnell politics.

Beyond the fact that Keller claimed to be married and the father of a child, almost nothing of importance is known about him. If indeed he was a 'doctor', as even the authorities were wont to address him, he may, as one chronicler has suggested, have been trained as a 'metallurgist'. He certainly had a profound interest in gold. While in Johannesburg he was of no fixed abode in the sense that his presence remained unrecorded in street directories. Likewise, he was never listed as an employee of any of the leading firms of gold assayers serving the mining industry.[28]

Keller's first and only known accomplice in illicit gold dealings on the Witwatersrand was Patrick Dennis O'Reilly. O'Reilly was a married man with four children who hailed from the adjacent Heidelberg district, part of the extended family bearing the same name spread across the Orange Free State. He and his close kinsman, Thomas O'Reilly, also of Heidelberg, were well connected in Afrikaner circles despite the fact that they were not particularly successful farmers and therefore led a somewhat chequered existence. In 1892, Thomas O'Reilly was successfully prosecuted for stock theft; by 1896 Pat was experiencing sufficient difficulty making a living off the land for him to leave and seek new opportunities in Johannesburg.[29]

When he and Keller first met briefly in Pretoria, O'Reilly was not a particularly good guide into the shadowy world of Rand illicit gold dealers, while Keller (alias 'Kelly'), if he was ever a 'metallurgist', was incapable of distinguishing bogus amalgam from the authentic article. On 21 January 1897, they along with J.J. Lennard, a confidence man who, when corresponding, chose to evoke the spirit of Robin Hood by signing his letters as 'Will Scarlet', were each sentenced in the Circuit Court in Pretoria to a year's imprisonment without hard labour for being found to be dealing in, and in possession of, false amalgam. It was a salutary sentence but one that neither of the purchasers, 'Dr. Leo Keller' or Pat O'Reilly, was destined to complete.[30]

Just five months into their sentence, an unusually well-financed and well-thought-through campaign for their early release took root in Johannesburg and, possibly, in Pretoria. In June, a petition began to circulate in public houses, supporting a plea for their release that would be forwarded to the State Secretary and ZAR Executive by a firm of 'Dutch' attorneys well versed in the Gold Law – J. Raaff and T.G. Kieser. The petition soon had over 200 signatures, which included many Afrikaner as well as English names but also did not want for names such as Abbot, Bright, Brophy, Cochrane, Cunningham, Gibson, Lorimer, O'Connor, Ryan and Wilkinson. Interestingly, the petition did not include the name of Sol Gillingham, arguably the leading figure in the Irish community, or that of a single member of the group of Fenians from Dublin whose departure had aroused the suspicion of Inspector Mallon only a few months earlier. Here was a petition anchored in ethnic politics but lacking names of the foremost Irish nationalists of the day. Strange. By August 1897, Keller – or was his real name, as seems likely, 'Kelly', with the 'Dr' a mere affectation, part of an alias? – and Patrick O'Reilly were both out of prison and back on the Rand.[31]

The pair's re-entry into Johannesburg coincided, almost to the month, with two of the leading Dublin Fenians – Griffith and MacBride – taking up positions in the reduction works of a prominent mine, and with what was possibly the single most active period in the history of the IGB trade on the Witwatersrand. But Kelly and O'Reilly were no longer partners, having gone their separate ways after the messy business with 'Will Scarlet'. Measured against what is said to have followed, Kelly was spectacularly successful, managing to accumulate thousands of ounces of gold over six months, between June and December 1897. O'Reilly's fortunes were mixed. He certainly penetrated to the very heart of the illegal trade, where he often encountered and also obtained valuable information about police secret agents such as Count De Sarigny and the state's counteroffensive against the dealers. The latter stood him in good stead when, in mid-1898, he was again prosecuted for illegal dealing and sentenced to three years' imprisonment and a fine of £200. Indeed, so sensitive was the information he possessed that, on request, he was again released from prison.[32]

Kelly, who could not conceivably have been working on his own, was probably obtaining amalgam or gold from networks that must have included Irishmen, possibly even the Dublin Fenians. By late 1897 it was clear that he and his unknown associates – men capable of thinking on a transoceanic scale – were ready to embark on an audacious export programme.

## Goodbye *Dorothea*

Built in America and registered first in 1834, the three-masted barque *Dorothea* started life as the *Columbus*, sailing between New York and Liverpool for the Black Ball Line. But when in 1845 her cabins became too small and outmoded for modern travel, she was converted from passenger service into a trader and thereafter passed through the hands of a series of European owners. She ended her working life as the *Ernestine*. As an elderly lady of the seas, who should perhaps have known better, she was, in the mid-1890s, lured south by the call of gold and into the company of the Irish. Her penultimate voyage was devoted to transporting iron rails for the east-coast line from Antwerp to Lourenço Marques but, on entering Delagoa Bay, the *Ernestine* struck a reef. She was freed with difficulty but had to be run aground, where she was abandoned and then sold as a hulk.[33]

When Dr Keller/Kelly first saw the *Ernestine*, she had lain neglected on the beach at Lourenço Marques for eighteen months and was far from seaworthy. Kelly purchased the ship for £500, renamed her the *Dorothea*, put her under an American flag and then spent a further £3 000 repairing her for the short journey south to Durban, where he planned on an entire refit for a far lengthier voyage to who knows where.[34] It was an enormous investment for a man who, only months earlier, had been languishing in the Pretoria prison until somebody had paid Raaff and partners to get him sprung, but it was presumably one commensurate with anticipated profits. What the master of the *Dorothea*, Captain Mathison, may not have known was that a large quantity of illegally acquired gold was rumoured to have been stashed aboard the ship shortly before she was set to depart.[35]

The *Dorothea* duly set sail but, on 31 January 1898, ran into heavy seas on a dark night off Cape Vidal on the coast of Zululand. The ballast shifted and the ship took on water, listing so badly that the bilge pumps would not work effectively. The captain ordered 'the masts and bulwarks to be cut away' and the *Dorothea* briefly righted herself. But by then she had retained so much water that abandonment was the only option. Boats were lowered and the scratch crew, put together from men of several different nationalities along with John Watts, 'a representative of the owners', were set afloat. They were rescued by passing vessels some time later and eventually found their way to Durban. There, the American consul took an interest in the well-being of the crew, and Mathison informed him that the ship was uninsured, a development that, given her undeclared cargo, was not surprising. Watts, however, was singularly unforthcoming. Beyond acknowledging that the ship belonged to 'Dr. Keller', he provided no details at all about the 'Rand syndicate' that owned the *Dorothea*, what the vessel was carrying or what her envisaged destination might have been.[36]

Informally, however, it was widely rumoured that Kelly had acquired the *Dorothea* to enable his 'firm' to export illegally acquired gold and that the cargo was worth a tidy sum. Back on the Rand the loss of the uninsured vessel occasioned dismay, perhaps even panic, among Kelly and his unknown partners. Members of the syndicate were forced to redouble their activities in the IGB business in order to raise the additional capital necessary to salvage the *Dorothea*'s hidden wealth, or risk having to abandon their longer-term plan to raise funds for whatever personal or political projects they had in mind. The buoyancy in the IGB trade, as we shall see, persisted right up to the time of Smuts's appointment and beyond that, but, predictably, neither the Chief Detective nor his agents saw fit to report directly or indirectly on the loss of the *Dorothea*, or on the scandal over the loss of gold sustained by unknown Johannesburg mines. That seemingly important duty was left to Ferguson's successor in the year that war broke out, 1899.[37]

According to the new Acting Chief Detective J. Watts, who was quick to establish official contact with his Natal counterparts, it was a matter of only weeks before Kelly, with one James Spittle and a half-dozen other unnamed partners, put together a new syndicate that attempted, unsuccessfully, to salvage what was said to be 32 000 ounces of gold. It was the first of at least two attempts by the original owners of the sunken wreck to rescue their project, but to no avail. Kelly overreached himself financially and soon fled to America, but the Natal government took sufficient interest in the wreck to make yet another fruitless attempt at salvaging the supposedly valuable cargo. Several further, equally unsuccessful attempts were made to recover 'hidden treasure'. In 1980 it was claimed, somewhat unconvincingly, that samples retrieved from the wreck had indeed been confirmed as being gold.[38]

But by mid-1898, Project *Dorothea*, whatever that might have been – a strictly criminal endeavour undertaken by a lone American-Irish marginal and a few friends, or one with more ambitious political objectives and embarked on in conjunction with the Irish Republican Brotherhood and a few well-placed Fenians working in Rand refineries – lay in tatters. But this does not exhaust the list of possible collaborators in the original venture. From what transpired later, it would seem that Ferguson and De Sarigny were also members of the syndicate operating in illicit gold. It is within this rather vague context that we now have to probe more systematically the role of the Fenians.

## Hello Conspiracy

*John MacBride (1868–1916)*

The British government believed John MacBride to be a serious risk to its interests long before he was based in Johannesburg, and well ahead of his leadership of the Irish Brigade that fought for the Boers in the South African War. Even before this 'Fenian agent' could leave the *Pembroke Castle* in Cape Town during the closing week of May 1896, he was intercepted by a police sub-inspector in plain clothes named Eaton, who was accompanied by an unnamed 'private detective'. By subterfuge the two men somehow managed to inspect MacBride's baggage and found that he had packed two revolvers along with an unspecified 'peculiar piece of machinery' for his long train ride to the Witwatersrand.[39]

It is unlikely that MacBride, a man who had served a political apprenticeship in the shadows of Dublin Castle, was unaware of the fact that his presence had attracted official attention. As suggested earlier, this dockside experience probably alerted him to the need to warn Griffith to enter the subcontinent via Lourenço Marques in Portuguese territory rather than take the more familiar and natural routing through Cape or Natal ports. There, several months later, like ships passing in the night, Griffith would have slipped past another budding Irish nationalist martyr, young Roger Casement, then still a junior official in the British consulate. But here again, regardless of how or why MacBride's warning was transmitted to Griffith, the authorities at the Cape were anxious to perform their imperial duty. The Prime Minister, Sir Gordon Sprigg, informed Sir Hercules Robinson, the Governor, about what had been found on the *Pembroke Castle*. The Governor, a man of wholly Irish descent, understood what was at stake. MacBride was followed to Johannesburg by a 'private detective', who, upon his arrival, made MacBride's presence there known to the Chief Detective.[40]

Ferguson *knew*, from day one of MacBride's appearance in the Transvaal in June 1896, that he was a 'Fenian agent'. He must also have realised when Griffith joined MacBride six months later that he, too, was probably an IRB member, and that if the pair of them were involved in the IGB trade it most likely had a political as well as an economic logic to it. Indeed, if the two newcomers *were* involved in the illegal trade it was unlikely to have been primarily for personal gain, since neither of them were big spenders or conspicuously wealthy. The chances were that *if* the Dublin Fenians were dealing in amalgam the funds were being channelled out of the country and into the coffers of the IRB abroad, for political purposes.

Ferguson, who had a 'coloured' wife to whom he was married by antenuptial contract, led a modest suburban existence when he was not in the office or away assiduously working the public houses.[41] He appears not to have betrayed the presence of an IRB cell on the Rand to his superiors, while the Dubliners for their part appear to have said nothing – good or bad – about a Chief Detective who was widely known to be corrupt. Could there have been a vestige of patriotism in some of Ferguson's actions, and could he later have had IGB dealings with the exceedingly well-placed MacBride and Griffith? The truth of the matter is that all of this is speculation; nothing is certain. That said, these are some puzzling silences at a time when the IGB trade was thriving and a shipload of gold had been lost on the Natal coast. Like Sherlock Holmes, we are left having to account for the dog that did not bark in the night.

It is no clearer how twenty-eight-year-old MacBride put bread on the table during the first few months of his stay on the Witwatersrand than it is in the case of Griffith, who trailed him by six months. The son of a storekeeper in County Mayo with family ties to the Gills, and a man who had himself twice been a shop assistant, MacBride made no attempt to set himself up in business or to obtain work in the lively local retail trade. Instead, the small redhead, who was later given the not wholly edifying nickname 'Foxy Jack' by friends, for a time concentrated on political work. Then, perhaps parading some elementary knowledge of chemistry that he had acquired during his time at Moore's Pharmacy, he found himself a position as an 'assayer' on a singularly profitable mine, the H. Eckstein-owned Robinson Mine, that was close both to town and to MacBride's political work.[42] Later, in 1899, with the outbreak of war looming, he seems to have changed employers, moved further west and secured himself a more senior position at Langlaagte 'Block B', an Irish redoubt where 'One-Armed Jack' McLoughlin, too, had once worked.[43]

Among those present at MacBride's meetings at the Johannesburg mines in 1898 – organised to help plan the celebrations marking the uprising of the United Irishmen a hundred years earlier – was the often contradictory and always enigmatic Robert Noonan. A Dubliner, an illegitimate child and a man given to changing his name and place of birth as circumstances demanded, Noonan later gained fame as the author Robert Tressell. As a house painter, socialist and trade unionist with a preference for the use of white labour during his time on the Witwatersrand, Tressell wrote *The Ragged Trousered Philanthropists*, which was later to achieve near-iconic status in the twentieth-century British labour movement. Noonan's presence on the organising committee and his ideology – more socialist than nationalist – may have reflected MacBride's broadly accommodating approach to anti-imperialist politics. There were others – not necessarily committee members – who were more tightly focused on the issue of Irish nationalism.[44]

Most commentators agree that it was probably MacBride who invited Griffith to join him on the Rand and, indeed, on the mines – in reduction works – just a few months before the *Dorothea* sank. If so, it may have been for some secret project that was to be of finite duration, one that, in the case of Griffith, came to an end a few months after the final, failed attempt by the ship owners to salvage her hidden cargo. But could the twenty-six-year-old Arthur Griffith, later an iconic figure in the nationalist struggle for Irish independence, the founder in 1907 of Sinn Féin and by 1922 the first president of the Irish Free State, have – like the young Stalin who once robbed banks to help fund the Bolsheviks' early revolutionary drive – been party to illegal gold transactions for political ends?

*Arthur Griffith (1871–1922)*

A wholly appropriate, easily understood fog of bewilderment has long since settled over the historiography of Griffith's strange stay in southern Africa. The sharpest analyst and undoubtedly the most careful chronicler we have of his short visit commences her narrative suitably intrigued: 'Why,' she asks in the first lines of an illuminating essay, 'did Arthur Griffith leave Ireland for South Africa in late 1896, especially as he had already fallen under the spell of his future wife, Maud Sheehan, a girl of a well-to-do family whom he had met through the Celtic Literary Society?'[45] Griffith's early biographers and friends – often the same people – have adduced reasons that have left even the most informed historians sceptical.[46]

Gus Byrne, a 'fellow Sinn Féiner', suggested later – quite implausibly – that Griffith was pushed to leave by economic hardship rather than pulled south by other attractions. Once in Lourenço Marques in January 1897, Griffith boarded the inland-bound train, stopping off only at Belfast in the eastern Transvaal to stay with unknown friends for a few days before continuing his journey into the heartland of the South African Republic. In Pretoria, Griffith, who bore a club foot, made no effort to find a job; instead he spent some months 'idling in pleasant Pretoria', the source of his livelihood 'somewhat hazy'. It was not the behaviour of a man in deep financial straits. Another close friend and biographer, Patrick Colum, correctly notes that it had never been Griffith's intention to emigrate, apparently conceding that there was also no overriding political reason for his leaving. He was more like a person undertaking a 'sojourn', a longish seasonal migration, one bracketed by time but, by implication, one built around achieving some undisclosed objective. Hard-pushed to find other, more credible reasons for his departure, historians have scrabbled around for possible explanations – a sense of adventure, the call of close friends or perhaps distant relatives (such as E.R. Whelan, another member of the Celtic Literary Society) or the chance to improve his health.[47] In the end, forced to settle for a rather unsatisfactory melange of motivations for Griffith's mysterious southerly migration, our best guide views it neutrally; she terms it a 'sabbatical'.[48]

The puzzle of how the earliest months of Griffith's sabbatical in Pretoria – from late January to the end of March 1897 – were financed only deepens when we note that, in April, he was invited by another Irishman, J.J. Lavery, to become part-owner and part-contributor/editor of the small *Middelburg Courant*. Six decades later, in the 1950s, yet another of Griffith's admirers, Judge Michael Lennon, commissioned some research in South Africa, which he used as the basis for an article he wrote commemorating the thirty-fifth anniversary of Griffith's death. Our own alert guide, however, spots the problem immediately: 'Lennon's claim that Griffith had a little money which he invested in the *Courant* is surprising in view of the fact that Colum notes that the presentation made to him on his departure [from Dublin] by his friends of the Celtic Literary Society helped to pay for his passage [south].'[49] Griffith, it seems, was – even at this early stage of his stay – obtaining funding from some other, unidentified source. It could have been MacBride.

The *Courant* was a modest-sized provincial newspaper. In addition to the town that lent it its name, it circulated in tiny Brugspruit and Belfast as well as in Pretoria and Johannesburg. The little town of Middelburg itself – a strange choice of residence for the urban Griffith – sat astride the east-coast line, enabling him easy movement between the Witwatersrand to the west and the fast-fading goldfields around Barberton and Lydenburg in the east, which he visited on at least one occasion for whatever reason. What was striking about the *Courant*, however, was the rather cavalier political line that its new part-owner took when addressing a small readership divided unequally between largely English-speaking imperialists on the one hand, and a few Afrikaner nationalists in high dudgeon after the Jameson Raid on the other. As Griffith himself later put it:

> It had been the policy of the *Courant* to please all parties, the English for preference. I explained to the owner that if he wanted me to edit the paper its policy must be one which would please myself… I eventually managed to kill the paper, as the Britishers withdrew their support, and the Dutchmen didn't bother about reading a journal printed in English.[50]

It was as if Griffith did not *care* about the money invested in the paper, or about its long-term success. It was the attitude of an irresponsible or undisciplined person, which he never was. It may, however, also have been the behaviour of a man who had been advanced a limited sum of money for a project by unknown others and who, for a time, while it suited their purposes, used the business – which straddled the line to Lourenço Marques – as part of a cover, for other ends.[51]

Factors other than Griffith's politics, however, contributed to the demise of the *Courant*, and after about six months in Middelburg, by the last quarter of 1897, he was back in Pretoria. He remained there until at least February 1898. Griffith was once more close to the Rand, the economic and political heartbeat of the country. But, once again, it becomes unclear how exactly he earned a living. Colum assumes that he must have survived by taking on casual jobs – something that would not be a problem if it did not run foul of Griffith's reputation among admirers, who tend to see him as having been in more regular employment, an almost 'saintly figure who sent most of his wages home to his family'.[52] Something about Griffith and his finances does not add up.

Nobody knows when, exactly, but it was in early 1898 – at the height of the boom in the illicit gold trade, near the closing months of the corrupt Ferguson era and just prior to the advent of the reforming Smuts administration – that Griffith moved across to Johannesburg, where he was again in close proximity to his raffish friend MacBride. Griffith was in charge of a cyanide vat in the reduction works at the Robinson Mine for several months in mid-1898. Here – even more so than MacBride, who would also have enjoyed comparative freedom of movement about the property – Griffith was strategically located to steal amalgam, should he ever have been tempted to do so. As one contemporary observer of the early recovery process on the Witwatersrand noted:

> It is well nigh impossible for gold to be stolen by strangers and casual visitors to the mine. The only person to extract, without attracting attention, sufficient gold to be worth taking away is the man who has long and uninterrupted access to the battery house, the cyanide vats and the closely-observed place where the raw gold is within reach.[53]

Such long hours of uninterrupted labour could, of course, be further extended if the man presiding over the cyanide vats had a reputation for being a touch awkward, or even unapproachable.

While on the mine, Griffith, a tough and self-disciplined man but one also capable of relaxing among friends, taking the odd drink and manifesting a sense of humour, appears to have embraced an image characterised by austerity, abstemiousness and political distance. It was his hero-worshipping friend Byrne who noted: 'The English miners thought Griffith unnatural because of his high standard of purity. No one dare utter an obscene remark or a double meaning word in his presence at any time. A nun in a cloister was not more chaste.'[54] Nor would Griffith's pro-Boer politics in the face of growing unrest among Uitlanders have endeared him to many of his fellow miners.[55] It was hardly the recipe for cultivating company among rough-and-tumble white workers either on site or off duty. Griffith, who was aware of this deficiency, apparently chose not to do anything about it and, years later, passed on his impressions of this to Byrne, Colum and others.

It was a strange environment indeed for an aesthetically inclined, poetry-loving, mystical ethnic nationalist more accustomed to chasing ideas with words than recovering gold with cyanide. Griffith, it seems, had moved quite easily from largely mental to manual labour – notwithstanding his foot – and was always above suspicion. Even more puzzling is the way in which, at a moment when most of his countrymen on the Rand were building up a head of steam to celebrate the centenary of the Irish risings of 1798, Griffith's own political temperature suddenly dropped to almost subcritical levels.[56] Yet again this development does not fail to attract the notice of our faithful guide: 'Griffith appears to have been rather a background figure at Irish celebrations,' she notes, 'and does not seem to have spoken either at St Patrick's Day functions or at the '98 banquet.'[57] Here, then, was a deeply political man intent on maintaining a low profile; a person hoping to go unnoticed.

But the mist of mystery that clings to Griffith and his finances refuses to lift. By mid-1898 he was in continuous employment and, although hardly earning a fortune, was better placed to make regular remittances to his family then than at almost any other time during his stay in South Africa. And so he did. But what is interesting about those payments – if we are to take a friend's chronicle at face value – is not so much the regularity of his remittances but their size. Perceiving Byrne's following observation literally is dangerous because, as our sharp-eyed guide warns, it may have been an in-joke, or part of a jibe at his own family on the part of a long-time admirer. Nevertheless, Byrne wrote: 'I had entered the Civil Service, and my sister month by month used to write of the large sums he sent home. My sister and his were inseparable friends.'[58] Once again, there seems to be a gap between Griffith's seemingly modest means and his apparent disbursements.

When all of these latter-day observations are placed back to back, an impression emerges of something sinister underlying Griffith's stay in South Africa. It is a view in accordance with Inspector Mallon's misgivings about the travels of the Dublin Fenians at the time of their departure from Ireland many months earlier. It is portrayed here that Griffith was moving about as a secret agent in ethically dangerous territory, that he was somehow operating in a zone of moral hazard and that there were veiled challenges to his integrity that increased rather than decreased as he approached his time on the Rand mines.

All of this could easily be dismissed as pure speculation were it not for the importance of an exchange that Griffith himself initiated with another journalist friend, James Stephens. On his return to Ireland from South Africa, Griffith had, in 1899, helped found and then edit the weekly *United Irishman*. That journal, rumoured to have been secretly funded by the Irish Republican Brotherhood, lasted from 1899 to 1906, when Griffith left to set up and edit *Sinn Féin*, a daily that ran until it was suppressed in 1915. One evening while out on a stroll, at a time when Griffith was experiencing difficulty in keeping the project afloat, he confided his innermost feelings to his brother scribbler and political sympathiser. It is a set of musings that may, inadvertently, have revealed how, amidst great financial temptation, Griffith had been an agent for the IRB in southern Africa, helping to raise funds and act as conduit for money that could have underpinned first the *United Irishman* and later *Sinn Féin*. As Stephens recalled it:

> 'This is the first time in my life,' [Griffith] said, 'that I feel a sort of regret, not a real regret,' he emphasised, 'a sort of regret that I have always insisted on being an honest man.'
>
> 'Why should you crave to be a thief on this particular night?' I enquired.
>
> 'I could have been a fairly wealthy man if I had the luck in those days to want to be dishonest.'

> 'So,' I queried encouragingly.
>
> 'In the Africa of those days,' he continued, 'men in my position were able to retire after a few years and buy theatres.'
>
> [At that point they were interrupted.]
>
> On the second step he resumed, 'Personally, I have never wanted to buy a theatre, but our paper would have had at least a chance to make its way and win its public. I am thinking of you men [the journalists] also,' he said.
>
> 'How do we set up a craving for dishonesty in you?' I marvelled.
>
> [At that point the pair were again interrupted.]
>
> We resumed our walk; and on the second pace:–
>
> 'If I had taken the chances that were all around me,' said Mr Griffith, 'I could have paid you writers a great deal more than I am able to pay you now.'[59]

Several now unanswerable questions leap out at the historian from this short exchange between Griffith and an admiring employee. Where exactly was this African temple of temptation on which he had so bravely turned his back? It was unlikely to have been in Pretoria, where he spent his days 'idling', nor, almost by definition, could it have been at Middelburg, where the *Courant* had to be abandoned due to financial debacles. It must surely have been at the Robinson Mine, where he worked in the reduction works surrounded by amalgam. And what, precisely, was the link between such funding available to pay journalists working on the ill-fated *Sinn Féin* and his ability not to pay them, but to pay them more? Does this not suggest that the basic supply of funds might itself originally have come from an African source? What are the chances of Griffith having accumulated, from remittances alone over, say, a nine-month period, sufficient funds to have supported first the *United Irishman* and later *Sinn Féin* for at least a decade, if not longer? Those projects would, surely, have required more substantial endowments.

What seems more likely is that both in South Africa and in Ireland after his return, Griffith's modest personal circumstances as well as his journalistic endeavours were being supplemented by an unknown, outside source of funding. If that is so, then it surely had to have come from within the innermost informal circles of the Irish Republican Brotherhood cell in which he and other Dublin Fenians were operating.[60] And, if that is the case, is it not possible, too, that Arthur Griffith – with or without the assistance of MacBride – both before and after the sinking of the *Dorothea*, was acting as an agent or conduit for gold amalgam skimmed from the Robinson Mine and sold for cash that sometimes found its way into IRB coffers via the eastern Transvaal and Lourenco Marques? Griffith certainly had no love of the mine owners, writing, 'There is perhaps no more heartless set of scoundrels in any part of the world than the rich men of the Rand.'[61] Might not such men invite retribution?

Would Griffith, painted in such saintly colours by his admirers and confronted by great wealth, not have been tempted to play Robin Hood and steal from the rich to give to the poor and the oppressed back home rather than merely line his pockets for personal gain? Is it at all possible that Arthur Griffith, part romantic, was the biggest Irish social bandit of all?

It is difficult now, peering through the haze of times past, to envisage the president of the Dáil Éireann as a young man in his mid-twenties who might have interacted with bandits, bartered with dealers over amalgam or participated in weird pirate-like schemes in which three-masted ships set sail on the ocean blue to transport stolen gold to distant ports – all for motives that were not wholly sound in moral terms. Surely only a sublime flight of fancy could connect the younger Griffith to an all-action nationalist man; a man who, although playing a minor part with the Dublin Volunteers during the Howth gun-running of 1914, did not participate directly in the famous Easter Rising of 1916.

Perhaps. But then again, perhaps not. Griffith, no less than John McLoughlin and the Lancastrians who made up the first Irish Brigade, was, in part, a product of the late Victorian literature to which he had been exposed as a child. As a boy, he took pride in his knowledge of ethnic tales and indigenous music and lyrics, including ballads, some of which celebrated the achievements of Irish highwaymen.[62] And it was Byrne who noted that Griffith had read his way 'through all the penny dreadfuls from *Blood on the Doorstep*, or *The Wicked Mother-in-Law* to *Sweeney Todd: The Demon Barber of Fleet Street*'.[63]

This underlying taste for adventure and crime at times surfaced in the columns of the tiny *Middelburg Courant* in which, on one occasion, Griffith ran a lengthy article on 'The Modern Pirates' – desperadoes who operated in Malay waters along the Chinese coast.[64]

As with many an ethnic nationalist, however, this unusual choice of subject may have revealed both a darker side to his personality as well as some unknown, but possibly unfortunate, personal experiences. Just a few months after the conclusion of his southern African adventures, in 1899 Griffith went on to use the columns of the IRB's new outlet, the *United Irishman*, to name the 'three evil influences of the century … Pirates, the Freemasons and the Jews'. Freemasons he may have known from Dublin and feared for whatever reason. 'Jews' he would certainly have encountered in Johannesburg, although in what capacity remains unclear – it may have been via some underworld dealings in illegally acquired gold amalgam. But where on earth could the young man have picked up personal experience of 'pirates'? It was, and is, a most unlikely concatenation of life's supposedly dark forces. The two categories based, in part, on religion could have been conjured from a Catholic nightmare, but the third – exclusively criminal and unambiguously secular – was hardly an analogue. Could Arthur Griffith have been haunted by the ghosts of 'pirates' who had somehow done him down? Was he plagued by the unsuccessful attempts at salvaging of the cargo of the *Dorothea*?

Nor were all Griffith's interactions with criminals confined to noisy meetings across printing presses where ink swirled up to meet type set in lead. Indeed, he provides us with the only known case of an advanced Irish nationalist drawn from the post-Jameson Raid era interacting with remnants of the old, proto-nationalist bandits of the Irish Brigade. He met them in the eastern goldfields around Barberton, again a venue astride the rail route to Lourenço Marques, and deemed them 'the most courteous ruffians I have ever known'.[65] Here, then, was the chaste, unapproachable workman of the Robinson Mine sharing drinks with men who, for all their genteel manners, had been or were part of a bandit grouping notorious for burglary, highway robbery, theft and, occasionally, murder. Griffith – should circumstance demand it – was capable of admirable flexibility. It was hardly the behaviour of 'a nun in a cloister'. Irish Brigade stragglers may not have been the only miscreants he ever met.

## The Good Fortune of the Mysterious 'Mr. A. Griffiths'

MacBride, who entered the South African Republic via Cape Town in mid-1896 to bury himself in expatriate Irish politics on the Rand, might have been lost to the colonial authorities, but he was certainly not forgotten. The Cape government, despite maintaining fairly close ties with the republican authorities north of the Vaal, continued to act as the eyes and ears of imperial authorities in London. In late January 1898, H.A. Jenner, Chief of Police in Cape Town, was alarmed by the sudden appearance in the city of three men – two unknown Frenchmen and an Italian – suspected of being 'anarchists', who split up before taking separate overnight trains bound for Johannesburg.

On 4 February 1898, Jenner, who could provide descriptions of the men but not their names, took the precaution of writing to his counterpart in Pretoria, warning him of the possibility that such mischief-makers might seek out Irish radicals on the Rand:

> A man named John McBride, who was a member of the Dynamite and Fenian Societies came out here in May 1896. We at that time communicated with Chief Detective Ferguson, who will no doubt be able to give you all information where this man is to be found and what he is doing, as he will no doubt be busy should any plot be hatching.[66]

Jenner, however, had written to a part of the ZAR administration that was by then – the closing months of the pre-Smuts era – in an advanced state of corruption and decay. Ferguson made some desultory enquiries about the anarchists, who, he claimed, may have been spotted in Bloemfontein. Surprisingly, he made no progress in tracking 'Foxy Jack' MacBride, who was then employed at the Robinson Mine, where he was in daily contact with amalgam and, should he so wish, men managing large supplies of dynamite.

Nobody bothered to reply to Jenner. But the Chief of Police in Cape Town was not about to be fobbed off. On 4 May, he wrote again to Pretoria, this time downplaying his concerns about anarchists but enquiring about 'Fenians' in general, and one in particular. He reminded the Commissioner about the earlier, unanswered letter and continued, 'I would like to hear if you have any idea what became of these men [the anarchists], also if the man McBride is still in the Transvaal.'[67] Could it be that after the loss of the *Dorothea* British counter-intelligence, working through its official channels in the Cape and Natal, had renewed its interest in those members of the Irish Republican Brotherhood based on the Witwatersrand?

This time there *was* a response, a remarkably quick and clear-cut one, but in the form of a mere interdepartmental memo from Chief Detective Ferguson, who, when asked in a note on 9 May from his Commissioner whether he bore any knowledge of MacBride, replied in writing two days later with what could only have been a categorical lie: 'I know absolutely nothing about McBride.'[68] Far more likely was that the Chief Detective knew MacBride and Griffith only too well, and that he had risked maintaining a silence about the former's political agitations because, if probed further, it could have linked them all, including Kelly, to illicit gold buying and ultimately tie them to the uninsured cargo of the *Dorothea*. Perhaps considerations arising from within this same dark nexus informed Griffith's decision later that year to maintain a low profile during the Irish centenary celebrations.

Within days of Smuts assuming office in June 1898, the Chief Detective – apparently unaware that the new State Attorney was putting in place a parallel, secret structure within the police that had him as a principal suspect – set out to trap Count De Sarigny and James Spittle.[69] Why Ferguson chose to move at precisely that moment is uncertain. It may have been part of an attempt to demonstrate to Smuts that, contrary to reputation, he was actively pursuing IGB dealers. Or, with the syndicate behind the *Dorothea* falling apart fast after a costly but failed attempt to recover the cargo, he may have wanted to make a pre-emptive strike against those who knew of his own involvement in the IGB trade. We may never know; it was all smoke and mirrors.

Ferguson procured 300 ounces of amalgam worth about £400 from officials at the Robinson Mine on 14 June 1898.[70] Three days later, De Sarigny, whose title and country of origin remain a mystery, was arrested along with Spittle. But it was by no means clear that the gold obtained by Ferguson from the Robinson Mine had found its way into the hands of the supposed dealers, or back to the offices of the Public Prosecutor. The case was pushed firmly to the back of the official cupboard. Its underlying political considerations were apparent within days, however, members of the Second Volksraad, the house devoted to Uitlander – immigrant – affairs, taking an interest in the matter.[71] With one arm of the state acting against the other it was all an embarrassing mess and, not surprisingly, Smuts eventually decided to drop a prosecution that would have revealed not only the ineptitude of the state, but dubious dealings by several of his senior officers. The fallout came in the form of a long-standing political scandal actively promoted by opponents of the Kruger government that lasted right up until the outbreak of war.[72]

From the moment the Ferguson-De Sarigny operation went sour, Smuts, under pressure organising initiatives against crime syndicates involved in illicit liquor sales, prostitution and white slavery, accelerated confidential enquiries into the activities of the Chief Detective and the office of the Public Prosecutor, F.E.T. Krause. At first, he used Detective J.W. Treu to search for possible links between Ferguson and the major IGB syndicates, but it later became apparent that Treu may have had a vested interest in dislodging Ferguson, whose position some claimed he wished to assume. Treu was replaced by another agent, Crawford. But, even so, bad blood persisted between two rival factions of policemen. In January 1899, Treu underwent a preliminary examination for conspiring to murder the former Chief Detective. The state's case was led by none other than Dr F.E.T. Krause, whose own name was mentioned frequently during proceedings in relation to Ferguson's official doings. The case against Treu was eventually dropped, but not before Ferguson, in turn, was found guilty of threatening Treu.[73]

Between June 1898 and February 1899, as Smuts's anti-corruption campaign slowly gathered momentum, competing, treacherous factions within the police and the Public Prosecutor's office – with the principal actors all seemingly implicated in the issuing of permits and the illicit trade in gold – were involved in cases of assault, bribery, conspiracy to assassinate, theft and the purloining of material evidence.[74] And, running right through this conspiratorial and violent underworld was yet another small but significant band of Irishmen, or men of Irish descent, bearing names such as Beatty, Doyle, Ferguson, O'Flaherty, O'Reilly and Poole. Yet Arthur Griffith – refinery worker, a man with a journalist's eye, someone deeply involved in Irish expatriate politics at the time of the centenary celebrations, a person renowned for his memory who would later recall many, far less interesting developments that took place during his southern African stay – appears to have remembered nothing at all of these extraordinary events.[75] Nor, for that matter, did that other famous refinery worker and nationalist icon, John MacBride.

In the weeks *before* he was transferred to the liquor squad, J.W. Treu managed to worm his way into the margins of what had once been a major IGB syndicate but that, by then, was close to complete collapse. On 11 July, he wrote to Smuts outlining the role played by Ferguson and other minor figures in a series of betrayals, plots and counterplots that revolved around gold. It would have done justice to a modern spy novel. Treu drew attention to, among other things, the true identities of some of the aliases in use; the unlawful issue of a police revolver; sex scandals, including one that involved Ferguson arresting his rival, Patrick O'Reilly; and the roles of various Continental 'speculators'. In passing, he made mention of 'the *Dorothea* business' but, unfortunately for historians, failed to commit details to paper.[76] The *Dorothea* affair was the elephant in the room, but raised issues so fraught that nobody uttered so much as a whisper.

The new sense of direction and purpose for the State Attorney and his secret operatives was welcomed at the head offices of Consolidated Gold Fields and H. Eckstein and Company. But other mining houses remained sceptical after the De Sarigny debacle. At Gold Fields, however, Henry Birkenruth and Major Sapte forged ahead and drew in their own agents, including former ZARP Carl Hartung, whose past had by then been thoroughly probed. Hartung's first task was to identify leading members of the IGB syndicate he had fallen foul of as a prelude to persuading the state to issue a warrant for their arrest. Today this would be termed a joint 'sting' operation.

On 29 June, Sapte, enthusiastic about what he and others had elicited from their debriefing of Hartung, wrote to the State Attorney. He suggested that the puritanical Smuts personally interview Hartung to satisfy himself of the man's bona fides and character – a stiff test indeed. So confident was Sapte that Hartung would pass this test that he went on to suggest to Smuts that, if he were agreeable, he should then

> ... grant him a warrant made out for the arrest of a man named A. Griffiths whom Hartung says he can arrange to arrest with a large amount of amalgam on him. Hartung stated that he could get such a warrant from the Public Prosecutor, Dr. Krause, but I personally feel that it would be best to avoid in any way asking for any assistance from the officials here [in Johannesburg] until arrest has actually taken place.[77]

The next morning, having had the chance to think through the matter more carefully, Sapte again wrote to Smuts: 'I certainly trust that the Government will see their way to allowing Hartung to trap the man, A. Griffiths …' This was to be done on a no-cost-to-industry-or-state basis because, if it proved successful, it would 'allow him to trap others'.[78] The major's confidence in Hartung grew. So convinced were he and his colleagues about the soundness of the information they had been supplied that, a week later, on 6 July, Sapte wrote to the State Attorney yet again, urging him to give immediate attention to Hartung's offer to help trap the 'illicit gold dealers'. But Smuts, concentrating on Ferguson and under pressure as State Attorney, got his secretary to reply. The secretary noted that, although the State Attorney had made no decision, the matter was still under consideration.[79] Nothing happened. But still Sapte – about to depart for Europe – would not let go. On 16 July, amidst IGB dealings that continued to flourish via certain individuals despite the disintegration of the largest IGB syndicate on the Rand, he made a last effort to get Smuts to agree to the deployment of Hartung in a joint operation.[80] But somewhere along the line, between Sapte's travels and Smuts's unrelenting focus on Ferguson, the case of 'Mr. A. Griffiths' fell between the cracks.

But who was the elusive 'Mr. A. Griffiths'? It is possible that the first, faint clue lies in the very manner in which his name was recorded in confidential company and police correspondence. It was unusual for those suspected of being involved in underworld activities to be addressed with the honorific prefix 'mister'. Suspected criminals were usually referred to simply by their surnames, or by their first names along with family names or aliases. 'Mr. A. Griffiths' was clearly a cut above your normal gangster or ruffian; more of a gentleman – possibly even an educated man slightly out of place amidst the untutored lower-class company or semi-skilled workers generally found around the margins of the illegal gold trade. Could he have been a bespectacled, well-spoken journalist who suddenly found himself in an unaccustomed role? It is not clear, but it's certainly worth puzzling over.

Historians will, correctly, point to the fact that the person Consolidated Gold Fields was after was said to be 'Griffiths' rather than 'Griffith'. That on its own should not, however, be a source of too great consolation. In the very letter that the major wrote first naming his chief suspect, he – or the secretary who typed his letters – misspelt the names of two others, including Hartung's second name, 'Johan', which was rendered incorrectly as 'Johann' with a double 'n'. In terms of accuracy there really was – and is – not much to choose between 'Griffith' and 'Griffiths'.

Other questions remain. In 1898, the local street directory listed the presence of no man by the name of Griffith or Griffiths. Represented in whatever fashion, 'Griffith' or 'Griffiths' was not a common name in Johannesburg at the time. Moreover, the man allegedly close to the heart of the leading IGB syndicate, the one that had other prominent Irish names in it such as O'Reilly, was not known only as 'Griffiths' but bore the same initial as the unfortunate Arthur Griffith. What were the chances of there being not one but perhaps two men named 'Griffith' or 'Griffiths' in town who bore the same initial? And, if there was more than one 'A. Griffith' or 'A. Griffiths' in Johannesburg, how many happened to work in the reduction works of a singularly profitable mine where a very close friend worked as an assayer on the same property?

No more was heard of the elusive 'A. Griffiths' who excited so much interest among top officials of a leading mining company over the winter months of 1898, and who enjoyed the singularly good fortune of being ignored by an overworked State Attorney intent on getting rid of his Chief Detective. Nor, for that matter, is much more known about the strangely low-key Arthur Griffith during the closing months of his stay on the Witwatersrand. He stayed on for the centenary celebrations in October, but then, at some unidentified point in late spring or early summer, quietly took leave of the mine. Our most trusted guide to his movements in southern Africa is, once again, suitably quizzical. 'Why Griffith gave up the life of an expatriate Irishman,' she notes pertinently, 'is uncertain.'[81]

Deliberately avoiding the popular routes home that left from the Cape or Natal, Griffith made his way to the coast through the same eastern goldfields where he had once met up with remnants of the old Irish Brigade. He was, it is speculated, motivated by William Rooney's plea to return home to start up a newspaper, the *United Irishman*. In passing, it is interesting to note that while a good deal of other correspondence surrounding Arthur Griffith's life has survived, the communication between him and his closest friend, Rooney, covering his extended stay in southern Africa has not. Had it endured it might have provided additional clues as to the nature of his stay in Johannesburg. He left Lourenço Marques, the last port seen by the crew of the old *Dorothea*, aboard a modern Dutch ship that took him back to Europe via the wonder of the Suez Canal. What Griffith had sent ahead of him, or what he took with him, nobody knows.

Looking back, however, it would seem that an extraordinary concatenation of coincidences linked the last of the stragglers of the old Irish Brigade to the arrival of the most important of the Dublin Fenians on the Witwatersrand between 1897 and 1898. It was almost as if the old proto-nationalist 'social bandits' of the Irish Brigade were consciously handing over the baton of crime-as-politics to the new 'advanced nationalists' who were more versed in politics-as-crime. That elusive missing link, if ever found, would produce extraordinary, global continuities in the history of displaced anti-imperialist struggles and modern Irish nationalism. Perhaps Arthur Griffith, founder of Sinn Féin and the first president of the Irish Free State, a man who had met and interviewed another activist with great political ambition, territorial designs and a taste for bandit-like adventures, Cecil Rhodes, turned out to be southern Africa's most successful social bandit of all.

# Conclusion: The Irish Brigade and Anti-Imperialist Struggles in Retrospect

> For what are states but large bandit bands, and what are bandit bands but small states?
>
> – St Augustine, *City of God*

John MacBride was among several ardent middle-class, Rand-based nationalists who, on the eve of the South African War, helped to mobilise, organise and shape the Irish Transvaal Brigade that took to the field on the side of the Boers. The term 'brigade', however, was not 'a military reality but a romantic allusion to the Irish Brigade of Wild Geese who had fought as part of the French army in the eighteenth century'.[1] As an explanation for the official designation of a band of fighting men, this seems correct. The politically committed Fenians who headed and named the Brigade were unlikely to have been inspired by, or even broadly sympathetically disposed towards, its eponymous underworld predecessor on the highveld – the other 'Irish Brigade' of 'Captain Moonlight' and John McLoughlin.

That noted, however, we probably also need reminding that the Irish members of Parliament in the Palace of Westminster in Victorian times were said, too, to constitute an 'Irish Brigade' and that *their* role was hardly unproblematic, involving, as it did, elements of collaboration with, as well as resistance to, imperial power. Irish MPs had to conduct their struggle both within the system and against it. The men that came to make up 'Captain Moonlight' and John McLoughlin's foot soldiers of crime occupied similarly ambiguous, compromised positions as Irishmen in a British Army fighting imperial causes. In southern Africa, no less than in Westminster, the connotations of 'Irish Brigade' were not necessarily unambiguous, nor could they with absolute certainty be correlated to a political consciousness characterised by out-and-out anti-imperialist sentiments.

By 1899, the term 'Irish Brigade' was a symbolic designation as likely to be infused with a measure of confusion and uncertainty as most other ethno-nationalist nomenclature.

But if there was a clear-cut division in the minds of the Fenian founders of 'MacBride's Brigade' between that brigade and its more prosaic criminal predecessor, was this distinction equally clear to the rank and file of the Irish Transvaal Brigade? MacBride's Brigade might have presented itself as an entirely new military unit informed by political commitment, but upon closer examination one is bound to ask whether its origins were perhaps not a little more complex. In short, was there a total rupture between the proto-nationalism of the earlier, criminal 'Irish Brigade' and the later advanced nationalism that defined the leadership of MacBride's own brigade? The paucity of surviving documents renders a definitive answer impossible, but the temptation to speculate is utterly irresistible.

First, we know of at least one occasion between 1897 and 1898 when an advanced nationalist – none other than the future first president of the Irish Free State, Arthur Griffith – met members of the original Irish Brigade in the goldfields of the eastern Transvaal. What the nature of his business with the former bandits was is impossible to know. It may have been a purely social interaction predicated on a chance encounter. It would, however, also appear that Griffith's flow of personal income while in southern Africa was inexplicably erratic and that while working in the reduction works of a Rand gold mine he was, by his own admission, exposed to the temptations of dishonesty. If he was involved in illicit gold buying – as a mysterious 'A. Griffiths' was suspected of being at the same time – then it would seem that Griffith was merely acting as the conduit of funds for Irish Republican Brotherhood projects back in Ireland. If he and other advanced nationalists were engaged in unlawful actions, it is likely that they – like the young Joseph Stalin – were interested in ways in which criminal activities could assist in underwriting politics, whereas the original Irish Brigade members, proto-nationalists, were more interested in crime than in politics. And if that is true, then it may, at very least, demand a modest reassessment of the role played by Fenians in South Africa during the mid-1890s in the funding of IRB cultural and political projects back in Ireland.[2]

Second, was it possible for 'Foxy Jack' MacBride and others to mobilise more than 200 Irishmen – many of them drawn from the Witwatersrand –

without encountering elements of the earlier dispensation? It seems unlikely, even more so when we are reminded that several highveld Irishmen joined other commandos directly under the control of Boer generals. In October 1899, a journalist hostile towards the Boer republican cause observed members of the Irish Transvaal Brigade making their way to the railway station. He recorded that informants had told him that the group was made up, almost entirely, of 'loafers' leavened by some of 'the worst sweepings of Johannesburg'.[3] We also know that later both the British and the Boers, when hard-pressed, did not hesitate to recruit men from prisons to advance their causes. Given this, it would not be surprising to find a few members of the old Irish Brigade, men with imperfectly developed political sentiments, fighting for the republican cause.[4]

Third, it is noteworthy that a small but significant number of Irishmen attached to MacBride's Brigade or other Boer commandos were designated either as 'dynamitards' or assigned to 'dynamite squads'. Deneys Reitz claimed that there was 'an Irish love of explosives' and noted how, in Smuts's raid south into the Cape Colony, two Irishmen distinguished themselves by the creative use to which they put dynamite.[5] Former miners constituted one reservoir for such talents, but another source would surely have been those hardened miner-gangsters familiar with the darker arts of safe-lifting and blasting.

Fourth, the latter stages of the South African War were famous for the large-scale employment of guerrilla tactics as epitomised by General De la Rey – a man whose kinsman 'Groot Adriaan' had, it was said, himself once been a *vrijbuiter* – a freebooter.[6] As an art form guerrilla warfare demanded adaptability, the capacity to spring surprises and an intimate knowledge of the environment and its natural resources. Such innovative forms of resistance were ideally suited to the Boers, but they also called forth skills and tactics that would have been familiar to the urban-gangsters-cum-rural-brigands of the first Irish Brigade.

But since we are unable to identify or retrieve the names of known criminals in MacBride's Brigade, we are left to view it as a product of the advanced nationalists rather than of the proto-nationalists of 'Captain Moonlight' or John McLoughlin. Yet again, we are left staring at a profile of post-Jameson Raid Irishmen that seems hopelessly skewed in the direction of the middle classes and professional skills, one almost unnaturally divorced from the altogether more turbulent early history of the Irish on the Witwatersrand. It is a picture reinforced in the sparse existing literature that pushes to the fore the Irish-born in South Africa as 'a small elite band' of men possessing technical skills who were extracted largely from Ulster and Leinster.[7] While the outlines of this portrait appear to be accurate enough, the failure to capture other sources of light coming from the Lancashire- or South African-born Irish limits our appreciation of the underlying historical continuities at work.

If most or all Irish bank robbers, burglars, highwaymen and safe-lifters and blasters had indeed left the Witwatersrand by the outbreak of war in 1899, then they must have done so at some point *after* the Jameson Raid, by which time the region was more thoroughly integrated into the emerging southern African railway system. It is possible, even likely. But, if so, it is yet another topic that begs for additional research into the global migratory patterns of Victorian underworld figures manifesting strong ethnic identities. What is clearer, however, is that at the time of the Jameson Raid itself the political consciousness and social background of Irishmen on the Witwatersrand was probably more mixed than it appears to have been when MacBride formed his brigade.

When Jameson launched his raid on behalf of the mine owners over the closing days of December 1895 and the first week of January 1896, men from the various anglophone ethnic minorities on the Rand mobilised themselves into 'brigades', either to defend their own lives and property or to support Boer commandos in defence of Johannesburg, should the need arise. This mustering gave rise to a surprising array of groupings that reflected the heterogeneity of the town's small white population, with men drawn from, among others, America, Australia, Cornwall, Cumberland, Durham, Northumberland, Scandinavia and Scotland. Others formed part of 'mixed' brigades such as the 'Afrikanders' and the 'Devil's Own'.[8]

Amidst all this ethnic *Sturm und Drang*, unknown organisers mobilised over a hundred Irishmen into a 'brigade' at a time when the town still housed a fair number of Irish of doubtful character.[9] Again, as with MacBride's Brigade, it is difficult to conceive of any such unit being formed without it attracting at least some Lancashire-Irish stragglers from the McLoughlin era.

If this were so, then the political commitment of the 'Irish Brigade' that was raised at the time of the Raid may well have been leavened by the presence of some less committed, more opportunistic elements behaving in ways customarily associated with gangsters at times of war. In this regard it is instructive to note that the leading historian of the Irish in South Africa writes that, while the Brigade drilled along with other 'brigades', it was not always easy to tell who it supported – invading imperialists or defending Boers.[10]

It seems entirely plausible, but impossible to prove, that a thread of Irish criminality runs all the way from the earliest days of the Rand through the mid-1890s and into the South African War. If true, it is hardly a startling conclusion; most armies, insurrections and wars have similar rusty threads pervading them. In the same speculative mode, however, it is far more interesting to ask a question that is almost entirely counter-intuitive – namely, could the very *idea* of the Jameson Raid itself, in some modest way, have been inspired by the earlier actions of 'Captain Moonlight' or John McLoughlin's notorious 'Irish Brigade'? Is it not possible that banditry formed part of the logic of politics of the region and the times, and that by examining the largely concealed grammar of brigandage we may better understand the dynamics of banditry and power? What happens if – just for the moment – we set aside what we know about Cecil Rhodes, the Reform Committee, and the Jameson Raid and its sad history, and, instead of viewing it solely as an attempted *coup d'état* led by a mine owner with imperialist ambitions, we see it as but a bungled bandit raid orchestrated by an adventurous frontiersman?

In short, was not 1895–96 perhaps a defining moment in the history of the Witwatersrand in a rather novel sense, in that it marked a turning point where the criminals in McLoughlin's Irish Brigade shed their identity as gangsters to be seen more as 'social bandits', and Jameson's raiders – ostensibly made up of 'politicals' – emerged as something more akin to brigands?

Taken at face value the Jameson Raid comes across as a slightly insane and wholly criminal incursion by 400 armed men on horseback into a neighbouring state in an attempt to acquire valuable territory. The adventure was authorised by a visionary bandit-prince who, by the time the invasion was under way, had already successfully concluded two other 'private wars' in the subcontinent – in Manicaland and Matabeleland.[11] Those interested in the reasons behind these military campaigns will, no doubt, point to the need to understand Rhodes's lofty imperial motives as a reason for such expeditions. That may well have been a consideration, but we also know from other sources – including some of his closest friends – that not all of Rhodes's interactions with brigands and mercenaries were either so disinterested or so innocent.

Oral tradition has it that, at some point in the 1880s, Rhodes personally commissioned the well-known bandit Scotty Smith to invade and smash up Free Town, the small village on the Free State side of the Griqualand West border that was devoted almost entirely to the illegal trade in diamonds. Smith and his gang, it is claimed, routed the dealers and were paid for their efforts by the De Beers Company. If this tale, which has a ring of truth to it, can be verified, then – as we shall see – it was not the only occasion on which companies controlled by Rhodes resorted to the use of brigands to ensure their economic interests.[12] In this way the mine owners and the bandits joined forces to enforce what Karl Marx once termed 'primitive accumulation' in the very earliest phases of capitalist development.

The Jameson Raid, led by the swashbuckling Leander Starr Jameson commanding troopers of rather indifferent quality, was launched from Pitsani, in Bechuanaland – a point of departure located in the backyard of the two short-lived Boer-bandit 'republics' of Stellaland and Goshen, which were eventually united and incorporated largely into the Cape Colony. The raiders themselves, who were supposed to have been supported by a full-scale spontaneous uprising of foreigners – Uitlanders – in Johannesburg, were defeated and rounded up by armed Boer commandos after a series of skirmishes around Krugersdorp, Luipaardsvlei and Randfontein; that is, in the same hilly terrain – such as the Alexandra Kloof and nearby mountain ridges and vleis – most favoured by the Witwatersrand's very own white brigands – bank robbers, highway robbers and safe-lifters.

In line with St Augustine's observation, Jameson's raid was but a failed attempt by bandits to secure themselves a state, and it was recognised as such at the time. In London, the *South Africa Magazine* commented on the raiders, suggesting, 'We know they were wrong, and we know, too, that being disavowed by their Government, they can be hanged like dogs by the victors, who are entitled to treat them as mere brigands.'[13]

The raiders were defeated by the forces of a larger but vulnerable state whose own defensive capacity, in the form of men on horseback, was organised along lines that most nineteenth-century brigands would have recognised all too easily. What underlay Jameson's hopes for a successful invasion, however, was the disdain that he and fellow conspirators had developed for the Kruger state over the months leading up to the raid.

The conspiracy that led to the Jameson Raid was refined in the Cape during the latter half of 1895 by Rhodes, a man who took a considerable interest in Irish politics at Westminster.[14] In plotting the raid, he moved in concert with Joseph Chamberlain in Whitehall and a host of other leading political actors throughout southern Africa.[15] By October, his chief lieutenant, Jameson, was sufficiently contemptuous of Boer fighting prowess to boast to Hans Sauer – supposedly a reluctant latecomer to the Reform Committee – 'I could drive them out of the Transvaal with five hundred men armed with *sjamboks* [whips].'[16] It was a thought that would not have been lost on the canny but unpredictable Sauer, who later played the role of a bemused and hesitant participant in the Reform Committee's opportunistic skulduggery.

Sauer, one of Rhodes's closest friends and business associates, was a doctor and lawyer who had qualified in Edinburgh and London. He was also a man who Rhodes once jokingly referred to as a 'genial ruffian' at a time when the word 'ruffian' was more directly linked to crass criminal activity than it is today.[17] Hans Sauer was no stranger to the notion of annexing foreign territory. In 1883, he and Oscar Sommershield, then a partner in Jameson's Kimberley medical practice, were on a hunting expedition in Mozambique when they seized Inhaca Island from a Portuguese officer and a small number of men, annexing it in the name of the British Empire. If it was but a part of an extended two-day drunken prank, then the sequel was decidedly more serious. He and Sommershield fled but were pursued by a Portuguese patrol, captured, held in Lourenço Marques and released only after a great deal of behind-the-scenes diplomatic activity in three European capitals.

In Johannesburg, where Sauer was for many years District Surgeon, he was directly exposed to the vulnerabilities of the Kruger state's prison system, as he was called upon to oversee the administration of lashes, including those inflicted on white inmates.[18] Indeed, he would have supervised the flogging of several of the more troublesome elements of the Irish Brigade, including William Kelly. Sauer would have known how hard the state, which had had to mobilise the State Artillery as well as a burgher force, was pressed during 1891 when the Irish Brigade virtually laid siege to the prison in Pretoria. And if he did not learn about it from his own, official sources, then his younger brother would surely have told him since, as we have already noted, it was H.B. Sauer, along with J.W. Leonard QC, who in a fit of imperialist solidarity rushed to the legal defence of Hugh McKeone and William Cooper, then in their eleventh hour.

Hans Sauer had as good an idea about the limits of the Kruger state's capacity to counter an armed offensive at short notice as any man on the Reform Committee. McLoughlin's Irish Brigade had demonstrated this weakness to his brother as well as to other Jameson Raid conspirators at close quarters. Hans Sauer also knew, at first hand, about the state's inability to enforce the law in the bandit badlands around Krugersdorp in the late 1880s. Indeed, such was his contempt for the limitations of state agencies that he once recruited a platoon of mercenaries to protect his and Rhodes's mining rights. When the Pretoria High Court proved singularly incapable of defending their property against claim-jumpers, Sauer later recalled with some relish:

> I was obliged to organise a protective force to look after our claims, it was known as Sauer's Irish Brigade and was quite efficient, much more so than the Diggers' Committee. The principal argument used by the Brigade was the Irish *shillelagh*, and after one or two encounters with it the jumpers left our property severely alone.[19]

It would surely not be stretching the bounds of credibility too far to suggest that, of all the Rand's 'Irish Brigades', Hans Sauer's was the most likely to have contained within its ranks some of 'Captain Moonlight's' original veterans, men who had seen criminal action at Eureka City, along the Komatipoort railway line, at Lourenço Marques and during the invasion of Johannesburg in early 1888. And, if that is conceded, is it truly so far-fetched to suggest that, if not McLoughlin's 'Irish Brigade' itself, then the widespread activities of 'social bandits' in the South African Republic during the pre-rail era might have contributed to Hans Sauer and – ultimately – Cecil Rhodes's idea that a band of armed guerrillas, led with sufficient determination and stealth, might be in a position to overwhelm the Kruger state?

Put another way: if the members of McLoughlin's early Irish Brigade were but rootless brigands in search of capital to support heady lifestyles of short-term consumption, were not Jameson's raiders but the representatives of grand capitalists bent on banditry to secure them a state that would guarantee the long-term privileges of an imperial ruling class? Both sets of men, armed and on horseback, were made up of hopeful brigands – the one lot harking back to a rural Irish world already lost, intent on *breaking* the law; the other – English – set on *making* the law in an industrialising imperial world waiting to be won. The bandits of the Irish Brigade never encountered the brigands of the Jameson Raid, although they shared a common enemy in the shape of the Kruger state and its forces. Yet each would have known of the other and, as men fixed on brigandage, albeit to different ends, would perhaps have shown grudging respect for one another.

In the same way, the X-ray of honesty needs to be made to play across the social composition of not only the much-vaunted and subsequently mythologised Pioneer Column that, under Frank Johnson, took occupation of Mashonaland in 1890 to lay the foundations of Rhodesia, but those who followed.[20] We need reminding that, while most of those who enlisted in the Pioneer Column were deliberately drawn from eminent families across southern Africa to provide as much political cover as possible should things go wrong, the push north also took place at precisely the moment that the Witwatersrand was slumping into depression. This meant that, while the base of Rhodes's infant white state may have been formed by many men of impeccable social origins, it was soon seasoned by a sprinkling of doubtful characters – those readily encountered in frontier societies all across the southern plateau.[21] Rhodes, Jameson and Sauer were not only capable of acting as brigands in their own right, but were quite content to work with bandits when the occasion demanded it. Mark Twain, who knew that business and crime were often to be found within hailing distance, wrote pointedly about 'Rhodes and his Chartered Company of highwaymen'.[22]

Perhaps the moment has arrived for us to reconsider the history of mineral-rich southern Africa not so much as the exclusive playground of competing British imperial and Afrikaner nationalist forces – even if that remains the primary driver of subsequent interpretations – but from a perspective that makes more allowance for the less planned or predictable outcomes of actions by bandit bands, black and white, in Basotholand, Goshen, Griqualand West, Natal, the northern Cape, the Orange Free State, Stellaland and the South African Republic. By turning our backs on the frontier histories of brigandage during the era of rapid industrialisation, have we perhaps not lost a 'way of seeing' and understanding the South African state's complex origins?

In the same spirit, it might be noted that a new generation of young researchers needs to set out and snatch the social history of certain strategically situated small border towns – some of them satellite outposts located firmly within the orbits of larger mining centres – from the shadows of obscurity. In the age of the horse economy – the pre-railroad era – Boshof, Christiana, Free Town, Komatipoort, Kuruman, Ladybrand, Mafeking, Vryburg and Zeerust were all wired into the functioning of the greater regional economic system that sheltered the diamond- and gold-mining centres in ways that are now all but forgotten. Between them, these small towns saw proportionately as many cattle rustlers, coach robbers, highwaymen and illicit diamond and gold buyers as did Barberton, Johannesburg and Kimberley.[23] It is not so much the want of sources that prevents the emergence of such studies as the want of adequately primed historical imaginations. If we are to produce a historiography that will slip the grip of the old racist nationalists and avoid the claws of the greedy, venal new, we need to actively subvert the notion of South African exceptionalism by setting our social experiences in broader, comparative perspectives.

Be all that as it may, if we peer back into the darker recesses of the era immediately before the Jameson Raid, when there were said to be about a thousand Irish in Johannesburg, we can see the ghostly outlines of scores of men who were anything but conventional, well educated or disposed to associate themselves with a grand cause, be it Boer-nationalist or any other. Indeed, at a time when politics and pro-imperialist ideology were actively recasting many of the Rand's anglophone, Uitlander elements as English-speaking 'South Africans', the 'Irishness' of many such underworld figures was barely discernible. Anglicisation was a process indirectly facilitated by the arrival and extension of the railways on the Witwatersrand, between 1892 and 1895, a development that assisted in integrating the trans-Vaal into an emerging regional economy.

But, if we strain our eyes yet more and somehow manage to penetrate beyond the mists enveloping the depression of 1890–92, we can catch a glimpse of the deserters from the British Army who went on to shape the Irish Brigade. A loose-knit criminal band founded in the lowlands of the eastern Transvaal, the Brigade grew to thrive briefly on the southern highveld while the horse rather than the train dominated the transport of diamonds, gold and people. And, amidst scores of others, we can suddenly see the larger-than-life profiles of that small clutch of Lancashire- and southern African-born Irish Brigade members who, for about sixty months starting in the late 1880s and continuing well into the 1890s, rose to the very top of their professions as amalgam thieves, store burglars, bank robbers, highwaymen and safe-robbers.

It is perhaps also against this backdrop – the emergence of the Irish Brigade as a force in early organised crime on the Witwatersrand and the resulting crisis in the South African Republic's prisons, in which the Lancashire-Irish played a leading role – that we need to revisit State President S.J.P. Kruger's almost legendary hostility towards Johannesburg's immigrant mining population, suspicions that came to be realised largely during the Jameson Raid.[24] In a speech delivered at an emotional independence day celebration at Paardekraal, Krugersdorp, in July 1891, the President told an audience of over 10 000 that even the 'murderers and thieves' among them were eligible for God's forgiveness.

This tart observation followed the earlier, 1888 invasion of Johannesburg by criminal Irish, which had seen three people murdered over one weekend and much theft. It came about a year after the attempted breakout and fatal shooting of one of the priest-robbers at the jail in Potchefstroom in June 1890, which, in turn, preceded the more dramatic siege of the Pretoria prison by barely four months. It came just two months after John McLoughlin's attempted murder of Henry Higgins in a Johannesburg bar, and in the midst of the Irish Brigade's onslaught against the property of the mining companies and state – some of it in Kruger's very own Rustenburg constituency.

The President's description of some among his audience might have come across as being something of an exaggeration. It certainly angered Witwatersrand-based imperialists, who, later, used it to whip up public support for the South African War. But it can hardly be dismissed as being without foundation. Nor can it be portrayed simply as part of some quaint but rather archaic form of cultural oppression by an uncomprehending State President who, along with many other unthinking Boer yokels, was largely in the thrall of the Old Testament.[25]

Today, the names of Charles Harding, Jack McCann and the McKeone brothers, along with that of John McLoughlin and others like John Brown, lie buried beneath the sands of time – unrecognised, unloved and unwanted. In their heyday, however, when Johannesburg was no more than a mining camp on public diggings in a short-lived open economy, a few of them were seen as criminal heroes or outlaw legends; as men who, although motivated ultimately by self-interest, were striking back at the financial might of the emerging mining houses and the power of the state as exercised through the offices of the mining commissioners. At the height of its quasi-military challenge, the Irish Brigade severely tested the legal, police and prison systems of the state, contributing to the political vulnerabilities of the Kruger administration in the period leading up to the Jameson Raid. The foundations of the Zuid Afrikaansche Republiek were tested from below, by Irish brigands and their largely silent collaborators among the self-employed and working men of the Witwatersrand, long before the mine owners were willing to attempt a coup from above. The criminal, the unemployed and the workers showed the capitalists the way; the mine owners were the followers, not the leaders, of popular discontent.

In keeping with Hobsbawm's warning many years ago, hardly any of the great names of the first Irish Brigade's 'social bandits' have survived 'the transition from agrarian to industrial society'. Where they have done so, they tend to be presented as just so many 'colourful' characters, 'eccentric' criminals adding 'flavour' to the imagined life of vanished frontier societies in a male world. Even in death, their ghostly reputations are kept in chains and made to do hard labour in the pages of glossy magazines and popular histories. They are forced to toil in the dungeons of a state-sponsored heritage industry, working for ideological rent-seekers who, in the never-ending quest for cash and converts to rebranded nationalism, suck the lifeblood from more authentic history until it is left anaemic and emaciated.[26]

Social bandits deserve better. Some *were* just deeply antisocial, maladjusted and violent men, members of a masculine cult capable of heinous crimes, unable to relate to women in meaningful ways. But most were drawn, if not directly from small-scale agrarian societies, then from alienated manufacturing centres in which the real and supposed virtues of a rural social order were within easy reach of living memory. Opportunistic – often criminal – economic refugees from the first Industrial Revolution, these Irishmen found themselves locked into yet another society undergoing fundamental transformation. For a second time they lived through the history of ethnic, political and religious marginalisation, migrancy and urbanisation. Uncertain whether to look back to an imagined agrarian past in Ireland or forward to an industrial future on the Rand mines, they ended up doing both – as urban gangsters and rural brigands preying on black and white workers alike.

But, like most men who march to the beat of a different drum, they were not devoid of behavioural codes, ideas of friendship, bonds of honour or visions of a more justly ordered society – values that ordinary men and women, appreciating their responses and vulnerabilities, were occasionally willing to identify with and sometimes applaud. The outlaw heroes of the southern highveld were no cardboard cut-outs worthy only of decorating the backdrops to small mining towns of a bygone era. They were men with 'straight backs'; they were 'outlaw legends' and 'social bandits', the discards of an old Ireland who stubbornly refused to be incorporated into a new and expanding British Empire. The riff-raff of the Irish Brigade deserve to elbow their way forward through the crowd and take up their rightful place at the head of the parade, alongside many other ordinary Irishmen that made up 'Foxy Jack' MacBride's Brigade. Together they should march through the pages of Irish and South African history. They help complicate an already rich history and, perhaps for that reason alone, we should salute them.

# Note on Sources

## Archives

This study is, for the most part, based on documents housed in the National Archives of South Africa in Pretoria. But this book is not supported at its end by the usual list of principal sources. The interested reader, student or professional historian is asked to refer to the notes for each chapter should he or she wish to take aspects of these studies further or verify the evidence used. A short explanatory note on the principal primary sources used in this study may, therefore, be helpful.

Reconstructing the careers of bandits and professional criminals during the era of mineral discoveries in the southern African interior is a daunting task. This is especially so in the case of the South African Republic, where a hard-pressed administration was called upon to deal with the effects of an economic and social revolution as well as an attempted *coup d'état* in the mid-1890s. With minor exceptions, there are no continuous runs or major collections of documents pertaining to the police (ZARPs), the proceedings of the landdrosts' or higher courts, or the administration of prisons. Brigands, black or white – the Jameson Raid aside – were never the subject of commissions of enquiry or occasional, dedicated official reports. The few surviving records of the Chamber of Mines and the gold-mining companies of the day are equally disappointing for the period before the South African War of 1899–1902.

For the historian in search of a starting point it is therefore necessary to embark on a systematic reading of the daily press on the Witwatersrand during the period circa 1886–99 (see 'Newspapers' below). The newspapers of the day – now in a state of terminal decay as befits a country where the rulers have but a passing interest in history that cannot be harnessed readily to political projects – provide an unparalleled source for those seeking to document the frequency, nature and trajectories of non-corporate brigandage on the mineral frontiers. Once the dates and places of incidents of banditry have been retrieved from press reports, along with the names of the persons involved and reports of preliminary examinations or cases heard in the landdrosts' courts, it is possible to switch languages, from the luxury of seeing printed English on microfilm to the poor-quality Afrikaans-Dutch cursive found in the surviving primary documentation of the state archives.

The correspondence of various State Attorneys (SP) contains letters, marginalia and memos to local Public Prosecutors that sometimes offer insights into how banditry was dealt with and viewed by senior officials in the law-enforcement agencies of the Kruger state. As State Attorney, J.C. Smuts alone appears to have had a clear understanding of the nature of organised crime, and he put into place measures to counteract a corrupt and ineffectual police force and Public Prosecutor's office in Johannesburg. Unfortunately, he took office only after the heyday of the Irish Brigade, but his 'Secret Minutes' nevertheless provide us with the clearest picture we have of illicit gold buying after 1898. The files of his colleague, State Secretary Dr W.J. Leyds (SS), the official who routinely dealt with incoming or outgoing requests for extradition, occasionally provide good accounts of the principal offences attributed to those wanted for brigandage, theft and other crimes against property. The detailed criminal and prison records of individual bandits, however, are often best recovered via the numerous pleas for remission of sentences directed to Kruger's Executive Council (UR). Many of these submissions, supported by the poacher-turned-gamekeeper Thomas Menton, offer detailed information about behaviour in prison and criminal offences that cannot be found elsewhere.

Where pertinent, archival collections housing official documents relating to other, pre-Union states were consulted in Bloemfontein, Cape Town and Pietermaritzburg. Here, too, relevant details are set out in the notes.

## Newspapers

A wide range of English- as well as Afrikaans-Dutch-medium daily and weekly newspapers in the Cape Colony, Orange Free State, Natal and South African Republic were examined to put together this composite exploration of banditry on the southern African highveld. Not all periodicals, however, were explored in equal depth or for the full period covered by the study. The *Cape Times*, *De Express en Oranjevrijstaatsche Advertentieblad* (bilingual), *Diamond Fields' Advertiser* and *Natal Witness*, for example, were consulted only when examining the exploits and fate of particularly prominent 'criminal heroes' such as the brothers McKeone, John and Hugh, or 'One-Armed Jack' McLoughlin in order to establish their movements and to try to discover in what ways and how widely their reputation as brigands had spread.

A study focused primarily on the terrain north of the Vaal, however, demands a more directed and disciplined approach to a reading of the press in the South African Republic for the period after 1886. In Johannesburg the *Star* – voice of the mine owners – aside from being a vocal critic of any failings of the Kruger administration's judicial, penal and policing systems, faithfully recorded most serious incidents of gold amalgam theft and safe-robbery. The view of the common man – and the citizenry *was* overwhelmingly male – is best recovered from the *Standard & Diggers' News*, an organ broadly sympathetically disposed to both the government and the rapidly emerging white working class.

This Rand-centric approach, however, has to be counterbalanced by paying attention to Pretoria-based sources, which, aside from sharing the capital city with the Kruger administration that represented largely rural constituents, often also reported more fully on developments in adjacent areas of regional importance, such as Rustenburg. The *Volksstem* could be relied upon to reflect the views of the Executive Council, the Chief Justice and members of the Volksraad with reasonable accuracy. So, too, could the *Press*, although on occasion it could also be critical of a sometimes faltering administration. These views, in turn, need to be offset through a reading of *Land en Volk*, which was almost always critical – sometimes acidly so – of the government. Newspapers based in the smaller centres through which Irish Brigade members passed at various moments – such as the *Barberton Herald* or the *Potchefstroom Budget* – also provide invaluable information on specific incidents of assault, brigandage and theft.

Archival and newspaper sources have been supplemented by information drawn from a fairly small but important set of more or less contemporary accounts that, along with other secondary sources, are listed in the select bibliography that follows.

# Select Bibliography


Akenson, D.H. *The Irish Diaspora: A Primer*. Belfast, 1993

Blackburn, D., and W.W. Caddell. *Secret Service in South Africa*. London, 1911

Bourke, J. 'Irish Masculinity and the Home, 1880–1914', in M. Cohen and M.J. Curtin (eds). *Reclaiming Gender: Transgressive Identities in Modern Ireland*. New York, 1999

Bulpin, T.V. *Lost Trails of the Transvaal*. Cape Town, 2002

Cohen, L. *Reminiscences of Johannesburg and London*. Johannesburg, 1976

Coohill, J. *Ireland: A Short History*. Oxford, 2005

Crummey, D. (ed.). *Banditry, Rebellion and Social Protest in Africa*. London, 1986

Curror, W.D. (revised and enlarged by H. Bornman). *Golden Memories of Barberton*. Barberton, 2002

Davies, A. *The Gangs of Manchester: The Story of the Scuttlers, Britain's First Youth Cult*. Preston, 2008

Davies, A., and S. Fielding (eds). *Workers' Worlds: Cultures and Communities in Manchester and Salford, 1880–1939*. Manchester, 1992

Dominy, G. 'More than just a "Drunken Brawl"? The Mystery of the Mutiny of the Inniskilling Fusiliers at Fort Napier, 1887', in D.P. McCracken (ed.). *Southern African-Irish Studies Vol. 1*. Durban, 1991

Greenall, R.L. *The Making of Victorian Salford*. Lancaster, 2000

Hobsbawm, E.J. *Primitive Rebels*. Manchester, 1959

—. *Social Bandits*. Harmondsworth, 1972

Jeffery, K. 'The Irish Military Tradition and the British Empire', in K. Jeffery (ed.). *'An Irish Empire'? Aspects of Ireland and the British Empire*. Manchester, 1996

Johnson, M. 'Violence Transported: Aspects of Irish Peasant Society', in O. MacDonagh and W.F. Mandle (eds). *Ireland and Irish-Australia: Studies in Cultural and Political History*. Kent and Surry Hills, 1986

Kidd, A. *Manchester: A History*. Lancaster, 2006

Klein, H. *Stage-Coach Dust: Pioneer Days in South Africa*. London, 1937

Kooistra, P. *Criminals as Heroes: Structures, Power and Identity*. Bowling Green, Ohio, 1989

Kubicek, R.V. *Economic Imperialism in Theory and Practice: The Case of South African Gold Mining Finance, 1886–1914*. Durham, North Carolina, 1979

Lezard, A. *The Great Gold Reef: The Romantic History of the Rand Goldfields*. New York, 1937

Lowe, W.J. *The Irish in Mid-Victorian Lancashire: The Shaping of a Working-Class Community*. New York, 1989

Mabin, A., and B. Conradie (eds). *The Confidence of the Whole Country: Standard Bank Reports on Economic Conditions in Southern Africa, 1865–1902*. Johannesburg, 1987

McCracken, D.P. *MacBride's Brigade: Irish Commandos in the Anglo-Boer War*. Dublin, 1999

—. *Forgotten Protest: Ireland and the Anglo-Boer War*. Belfast, 2003

—. *Inspector Mallon: Buying Irish Patriotism for a Five-Pound Note*. Dublin, 2009

McCracken, P.A. 'Arthur Griffith's South African Sabbatical', in D.P. McCracken (ed.). *Ireland and South Africa in Modern Times, Southern African-Irish Studies Vol. 3*. Durban, 1996

McGarry, F., and J. McConnel. *The Black Hand of Republicanism: Fenianism in Modern Ireland*. Dublin, 2009

McGrath, D. 'Violence and Lawlessness on the Western Frontier', in T. Gurr (ed.). *Violence in America, Volume 1: The History of Crime*. New York, 1989

Metrowich, F. *Scotty Smith: South Africa's Robin Hood*. Cape Town, 1970

Meyer, R.E. 'The Outlaw: A Distinctive American Folktype', *Journal of the Folklore Institute* 17, 1980, pp. 94–124

O'Malley, P.O. 'Social Bandits, Modern Capitalism and the Traditional Peasantry: A Critique of Hobsbawm', *Journal of Peasant Studies* 6 (4), 1979, pp. 489–501

Roonan, B. *Forty South African Years: Journalistic, Political, Social, Theatrical and Pioneering*. London, 1919

Sauer, H. *Ex Africa*. Bulawayo, 1973

Seal, G. *The Outlaw Legend: A Cultural Tradition in Britain, America and Australia*. Cambridge, 1996

Steckmesser, K.L. 'Robin Hood and the American Outlaw', *Journal of American Folklore* 79, 1966, pp. 348–355

Tosh, J. 'What Should Historians do with Masculinity? Reflections on Nineteenth-Century Britain', *History Workshop Journal* 38 (1), 1994, pp. 179–202

Turrell, R.V. *Capital and Labour on the Kimberley Diamond Fields, 1871–1890*. Cambridge, 1987

Van Onselen, C. *The Small Matter of a Horse: The Life of 'Nongoloza' Mathebula, 1867–1948*. Pretoria, 2008

Williams, T.D. (ed.). *Secret Societies in Ireland*. Dublin, 1973

# Acknowledgements

I am the accused in this case and I suppose it is necessary to state that any of the errors of fact or interpretation that remain in this study do so despite the assistance of the people whose names are listed below. Some individuals may have been unwitting accessories before the fact of the book and many during the research, but none after the fact. Responsibility for any shortcomings in this history lie with me.

I am happy to acknowledge the generous assistance, but also the innocence, of D. Ambrose, E. Ashton, K.S.O. Beavon, J. Berg, H. Bornman, B. Bozzoli, L. Chernis, B. Conradie, T.J. Couzens, G. Dominy, G. Dunstall, R.M. Godsell, R. Grantham, A. Grundlingh, G. Hendrich, J. Higginson, B. Housdon, R. Kaplan, E. Katz, P. Pearson, F.J. Pretorius, M. Shain, J.D. Sinclair, N. Stassen, P.J. Stickler, L. Swanepoel, A. van der Walt and D. Wall.

It would be remiss of me if I were not to single out and thank most sincerely Deborah Green in Stockport, Janie Grobler in Barberton and Cecilia Jacobs in Pretoria for research assistance provided throughout the duration of this awkward and, at times, disjointed project. Donal and Patricia McCracken were extremely generous in providing me with encouragement and access to primary data in their possession.

I have an even larger debt, however, and that is to fellow historians whom I know to be better read and more informed than I. It has been my good fortune, over very many years, to have benefited from the critical comments, insights and support of many colleagues. Two, in particular, epitomise the very best that this profession has to offer. Nobody can ask for better intellectual company, more loyal friends or more stimulating critics than Ian Phimister and Paul La Hausse de Lalouvière.

Last, but by no means least, I wish to thank senior colleagues at the University of Pretoria. Most researchers in my field need little more than time to read and glean a few ideas, and a pen and paper to record their findings and interpretations. It is a sad fact that in most modern universities, where there is so much glib talk about the need for in-depth, quality research, few get it. Over a decade, three different vice chancellors and a deputy vice chancellor, Prof. R. Crewe, have afforded me the ideal conditions in which to undertake research and to write. No social scientist could ask for more by way of material support or time than I have been accorded to pursue my interests in global social history. My debt to the University of Pretoria is immense and I am pleased to acknowledge it.

Charles van Onselen
University of Pretoria
May 2010

# Notes

**CHAPTER 1**

1. For the wider context see J. Coohill, *Ireland: A Short History* (Oxford, 2005), pp. 33–34.
2. Ibid., pp. 39–56, 49–51 and 83–88.
3. See S. Clark, *Social Origins of the Irish Land War* (Princeton, 1979), pp. 79–83; J. Kelly, *That Damn'd Thing Called Honour: Duelling in Ireland* (Cork, 1996), pp. 1, 24 and 253; and M. Johnson, 'Violence Transported: Aspects of Irish Peasant Society', in O. MacDonagh and W.F. Mandle (eds), *Ireland and Irish-Australia: Studies in Cultural and Political History* (Kent and Surry Hills, 1986), p. 141.
4. See S. Dunford, *The Irish Highwaymen* (Dublin, 2000); Clark, *Social Origins of the Irish Land War*, p. 82; and Johnson, 'Violence Transported', in MacDonagh and Mandle, *Ireland and Irish-Australia*, pp. 145–146.
5. See especially 'Introduction', in T.D. Williams (ed.), *Secret Societies in Ireland* (Dublin, 1973), pp. 7–8, and, in the same volume, M. Wall, 'The Whiteboys', pp. 14–25.
6. See Clark, *Social Origins of the Irish Land War*, pp. 82–83; and T. Fennell, *The Royal Irish Constabulary* (Dublin, 2003), pp. 9–93.
7. Clark, *Social Origins of the Irish Land War*, p. 112; Coohill, *Ireland*, pp. 58–79; and W.J. Lowe, *The Irish in Mid-Victorian Lancashire: The Shaping of a Working-Class Community* (New York, 1989), p. 8.
8. For the continuities of Irish culture in new working-class settings, and the very particular way in which it contributed to the utilisation of unskilled labour in the Industrial Revolution, see E.P. Thompson, *The Making of the English Working Class* (Harmondsworth, 1968), pp. 469–485.
9. See Coohill, *Ireland*, pp. 67–68; A. Davis and S. Fielding (eds), *Workers' Worlds: Cultures and Communities in Manchester and Salford, 1880–1939* (Manchester, 1992), pp. 11 and 26–27; Lowe, *The Irish in Mid-Victorian Lancashire*, pp. 13 and 34; and F. Neal, *Black'47: Britain and the Famine Irish* (New York, 1998), p. 9.

10. See A. Kidd, *Manchester: A History* (Lancaster, 2006), pp. 16–17, 24 and 119, which offers a fine exposition of local economic diversity. On the decline in importance of the immigrant Irish to the cotton industry see Lowe, *The Irish in Mid-Victorian Lancashire*, p. 81.
11. See especially R.L. Greenall, *The Making of Victorian Salford* (Lancaster, 2000), pp. 169 and 231; Lowe, *The Irish in Mid-Victorian Lancashire*, p. 13; and Kidd, *Manchester*, p. 102.
12. See G. Messinger, *Manchester in the Victorian Age: The Half-Known City* (Manchester, 1986), p. 177; Lowe, *The Irish in Mid-Victorian Lancashire*, pp. 34 and 147; and R. Roberts, *The Classic Slum: Salford Life in the First Quarter of the Century* (Harmondsworth, 1973), pp. 22 and 110.
13. See Davis and Fielding, *Workers' Worlds*, p. 27; Kidd, *Manchester*, p. 122; and Lowe, *The Irish in Mid-Victorian Lancashire*, p. 70.
14. See, for example, Messinger, *Manchester in the Victorian Age*, pp. 22–23.
15. Lowe, *The Irish in Mid-Victorian Lancashire*, pp. 127–128.
16. See especially A. Davies, *The Gangs of Manchester: The Story of the Scuttlers, Britain's First Youth Culture* (Preston, 2008), pp. 47, 73–75 and 137, but also A. Davies, '"These Viragoes Are No Less Cruel Than the Lads": Young Women, Gangs and Violence in Late Victorian Manchester and Salford', *British Journal of Criminology* 39 (1), Special Issue, 1999, pp. 72–89, and J. Burchill, '"The Carnival Revels of Manchester's Vagabonds": Young Working-Class Women and Monkey Parades in the 1870s', *Women's History Review* 15 (2), 2006, pp. 229–252.
17. Davies, *The Gangs of Manchester*, p. 17.
18. The content and context of some of the Victorian ideology of masculinity is neatly laid out in J. Tosh, 'What Should Historians do with Masculinity? Reflections on Nineteenth-Century Britain', *History Workshop Journal* 38 (1), 1994, pp. 179–202.
19. See Davies, *The Gangs of Manchester*, pp. 39–41 and 75, or as 'Russians' and 'Turks', p. 77.
20. See M. Luddy, '"Angels of Mercy": Nuns as Workhouse Nurses, 1861–1898', in G. Jones and E. Malcolm (eds), *Medicine, Disease and the State in Ireland, 1650–1940* (Cork, 1999), pp. 102–117.
21. J. Bourke, 'Irish Masculinity and the Home, 1880–1914', in M. Cohen and M.J. Curtin (eds), *Reclaiming Gender: Transgressive Identities in Modern Ireland* (New York, 1999), pp. 93–106.
22. From George Meredith's *Diana of the Crossways*, a novel set amidst Peel's Corn Laws of 1845, but published in 1885.
23. D.H. Akenson, *The Irish Diaspora: A Primer* (Belfast, 1993), p. 143.

24. See G. Dominy, 'The Imperial Garrison in Natal with Special Reference to Fort Napier, 1843–1914: Its Social, Cultural and Economic Impact', unpublished D.Phil. thesis, University of London, 1995, p. 60 (hereafter, 'The Imperial Garrison').
25. Lowe, *The Irish in Mid-Victorian Lancashire*, p. 193.
26. Dominy, 'The Imperial Garrison', pp. 126 and 246–248.
27. On the image of the 'hard man' see especially C. Emsley, *The English and Violence since 1750* (London, 2005), pp. 35–36.
28. Dominy, 'The Imperial Garrison', p. 135.
29. Ibid., p. 376.
30. Ibid., pp. 275 and 280.
31. Ibid., p. 312.
32. Ibid., pp. 258 and 376.
33. Ibid., pp. 143–160, 286–287 and 407. Also, G. Dominy, 'More than just a "Drunken Brawl"? The Mystery of the Mutiny of the Inniskilling Fusiliers at Fort Napier, 1887', in D.P. McCracken (ed.), *Southern African-Irish Studies Vol. 1* (Durban, 1991), pp. 56–72.
34. See F. Metrowich, *Scotty Smith: South Africa's Robin Hood* (Cape Town, 1970), pp. 1–38; and on O'Reilly, see H. Klein, *Stage-Coach Dust: Pioneer Days in South Africa* (London, 1937), pp. 55–60.

**CHAPTER 2**

1. See United Kingdom (UK), National Archives (NA), London, Kew, WO (War Office) Vol. 16/1718, South Lancashire, List of 'Men Became Ineffective', covering the year 1886. See also UK, NA, London, Kew, WO Vol. 16/1211, 6th Dragoons, Deserters, as recorded on Form 32.
2. See UK, NA, London, Kew, WO Vol. 16/1716, Book 3, April–Sept. 1883, and WO Vol. 16/1717, April–Sept. 1884, for Hutchings' and O'Brien's early military career and misadventures.
3. For a biography on John McLoughlin, see C. van Onselen, *Showdown at the Red Lion: The Life and Times of Jack McLoughlin* (Johannesburg & Cape Town, 2015). On the McLoughlin family in Manchester see, for example, *United Kingdom Census 1871*, 2–3 April, Schedule 151, Manchester, sub-district of St Cross, Ancoats.
4. See 'Daring Robbery at the Convent', *Potchefstroom Budget*, 28 June 1890.
5. See 'A Chequered Career', *Potchefstroom Budget*, 6 Aug. 1890. There were successful, masked highwaymen operating in the De Kaap Valley well before the Irish Brigade ever appeared there. See, for example, T.V. Bulpin, *Lost Trails of the Transvaal* (Cape Town, 2002), pp. 352–353.

6. See, for example, W.D. Curror (revised and enlarged by H. Bornman), *Golden Memories of Barberton* (Barberton, 2002), p. 67.
7. As a retrospective in the *Barberton Herald* of 2 Dec. 1887 put it: 'Those were good days, when hills round and above Barberton were alive with noise and industry. Sunday was no day of rest, the nights were simply a period of darkness, not a season for repose. Day and night there was one continuous volley of blasting. If a man wanted employment there it was at hand and he could fix his own remuneration.'
8. 'Eureka City', *Barberton Herald*, 1 March 1887.
9. On J. Carroll of Greengate, Salford, as a 'scuttler' see Davies, *The Gangs of Manchester*, p. 54.
10. See 'The Irish Brigade', *Barberton Herald*, 1 March 1887; and, for the 'scuttling' analogue in terms of Dwyer's behaviour towards the court, Davies, *The Gangs of Manchester*, pp. 240 and 282.
11. See T. Coleman, *The Railway Navvies* (Harmondsworth, 1982).
12. See, for example, L. van Onselen, *Head of Steel* (Cape Town, 1962), pp. 92–93.
13. See B. Roonan, *Forty South African Years: Journalistic, Political, Social, Theatrical and Pioneering* (London, 1919), pp. 107–113; Van Onselen, *Head of Steel*, p. 93; and T.V. Bulpin, *Storm over the Transvaal*, (Cape Town, 1955), p. 42.
14. Roonan, *Forty South African Years*, p. 116.
15. Roonan, *Forty South African Years*, p. 119; Bulpin, *Storm over the Transvaal*, p. 45.
16. Roonan, *Forty South African Years*, pp. 119–120; and Bulpin, *Storm over the Transvaal*, p. 45.
17. Roonan, *Forty South African Years*, pp. 112–114; Bulpin, *Storm over the Transvaal*, p. 44.
18. Roonan, *Forty South African Years*, pp. 104–105, 110 and 120.
19. See 'Crime in Johannesburg', *Standard and Transvaal Mining Chronicle*, 18 Feb. 1888.
20. 'Shocking Tragedy in Johannesburg', *Standard and Transvaal Mining Chronicle*, 18 Feb. 1888; see also R. Crisp, *The Outlanders* (St Albans, 1974), p. 95.
21. 'Shocking Tragedy', *Standard and Transvaal Mining Chronicle*, 18 Feb. 1888.
22. See, for example, the leader on crime carried in the *Diggers' News and Witwatersrand Advertiser*, 27 June 1889. On the gap that opened between talk and action, however, see the cautionary leader on 'Public Indignation' in the *Standard and Transvaal Mining Chronicle*, 22 Feb. 1888. It is perhaps significant that this, the only recorded lynching of a black man in industrialising South Africa, was undertaken by a party of white men composed of anglophone rather than Afrikaner elements. There is a popular account of the lynching in Bulpin, *Storm over the Transvaal*, pp. 93–94.

23. See 'Shocking Tragedy', *Standard and Transvaal Mining Chronicle*, 18 Feb. 1888.
24. See 'Burglary at an Office', *Standard and Transvaal Mining Chronicle*, 18 Feb. 1888.
25. See 'The Recent Murder Case' and 'Further Arrests: A Strange Story', *Standard and Transvaal Mining Chronicle*, 22 Feb. 1888.
26. D.P. McCracken, *MacBride's Brigade: Irish Commandos in the Anglo-Boer War* (Dublin, 1999), p. 15.
27. *Standard and Transvaal Mining Chronicle*, 29 Feb. and 21 March 1888.
28. See the *Standard and Transvaal Mining Chronicle*, 28 March 1888.
29. See 'Detecting Detectives', *Standard & Diggers' News*, 1 Feb. 1895.
30. As is suggested in Curror, as revised by Bornman, *Golden Memories*, p. 89.
31. On the economic dimensions of the crisis see R.V. Kubicek, *Economic Imperialism in Theory and Practice: The Case of South African Gold Mining Finance, 1886–1914* (Durham, North Carolina, 1979), p. 43. The social consequences of the 1890–92 depression can be traced in various contexts in C. van Onselen, *New Babylon, New Nineveh: Everyday Life on the Witwatersrand, 1886–1914* (Johannesburg, 2001).
32. See 'South African Republic, 1889–1892', in A. Mabin and B. Conradie (eds), *The Confidence of the Whole Country: Standard Bank Reports on Economic Conditions in Southern Africa, 1865–1902* (Johannesburg, 1987), pp. 296–297.
33. 'A Dastardly Outrage', *Star*, 2 June 1890.
34. The role and importance of Friendly Societies on the Witwatersrand – a development that both preceded (Masons) and followed (Ancient Order of Druids, Buffaloes, Oddfellows, Rechabites and others) the establishment of the mine workers' union in 1892 – awaits its historian. See, for example, the *Star*, 29 Feb. 1888; *Standard & Diggers' News*, 27 Feb. 1891; and the *Star*, 10 Aug. 1893. On political associations and the overwhelmingly populist mood of the day by mid-1890 see A.A. Mawby, *Gold Mining and Politics: Johannesburg, 1900–1907* (Lampeter, 2000), pp. 87–105.
35. P. Kooistra, *Criminals as Heroes: Structures, Power and Identity* (Bowling Green, Ohio, 1989), p. 11.

**CHAPTER 3**

1. See, for example, 'Robbery of Specie', *Standard & Diggers' News*, 13 Aug. 1889; 'Daring Bank Robbery', *Standard & Diggers' News*, 21 Sept. 1889; 'Mysterious Robbery', *Star*, 23 Jan. 1893; and 'The Great Bank Note Robbery', *Standard & Diggers' News*, 27 April 1894. For an outline of some of the more important robberies that followed see A.N. Wilson, 'The Underworld of Johannesburg', in A. Macmillan (ed.), *The Golden City: Johannesburg* (London, 1933), pp. 163–165.

2. For references to the world as portrayed by Bret Harte see, for example, items carried in the *Standard & Diggers' News*, 21 Sept. 1889, the *Star*, 25 Jan. 1895, and the *Bulawayo Chronicle*, 1 Feb. 1895. Authors and journalists alike accepted that many of their readers would be familiar with the writings of Bret Harte, whose better-known publications included 'The Luck of Roaring Camp' and 'The Outcasts of Poker Flat'. See, for example, G. Trevor's comments on white bandits, including some drawn from the Celtic margins of Britain, in his *Forty Years in Africa* (London, 1932), p. 134, where he likens them to characters drawn from the writings of Harte.
3. Republic of South Africa (RSA), Barberton Museum, Hospital Register 1893, entry for 4 April 1893; and Grave Register, entry for 20 Oct. 1893. (My thanks to Janie Grobler for uncovering this source for me.)
4. RSA, National Archives of South Africa (NASA), Pretoria, Transvaal Archive Bureau (TAB), State Secretary (SS) Vol. 3067, Ref. R 13367/91, Chief Justice Kotze forwards telegram and letter from Mary McKeone, Johannesburg, 2 Nov. 1891.
5. Psychological factors that go into the making of criminal heroes are discussed in Kooistra, *Criminals as Heroes*, pp. 15–21.
6. This portrait of the McKeone family and its movements is built up from various fragmentary accounts, but three items drawn from the *Star* are central: 'In the Condemned Cells: Ten Minutes with Cooper and McKeone', 2 Nov. 1891, and 'Mrs. McKeone Speaks' on 3 and 9 Nov. 1891. But see also 'Attempted Rescue: History of Their Lives', *De Express en Oranjevrijstaatsche Advertentieblad* (a bilingual journal), 10 Nov. 1891 (hereafter, *De Express*). The idea that the McKeone brothers were mentally deranged did not escape observers at the time. See, for example, *Civis Americanus Sum* to the editor, 'McKeone Morally Irresponsible', *Star*, 3 Nov. 1891.
7. See, for example, 'Selling Counterfeit Diamonds', *Star*, 5 Nov. 1891.
8. The suitability of the far West Rand to banditry and brigandage is explored in some detail below; see Chapter 7.
9. Barsdorf must have been an early and very successful investor in mining properties. By the late 1890s, having left behind several large buildings bearing the family name in reef towns, he served as the Secretary to the Wool Exchange in London, while also acting as agent for the Witwatersrand Chamber of Mines. See RSA, Archives of the Chamber of Mines, Hollard Street, Johannesburg, Letter Book (1897–1898), Letters from the Secretary of the Chamber to A. Barsdorf Esq., dated 30 Sept. and 1 Oct. 1897 and 10 Jan. 1898.
10. See the *Star*, 'In the Condemned Cells: Ten Minutes with Cooper and McKeone', 2 Nov. 1891; 'Mrs. McKeone Speaks', 3 and 9 Nov. 1891; and 'Attempted Rescue: History of Their Lives', *De Express*, 10 Nov. 1891.

11. For Irish roughs in the district working as freelancers see, for example, H. Sauer, *Ex Africa* (Bulawayo, 1973), p. 136. On McCann, who, for a time in early 1889, was a barman at Connolly's Sportsman's Arms in Johannesburg and then Langlaagte, see RSA, KwaZulu-Natal Archives (KZNA), Pietermaritzburg, CSO Vol. 1213, File 1391/1889, Statement by Henry Charles Hartley, in the case of The State vs John ('Jack') McCann, Harry Fisher, Charles Hartley and George Mignonette, 22 Sept. 1888. For McLoughlin's long-standing affinity for Krugersdorp see, for example, 'Burglary at Rustenburg', *Standard & Diggers' News*, 21 May 1890, in which there is a devastatingly accurate description, only the name being missing, of McLoughlin. The Krugersdorp district was also the chosen refuge for both McCann and McLoughlin in 1894–95. See Chapter 7.
12. 'Circuit Court', *Star*, 1 Oct. 1889.
13. See K.L. Steckmesser, 'Robin Hood and the American Outlaw', *Journal of American Folklore* 79 (1966), pp. 348–355.
14. 'Circuit Court', *Star*, 1 Oct. 1889.
15. Even the bank officials later understood this, albeit imperfectly. See RSA, Standard Bank, Archives and Historical Services (A&HS), Johannesburg, ARCH 1/1/KGD, 'The Standard Bank of S.A. Ltd. in Krugersdorp', a fine summary of the branch's history compiled by L. Theunissen, July 1988, p. 5 (hereafter, Theunissen, 'Standard Bank, Krugersdorp'). See also, in addenda, 'Robbery at Standard Bank Krugersdorp, Report by Mr. F.B. Shotter', 4 Sept. 1889, p. 7 (hereafter, Shotter, 'Report on Robbery').
16. 'Circuit Court', *Star*, 7 Oct. 1889.
17. Ibid.
18. The robber '... is not the enemy of the king or emperor, who is the font of justice, but only of the local gentry, clergy or other oppressors' (Hobsbawm, *Social Bandits* [Harmondsworth, 1972], p. 43).
19. 'Circuit Court', *Star*, 7 Oct. 1889.
20. See McKeone's statement from the dock, 'Circuit Court', *Star*, 7 Oct. 1889. Here, then, were the classic ingredients for the making of a 'social bandit' evoking public sympathy. See G. Seal, *The Outlaw Legend: A Cultural Tradition in Britain, America and Australia* (Cambridge, 1996), pp. 9–11; or Hobsbawm, *Bandits*, p. 42: 'First, the noble robber begins his career of outlawry not by crime, but as the victim of injustice, or through being persecuted by the authorities for some act which they, but not his people consider criminal.'
21. Kooistra, *Criminals as Heroes*, p. 33.
22. Journalists were quick to spot the Johannesburg connection. The morning after the robbery, it was noted: 'What influenced the men to take the high road for Johannesburg is unknown, probably they were the members of a

gang having its headquarters here.' That 'gang' was, almost certainly, the Irish Brigade – a conjecture that is supported by the presence of Carroll and 'Crooked Nose' Jackson – but, in the first instance, see 'A Bank Robbed', *Star*, 30 Aug. 1889.

23. RSA, Standard Bank, A&HS, Johannesburg, Theunissen, 'Standard Bank, Krugersdorp': Extract from Krugersdorp Branch letter to the General Managers, Standard Bank, Cape Town, 30 Aug. 1889.
24. Tossel, it was said, was an American. Some of his early career was recorded by a man who was himself in Krugersdorp on the day of the robbery – see C.G. Dennison, *History of Stellaland* (Vryburg, 1928), p. 22. Others, however, disputed this and suggested that he was a West Country man from Devon who only affected an American accent. He, too, may have been a bit of a dreamer, a man drawn from Bret Harte country.
25. 'A Bank Robbed', *Star*, 30 Aug. 1889.
26. On 'Jackson', clearly not his real name, see RSA, Standard Bank, A&HS, Johannesburg, Theunissen, 'Standard Bank, Krugersdorp': Shotter, 'Report on Robbery', p. 7.
27. RSA, Standard Bank, A&HS, Johannesburg, Theunissen, 'Standard Bank, Krugersdorp': Extract from Krugersdorp Branch letter to the General Managers, Standard Bank, Cape Town, 30 Aug. 1889. See also 'A Bank Robbed', *Star*, 30 Aug. 1889.
28. RSA, Standard Bank, A&HS, Johannesburg, Theunissen, 'Standard Bank, Krugersdorp': Shotter, 'Report on Robbery', p. 6.
29. Ibid. On Ferguson's liking for gambling and low company, including that of the highwayman and safe-cracker Mike Hart, see the comments of a contemporary in L. Cohen, *Reminiscences of Johannesburg and London* (Johannesburg, 1976), p. 102.
30. RSA, Standard Bank, A&HS, Johannesburg, Theunissen, 'Standard Bank, Krugersdorp', p. 5.
31. On McKeone's operation see 'The Bank Robbery', *Standard & Diggers' News*, 3 Sept. 1889, and on the use of the stocks, 'The Row in Gaol', *Star*, 12 Nov. 1889.
32. Seal, *The Outlaw Legend*, p. 9.
33. See Hobsbawm, *Bandits*, p. 46.
34. 'Circuit Court', *Star*, 7 Oct. 1889.
35. Ibid.
36. 'Cooper and McKeone', *Star*, 9 Nov. 1891.
37. See RSA, KZNA, Pietermaritzburg, CSO Vol. 1213, File 779/1889, 'John Boswell alias John McCann, 1. theft at Johannesburg 2. escaping from gaol there 3. theft of a horse at Komati', 15 Feb. 1889.

38. See 'The Row in Gaol' and 'Excitement at the Gaol' in the *Star*, 12 and 13 Nov. 1889.
39. Turpin's tale can be traced in the following items in the *Gold Fields News*: 'Barberton Gaol', 21 Jan. 1891; 'Turpin and Smythe', 24 Jan. 1891; 'The Gaol Birds Recaptured', 28 Jan. 1891; and 'Escape of Jail Birds', 31 Jan. 1891. (My thanks to Janie Grobler for drawing these items to my attention.)
40. 'Mrs. McKeone Speaks', *Star*, 9 Nov. 1891.
41. See 'Cooper and McKeone', *Star*, 5 Nov. 1891; and 'Cooper and McKeone', *Cape Argus*, 6 Nov. 1891. He and Hugh McKeone later claimed to have legally accumulated about £2 000 – in ways that they did not disclose – which had been either hidden or invested somewhere in the Transvaal countryside. See, for example, 'The Condemned Men', *Star*, 31 Oct. 1891.
42. See 'In the Condemned Cells', *Star*, 2 Nov. 1891; and 'Cooper and McKeone', *Star*, 5 and 9 Nov. 1891.
43. The tale of the gardens and the gallows is recounted in 'Johannesburg and Pretoria Gaols: The Strengths and Weaknesses', *Star*, 15 March 1890.
44. See report carried in the *Diamond Fields' Advertiser*, 3 March 1890.
45. 'McKeone', *Diamond Fields' Advertiser*, 13 March 1890.
46. Some sense of the climate of opinion prevailing at the time – and its subsequent romanticisation as part of a general legacy in popular history – can be gauged from Bulpin's *Storm over the Transvaal*, p. 163: 'There [Johannesburg] he collected his horse, a famous black animal, and rode to Krugersdorp …' In McKeone's own version, recorded in a letter to his brother, he suggests that he (McKeone) went to Krugersdorp under cover of darkness and stole Brian Boru from the stables.
47. 'Dick Turpin at the Circus', *Diamond Fields' Advertiser*, 17 March 1890. On Fillis, see F. van Jaarsveld, *Frank Fillis: The Story of a Circus Legend* (Stellenbosch, 2007), p. 76.
48. See T.J. Couzens, *Murder at Morija* (Johannesburg, 2003), p. 181.
49. 'Johannesburg Notes: The Pursuit of McKeone', *Diamond Fields' Advertiser*, 7 March 1890.
50. This letter, one of several intercepted by the police, ostensibly from 'T.L. Roberts' (Jack McKeone) to 'Bertha' (Bernard McKeone), was reproduced in the *Star*, 21 March 1890.
51. 'The Chase after McKeone', *Star*, 8 March 1890.
52. These are the ideas of Michael Schudon (1979) as put forward by Kooistra in his *Criminals as Heroes*, p. 24.
53. Jack McKeone to Bernard McKeone, *Star*, 21 March 1890.
54. Bulpin, *Storm over the Transvaal*, p. 163.
55. Jack McKeone to Bernard McKeone, *Star*, 21 March 1890.

56. See 'Johannesburg Notes', *Diamond Fields' Advertiser*, 12 March 1890. Bulpin, in *Storm over the Transvaal*, p. 164, claims that the police were inebriated, but I have found no evidence to support this. Bulpin had an enviable eye for the importance of social history, keeping extensive notes from different sources for the many books he authored. But, since he failed to provide footnotes or other helpful notes to the sources of his published work, his observations frequently have to be treated with caution. He sometimes inserts descriptive detail into his accounts that cannot be substantiated readily from the most obvious primary sources. His work remains perennially popular, however, precisely because of his ability to spot and use telling examples to illustrate important themes in South African history.
57. Jack McKeone to Bernard McKeone, from Maama's village, 1 April 1890, as reproduced in the *Star*, 16 April 1890.
58. 'McKeone and Cooper', *De Express*, 10 Nov. 1891.
59. Jack McKeone to Bernard McKeone, *Star*, 16 April 1890.
60. It is difficult to make sense of the reported suicide, or an attempt at suicide, and its timing. Father Joseph Gerard reported on the matter as if the victim had succeeded in her intent – in which case it may not have been Martha McKeone. See the diary of Father Joseph Gerard, *Le Père Gerard Nous Parle, Vol. 3, Son Sejour a Sainte-Monique, 1876–1897* (Roma, Social Centre, 1970), entries for Jan. and Aug. 1890, which suggest that this attempt occurred around New Year, 1890. Jack McKeone, however, was writing about having seen his sister in April 1890. Moreover, some Witwatersrand press reports suggest that towards the end of 1891, when Hugh McKeone was under sentence of death at Pretoria, his sister (sometimes also portrayed as a woman being his mother's sister, i.e. his aunt) appeared to help plead for a reprieve. It will require additional research to determine the course of Martha McKeone's extraordinary life in greater detail. (I am indebted to Prof. David Ambrose for kindly making available to me copies of the relevant entries from Father Gerard's diary.) On Father Gerard's work in wider context see also Couzens, *Murder at Morija*, pp. 120 and 125.
61. Martha McKeone to Master John McKeone, 21 March 1890, as reproduced in the *Star*, 16 April 1890.
62. See Bulpin, *Storm over the Transvaal*, p. 164.
63. In 'McKeone and Cooper', *De Express*, 10 Nov. 1891, it is claimed, quite explicitly, that Chief Jonathan Molapo had the McKeone brothers and Cooper arrested and handed over to the authorities in Ladybrand. If this uncontested arrest and delivery did indeed take place, it somehow eluded official observation or recording. It does, however, fit with the theme of betrayal that underlies the making of outlaw legends – see, for example, R.E. Meyer, 'The

Outlaw: A Distinctive American Folktype', *Journal of the Folklore Institute* 17, 1980, p. 108. For a brief summary of the broader context of Basotho politics at this time see, for example, M. Wilson and L. Thompson (eds), *The Oxford History of South Africa* (Oxford, 1971), pp. 267–271.

64. 'Barsdor' is presumably the same person who, elsewhere in the press, is referred to as 'Baasdorf '.
65. J.L. McKeone to the Secretary of the Executive Council, Pretoria, 1 April 1890, as reproduced in the *Star*, 16 April 1890.
66. RSA, NASA, Pretoria, SS Vol. 2330, Ref. R 6093A/90 and R 515/90, State Attorney to State Secretary, 18 April 1890, requesting the latter to arrange for McKeone to be extradited. On the letters see the *Diamond Fields' Advertiser*, 23 April 1890.
67. RSA, NASA, Pretoria, State Attorney (SP) 26A, SPR, Telegram: State Attorney to Landdrost, Pretoria, 6 May 1890; and SPR 1488/90, Landdrost, Krugersdorp, to State Attorney, 17 May 1890.
68. RSA, NASA, Pretoria, DSP Vol. 21, Ref. SPR 2137/90, Telegram: Lieut. Heugh to State Attorney, 26 July 1890.
69. See especially RSA, NASA, Pretoria, SS Vol. 2479, Ref. R 11106A/90, for the accusations and counteraccusations that occurred among white prison staff.

**CHAPTER 4**

1. *Fifth Annual Report of the Witwatersrand Chamber of Mines, for the year ending 31 December 1893*, p. 5.
2. Blackburn and Caddell – who appear sometimes to have problems identifying the precise year in which certain of the events they describe occurred – are of the opinion that 1895 marked the apogee of highway robberies insofar as it affected black migrants. They may, however, have conflated the earlier, 1892 experiences of Cooper and McKeone into their account. They also appear to place too much emphasis on the law and fail to take cognisance of the role of the railway. Despite these reservations, however, they offer a generally informative account of the activities of highwaymen and their successors. See D. Blackburn and W.W. Caddell, *Secret Service in South Africa* (London, 1911), pp. 153–155.
3. See *Fifth Annual Report of the Witwatersrand Chamber of Mines, for the year ending 31 December 1893*, p. 5.
4. For an early example of the complaints about these problems see, for example, RSA, Archives of the Chamber of Mines of the Witwatersrand, Hollard Street, Johannesburg, Letter Book (1888), President of the Chamber of Mines to the State Attorney, Pretoria, 7 Aug. 1888.

5. On the economics of early gold transportation see *Annual Reports of the Chamber of Mines for 1889, 1890 and 1891* at pp. 11–12, 14 and 80–81.
6. See, for example, L. Cohen, *Reminiscences of Kimberley* (London, 1911), Chapters 7 to 10.
7. H. Klein, *Stage-Coach Dust*, p. 60. This incident may also have contributed to Jack O'Reilly wanting to obtain permission from the state to hire an island in the Vaal River from the state. See RSA, NASA, Pretoria, TAB, SS Ref. R 15967/93, Application for island number 34 in the Vaal River by Niemeyer & Marais, Pretoria, on behalf of H.J. O'Reilly. It seems possible, but improbable, that O'Reilly might have used the proceeds of his activities as highwayman to purchase a farm in the Klerksdorp/Potchefstroom district. See note 38 below.
8. On theft of bullion as a generic problem see, for example, H.A. Chilvers, *Out of the Crucible* (London, 1929), p. 64. Details of theft of bullion from state-guarded coaches seem difficult to come by for reasons that are not entirely clear.
9. See, for example, 'The Gang in the Country', *Star*, 15 Aug. 1890; and, for a later still robbery, Bulpin, *Storm over the Transvaal*, p. 165.
10. See 'Stage Robbery in the Transvaal', *New York Times*, 11 Dec. 1897; and A.P. Cartwright, *Valley of Gold* (Cape Town, 1973), pp. 124–125.
11. Hobsbawm, *Bandits*, p. 4.
12. See R.D. McGrath, 'Violence and Lawlessness on the Western Frontier', in T. Gurr (ed.), *Violence in America, Vol. 1, The History of Crime* (New York, 1989), p. 2. It is also in this tradition that it is reported of coach robberies undertaken in the De Kaap Valley by members of the Irish Brigade that '[t]he passengers were not molested or robbed as they concentrated on gold bullion and money carried by the coaches' (Curror, as revised by Bornman, *Golden Memories*, p. 67).
13. C. van Onselen, *The Small Matter of a Horse: The Life of 'Nongoloza' Mathebula, 1867–1948* (Pretoria, 2008), p. 21.
14. See, for example, highwaymen working around Heidelberg, as reported in the *Standard & Diggers' News*, 3 Feb. 1891. On De Koker and Van Greuning – subjects clearly worth exploring in greater depth – see, for example, *Standard & Diggers' News*, 31 May 1892.
15. United States of America (USA), Yale University Library, New Haven, AC 565, Box 7, Folder 75, Louis Cohen Scrapbooks, manuscript for his work on Johannesburg and Kimberley, p. 4.
16. On Van de Venter see, for example, 'Van de Venter Captured', *Star*, 8 July 1893, and 'Round the Camp', the *Gold Fields News* and *Barberton Herald*, 11 July 1893; and Bulpin, *Storm over the Transvaal*, p. 165. Van de Venter, whose

exploits are currently being researched, is, it is hoped, the subject of a forthcoming essay.

17. Sauer, *Ex Africa*, p. 138. On Hans Sauer and the Irish Brigade see also *Ex Africa*, p. 136; and Conclusion.
18. The link between Boers and 'Boer policemen' and armed robbery of blacks is another such link in need of more detailed examination. See, for example, the letter to the editor by 'Kaapenaar' in the *Star*, 5 Nov. 1891.
19. See, for example, 'A Highway Robbery', as reported in the *Star* of 30 June and 6 July 1893.
20. The robbery at the Smit farm and the attack on the miner are both reported in the *Diamond Fields' Advertiser*, 23 April 1890.
21. See R.V. Turrell, *Capital and Labour on the Kimberley Diamond Fields, 1871–1890* (Cambridge, 1987), pp. 177–179. Turrell is one of the few historians to have explored the small towns surrounding major mining centres in an attempt to identify altered regional crime patterns. But, even in the case of Kimberley, the need for more, potentially very rewarding social research is palpable.
22. On the Brown family of Manchester, see UK Censuses of 1861, 1871, 1881 and 1891, when Brown Snr was still alive and living with his third wife. On J.W. Brown see Manchester, Central Records, Police Court Registers, 12–13 June 1876, Record: J.W. Brown found guilty of theft, sentenced to one month with hard labour; 4 Jan. 1878, sentenced to two months hard labour for theft; and, along with McLoughlin and others, on 11 Dec. 1879 at the Quarter Sessions, six months hard labour for theft from pawnshops. On the latter see also *Manchester Evening News*, 12 Dec. 1878. For a further example of European highwaymen at work robbing whites in the Kimberley district see the *Diamond Fields' Advertiser*, 3 May 1890.
23. *Diamond Fields' Advertiser*, 3 May 1890.
24. For the Cape part of the legal proceedings see RSA, Cape Town, Cape Archive Depot (CAD), 1/KIM 1/2/1/1/9 Criminal Record Book p. 47, Case No. 161, The Queen vs Horace Edward Hicks, John Brown and John James 'European speculators'.
25. See, for example, the remarks made by the judge in the Kimberley High Court during the sentencing of Collis, a tailor, and McGiddy, a jockey, to eight years' imprisonment with hard labour for highway robbery; *Diamond Fields' Advertiser*, 10 May 1890.
26. Although we have only Hugh McKeone's word on this foray into Natal – see 'In the Condemned Cells', *Star*, 2 Nov. 1891 – it fits with what other newspaper evidence we do have.
27. See 'One Branch of their Activity', *Star*, 5 Nov. 1891.

28. RSA, NASA, Pretoria, TAB, SP Vol. 20, Telegram from Landdrost, Ladybrand, to State Attorney, 19 May 1890. See especially 'Their Previous Record', *Star*, 5 Nov. 1891.
29. 'McKeone's Brother gets Fifteen Lashes', *Star*, 13 May 1890.
30. RSA, NASA, Pretoria, TAB, SP Vol. 21, Landdrost, Ladybrand, confirms sentencing of H. McKeone and W. Cooper in Circuit Court.
31. See 'Their Previous Record' and 'In the Condemned Cells' in the *Star*, 9 Nov. 1891.
32. RSA, NASA, Pretoria, TAB, SP Vol. 22, Ref. 2739/90, Landdrost, Ladybrand, to Landdrost, Bloemfontein, 2 Sept. 1890.
33. The pair's Bloemfontein escapes and exploits are recounted in 'History of their Lives', *De Express*, 10 Nov. 1891; see also 'Their Previous Record', *Star*, 9 Nov. 1891.
34. 'Their Previous Record', *Star*, 9 Nov. 1891.
35. 'The Condemned Men', 'In the Condemned Cells' and 'Cooper and McKeone', *Star*, 31 Oct. 1891, 2 and 9 Nov. 1891.
36. See 'Cooper and McKeone' and 'Their Previous Record', *Star*, 3 and 9 Nov. 1891.
37. See 'Cooper and McKeone' and 'The Condemned Men', *Star*, 26 Oct 1891; and 'Cooper and McKeone', *De Express*, 10 Nov. 1891.
38. See RSA, NASA, Pretoria, TAB, SS Ref. R 2320/93: H.J. O'Reilly seeks to hire state-held land at Gatrand, in the Potchefstroom district. In the same year, during which he was also active as a highwayman, O'Reilly appears to have been involved in cattle rustling in the Heidelberg district, where he encountered Patrick Dennis O'Reilly – amalgam thief and part of the extended, indigenous O'Reilly clan based in the Orange Free State – see, among others, SP Vol. 35, SPR 192/93, Public Prosecutor, Heidelberg, re: sworn affidavits against fugitives Jamison (*sic*) and O'Reilly alias Miles.
39. RSA, SANA, Pretoria, TAB, SP Vol. 26A, Ref. SPR 1652/91 and SPR 1647/91. See especially the full account, in Afrikaans-Dutch, in 'De Hooggerechtshof ', *De Volksstem*, 22 Oct. 1891.
40. Not surprisingly, given the political storm that followed, the English-medium press failed to report on this incident as recounted in evidence before the High Court. The two best accounts are to be found in the Afrikaans-Dutch press: 'De Hooggerechtshof ', *De Volksstem*, 22 Oct. 1891, and 'De Doodvonnis', *De Express*, 10 Nov. 1891. Mrs Mary McKeone's version of the same events, in which the police were said to have deliberately insulted and provoked lads who had been left with their own revolvers for unknown reasons, is reported in 'Mrs. McKeone Speaks', *Star*, 9 Nov. 1891.

41. RSA, NASA, Pretoria, TAB, SP Vol. 26, Ref. SPR 1669/91, in which there is a request for a warrant allowing for the transfer of Cooper and H. McKeone from Klerksdorp to Pretoria.
42. See, among others, 'Cooper and McKeone', 'Cooper's Designs of Escape' and 'In the Condemned Cells', *Star*, 3, 6 and 9 Nov. 1891.
43. See, for example, 'Cooper and McKeone', *Star*, 20 Oct. 1891.
44. On Harding see 'Een Zakkenroller', *Land en Volk*, 10 Nov. 1891; and 'Joined by a Friend', *Star*, 14 Nov. 1891. On Brown, Todd and Sutherland see 'News from Pretoria', *Natal Witness*, 22 Oct. 1891.
45. RSA, NASA, Pretoria, TAB, Uitvoerende Raad (UR) Vol. 52, pp. 28 and 43. (I am indebted to Mr Cornelis Muller for helping to track the original resolutions of the Executive Council in this matter.)
46. See especially 'Attempt to Storm the Gaol', *Cape Argus*, 2 Nov. 1891.
47. 'Attempt to Storm the Gaol', *Cape Argus*, 2 Nov. 1891.
48. Ibid.
49. See 'News from Pretoria', *Natal Witness*, 28 Oct. and 4 Nov. 1891; and, on the mobilisation of civilians, two items entitled 'Cooper and McKeone' in the *Cape Argus* and *Natal Witness*, 5 and 7 Nov. 1891.
50. On the siege of the Pretoria state prison in 1891 as a possible contributory factor to the type of thinking that eventually led to the *idea* of staging a raid, as opposed to the Jameson Raid itself, in 1895, see Conclusion.
51. Unfortunately, there appear to be no surviving copies of *The Press*. The extract here is taken from F.R. Statham's 'Hanging by Proxy' as reproduced in the *Star*, 4 Nov. 1891.
52. 'Why not the Lash', *Star*, 4 Nov. 1891.
53. 'Justice in the Transvaal', *Natal Witness*, 31 Oct. 1891.
54. 'Hanging by Proxy', *Star*, 4 Nov. 1891.
55. See especially 'Cooper and McKeone', *Star*, 4 Nov. 1891.
56. See 'Mutiny in Pretoria Gaol' and 'Lash for Mutinous Gaolbirds', *Cape Argus*, 10 and 11 Nov. 1891.

**CHAPTER 5**

1. Curror, as revised by Bornman, *Golden Memories*, p. 196.
2. The growth of the Oddfellows with its distinctively Mancunian roots was particularly noticeable during the last three decades of the nineteenth century, when membership rose from 427 000 in 1872 to 597 000 in 1886 and had reached 713 000 by 1899 – see E. Hopkins, *Working-Class Self-Help in Nineteenth-Century England: Responses to Industrialization* (New York, 1995), p. 56.
3. See RSA, KZNA, Pietermaritzburg, CSO Vol. 1213, File 779/1889, 'John Bos-

well alias John McCann, 1. theft at Johannesburg 2. escaping from gaol there 3. theft of a horse at Komati', 15 Feb. 1889.

4. See D.P. McCracken, *Inspector Mallon: Buying Irish Patriotism for a Five-Pound Note* (Dublin, 2009), pp. 143–152, for a fine exposition of the dynamics of Irish informing and shadowing as it related to political, as opposed to criminal, policing.
5. On McCann's trial see also the *Diggers' News and Witwatersrand Advertiser*, 11 and 20 July 1889; and the *Star*, 18 July 1889.
6. A brief outline of Kelly's career on the Rand can be obtained from items in the *Star*, 23 Jan. 1892; *Standard & Diggers' News*, 27 Jan. 1892 and 30 May 1892; *Star*, 9 Aug. 1893, 10 Aug. 1893, 12 Aug. 1893 and 24 Sept. 1894.
7. On O'Brien's antecedents see, for example, *Standard & Diggers' News*, 17 Jan. 1890; and more especially 'A Chequered Career', *Potchefstroom Budget*, 6 Aug. 1890. RSA, NASA, Pretoria, TAB, SP Vol. 2458, Ref. SPR 10475/90, Telegram re: attempted escape of O'Brien, McLoughlin and Reid.
8. See 'Prostitutes and Proletarians, 1886–1914', in Van Onselen, *New Babylon, New Nineveh*, pp. 109–164; and, on the rise of Joseph Silver on the Witwatersrand, C. van Onselen, *The Fox and the Flies: The World of Joseph Silver, Racketeer and Psychopath* (London, 2007), Chapters 8 and 9.
9. See items in *Diggers' News and Witwatersrand Advertiser*, 27 July 1889; *Standard & Diggers' News*, 5 Dec. 1890 and 19 Feb. 1890; and 'Safe-Lifters in Dock', *Star*, 10 Aug. 1890.
10. *Standard & Diggers' News*, 1 Feb. 1890, and *Diamond Fields' Advertiser*, 3 May 1890.
11. See especially Kooistra, *Criminals as Heroes*, pp. 28–29.
12. See reports of safe-robbery and -blasting in the *Star* of 11, 15 and 18 Aug. 1890. A year later, it was still widely accepted in informed circles that enjoyed easy access to state officials that the plague of highway and safe-robberies sweeping the country was largely the product of a single gang. Although unnamed, this gang could only have been the Irish Brigade if one checks arrests, prosecutions and convictions of this class of offenders. See, for example, the comments of the Pretoria-based *The Press* as cited in the article by Statham, 'Hanging by Proxy', *Star*, 4 Nov. 1891.
13. On the robbery at Somers & Co., Rustenburg, see reports in the *Standard & Diggers' News*, 21 May 1890, and the *Star*, 24 May 1890.
14. See 'The Roodepoort Robbery: Still another Safe' and 'Safe Blasting Epidemic' in the *Star*, 11 and 15 Aug. 1890.
15. The *Star*, 15 Aug. 1890. On James Sutherland, see *UK Census 1851*, HO 107 225, Folio 488, p. 24, Sutherlands of 28 Lime Street, Ancoats; and, in *UK Census 1861*, the same family resident in adjacent New Cross. On William Todd,

see *UK Census 1871*, RG 10 4064, Folio 99, p. 30, William Todd, aged 19, 'French Polisher', held in District County Prison, Salford.

16. See 'Five Years for a Joke', 'The Authority of the People' and 'The Sutherland Case' in the *Star*, 22 Oct., 3 Nov. and 12 Nov. 1891. For a view from further afield, see 'Justice in the Transvaal', *Natal Witness*, 31 Oct. 1891.
17. See 'Potchefstroom News' in the *Standard & Diggers' News*, 28 June 1890; and 'Daring Robbery at the Convent' and 'The Convent Robbery' in the *Potchefstroom Budget*, 28 June and 2 July 1890.
18. RSA, NASA, Pretoria, TAB, SS Vol. 2458, Ref. R 10475/90, Telegram from Landdrost, Potchefstroom, to State Attorney, 26 July 1890.
19. Years later McLoughlin recounted how, in a subsequent visit, he attempted to avoid the nuns by meeting his sick brother in the hospital gardens – RSA, NASA, Pretoria, Witwatersrand Local Division (WLD), 377/1909, Rex vs Jack McLoughlin, p. 56 (hereafter, Rex vs McLoughlin, 1909).
20. See, among others, T.S. Jensen, B. Krebs, J. Nielsen and P. Rasmussen, 'Immediate and Long-Term Phantom Limb Pain in Amputees: Incidence, Clinical Characteristics and Relationship to Pre-Amputation Limb Pain', *Pain* 21 (3), 1985, pp. 267–278; K. MacIver, D.M. Lloyd, S. Kelly, N. Roberts and T. Nurmikko, 'Phantom Limb Pain, Cortical Reorganization and the Therapeutic Effect of Mental Imagery', *Brain* 131 (8), 2008, pp. 2181–2191; and V.S. Ramachandran and W. Hirstein, 'The Perception of Phantom Limbs', *Brain* 121 (9), 1998, pp. 1603–1630. (I am indebted to Prof. R. Kaplan for drawing this and other relevant literature to my attention.)
21. See 'Attempted Murder: Sunday Sport' and 'Attempted Murder', *Standard & Diggers' News*, 5 and 11 May 1891; and Rex vs McLoughlin, 1909, p. 71.
22. See 'Johannesburg Notes: Great Thefts of Amalgam', *Diamond Fields' Advertiser*, 9 April 1890; and items in the *Standard & Diggers' News*, 16 and 18 April 1891 and 5 May 1891.
23. On Hollander fencing goods stolen in Johannesburg in Boshof, see 'Life on the Witwatersrand', *Diamond Fields' Advertiser*, 28 Dec. 1887.
24. See Rex vs McLoughlin, 1909, p. 71.
25. See 'Attempted Murder: Sunday Sport' and 'Attempted Murder' in the *Standard & Diggers' News* of 5 and 11 May 1891.
26. See 'A Daring Attempt' and 'The Prison Breakers', *Standard & Diggers' News*, 22 and 24 June 1891.
27. Rex vs McLoughlin, 1909, pp. 64 and 72. See also L. Herschbach, 'Prosthetic Reconstructions: Making the Industry, Re-Making the Body, Modelling the Nation', *History Workshop Journal* 44, 1997, pp. 23–27. For an example of a miner – Tom Logan – losing both hands due to the use of unstable dynamite, see *Bulawayo Chronicle*, 19 July 1895.

28. See items in the *Standard & Diggers' News* dated 17 June and 24 Aug. 1892, and a short retrospective report on 3 Jan. 1893.
29. 'The Arrests', *Star*, 3 Jan. 1893. On Ferguson and Hart see Chapter 3, note 29.
30. The Rattray saga can be followed in reports carried in the *Star* dated 3 Jan. 1893, headlined 'Audacious Burglary' and 'The Arrests', and then in various subsequent accounts entitled 'The Safe Robbery', dated 5, 14, 16, 19, 21 and 22 Jan. 1893.
31. On Stevenson's family background see *UK Census 1871*, R 6, Piece 2820, Folio 57, entry on Stevensons of Rushy Pits, Hixon; and on Stevenson's troubled childhood and entry into the ranks of the North Staffordshires: UK, Staffordshire Record Office, CES/3/2/812, 'License on Discharge Register' (for Werrington Industrial School). On Stevenson's later career in Johannesburg, see, for example, 'A Slippery Customer', *Standard & Diggers' News*, 25 March 1892, and 'Boxing', *Star*, 9 Oct. 1893.
32. In Stevenson's earlier career, as Ferney alias Davidson, see 'A Slippery Customer' in the *Standard & Diggers' News*, 25 and 31 March 1892. It is interesting to note, in passing, how at about this time, when he was wanted for horse theft and was most closely involved with McLoughlin, Stevenson's reported alias approximated that of the famous Irish highwayman James Freney. Might the press have recorded his assumed name incorrectly?
33. See RSA, NASA, Pretoria, WLD, 377/1909, Rex vs McLoughlin, Affidavit by Sarah McNeil (née Fredericks) dated 24 Nov. 1906.
34. On the fight, in which Stevenson fought under the ring name 'Steele', see 'Steele vs Lobb' in the *Star*, 25 May 1893. Stevenson appears to have enjoyed fighting professionally – see also his appearance, under his own name, in 'Boxing', *Star*, 9 Oct. 1893. The changing relationships between McLoughlin, Stevenson and the two prostitutes can be traced in Rex vs McLoughlin, 1909.
35. C.R. O'Flaherty's position at Langlaagte is recorded in the RSA Archives of the Witwatersrand Chamber of Mines, Hollard Street, Johannesburg, Letter Book No. 5 (1890–1892), List of accredited representatives as at 30 Sept. 1892. For McLoughlin and Stevenson at work at Langlaagte, see RSA, NASA, Pretoria, WLD, 377/1909, Rex vs McLoughlin, Affidavit by Sarah McNeil (née Fredericks) dated 24 Nov. 1906.
36. See items in the *Star* of 24 May, 8 July and 22 Sept. 1893.
37. Rex vs McLoughlin, 1909, p. 68.
38. See 'The Pretoria Railway Robbery', *Star*, 18 April 1894, and *Land en Volk*, 31 Jan. 1895, but more especially Rex vs McLoughlin, 1909, evidence of Detective C.A. Mynott, pp. 3–5.
39. See K. Marx and F. Engels, *On Ireland* (London, 1971), p. 88. This extract came from a piece written by Marx in December 1858, which appeared in the *New*

*York Daily Tribune* on 11 Jan. 1859. It was a theme that Marx had raised earlier, in the 6 Jan. 1859 issue of the same newspaper, when he wrote, 'Thus, at this very moment, while giving vent to his virtuous indignation against Bonaparte's spy system at Paris, he [John Bull] is himself introducing it at Dublin' (*On Ireland*, p. 86).

40. In South Africa, white informers may have been among the first to have been killed by gangsters, but it was not long before the practice of killing *impimpi* – black informers – was also evident within the Transvaal prison system. Elements of informing and its consequences on the Witwatersrand can be traced in two articles by C. van Onselen: 'Jewish Police Informers in the Atlantic World, 1880–1914', *The Historical Journal* 50 (1), 2007, pp. 119–144; and 'Who Killed Meyer Hasenfus? Organized Crime, Policing and Informing on the Witwatersrand, 1902–08', *History Workshop Journal* 67, 2009, pp. 1–22.
41. See D.P. McCracken, 'The Death of the Informer James Carey', in D.P. McCracken (ed.), *Ireland and South Africa in Modern Times, Southern African-Irish Studies Vol. 3* (Durban, 1996), pp. 190–199.
42. On highwaymen, see *Bulawayo Chronicle*, 24 Aug. 1894; and on McLoughlin's presence in the region's capital, see, among several others, *Star*, 26 Jan. 1895, and *Bulawayo Chronicle*, 1 Feb. 1895.
43. Bulpin, *Storm over the Transvaal*, p. 244. As always with Bulpin, it is impossible to tell where precisely he found this information, but the broad outline, if not the detail, is probably factually sound.
44. USA, Yale University Library, New Haven, AC 565, Box 7, Folder 75, Louis Cohen Scrapbooks, manuscript for his work on Johannesburg and Kimberley, p. 17.
45. As cited in Kooistra, *Criminals as Heroes*, p. 21.
46. Rex vs McLoughlin, 1909, p. 7, evidence of Rosie Pietersen.
47. 'A Sensational Saturday Night', *Standard & Diggers' News*, 28 Jan. 1895; and 'Double Murder', *Star*, 28 Jan. 1895.
48. Rex vs McLoughlin, 1909, pp. 11–13.
49. Rex vs McLoughlin, 1909, evidence of Sarah McNeil (née Fredericks), pp. 12– 13, Jane Absalom, pp. 19–21, and E.G. Isaacs, pp. 24–26.
50. As Kooistra notes: 'These lawbreakers became heroes, in short, because they were heroic. While the actual content of their actions was illegal, their manner of conduct was inspirational. Their calmness in the face of danger, their courage and determination, and their fierce loyalty to friends and principle were things at which to marvel' (*Criminals as Heroes*, p. 23). Note how closely this formulation accords with J.L. 'Jack' McKeone's self-perception as outlined in his letter to the State Secretary.

51. Rex vs McLoughlin, 1909, p. 37, evidence of M. Goldberg. Goldberg's story, which started out in the most dramatic terms possible, moderated steadily as it passed through successive stages as press report, written statement to the police and, finally, as evidence in court before the Chief Justice fifteen years later. See, for example, 'A Sensational Saturday Night', *Standard & Diggers' News*, 28 Jan. 1895, in which the bullet 'grazed' him, and compare that with his evidence in court, by which time it 'whizzed past, over my head'.
52. Rex vs McLoughlin, 1909, evidence of Sah Badien Ben, p. 43, and Jeanette Jack, p. 44.
53. In Rex vs McLoughlin, 1909, at p. 34, Harry Lobb – who was present at the dinner – claimed that it had taken place at Rosenthal's, but in 'A Menace to the Town', *Star*, 30 Jan. 1895, Robert Ferguson, who claimed to be using information drawn from his own underworld sources, alleged that McLoughlin was 'supping off two soles at Pross's Café in Commissioner Street'. I have chosen to adopt Lobb's version – that of an honest crook rather than that of a bent detective.
54. See 'A Menace to the Town', *Standard & Diggers' News*, 30 Jan. 1895.
55. On McLoughlin's interest in press reports about his activities, see his evidence in Rex vs McLoughlin, 1909, p. 70.
56. See 'Commissioner Street Murder', *Standard & Diggers' News*, 28 Jan. 1895; and 'Where are the Police?' in the *Star* of 28 Jan. as reprinted on 2 Feb. 1895.
57. 'Commissioner Street Murder', *Standard & Diggers' News*, 28 Jan. 1895; see section on 'A Daring Safe Robbery'.
58. 'McLoughlin's Friends', *Star*, 28 Jan. 1895. It is clear from a later report carried in the *Star*, 'A Menace to the Town', 30 Jan. 1895, that it was Hollander who was doing most of the talking to the newspaper.
59. The *Star*, 2 Feb. 1895.
60. A Menace to the Town', *Standard & Diggers' News*, 30 Jan. 1895.
61. The entire subplot can be followed in 'A Menace to the Town', *Standard & Diggers' News*, 30 Jan. 1895; 'The Detective and the Murderer', *Star*, 30 Jan. 1895; 'Mr. Ferguson's Denial', *Star*, 2 Feb. 1895 (carrying the detective's letter of 31 Jan.); and the *Standard & Diggers' News*, 8 Feb. 1895. All of the above, which provides irrefutable evidence of Ferguson's presence in Johannesburg at the time, should be contrasted with the deliberately false, studiously tentative and factually incorrect evidence he presented at McLoughlin's trial fourteen years later; see Rex vs McLoughlin, 1909, pp. 52–53, evidence of Robert Ferguson. Not surprising, then, that Louis Cohen, a contemporary of Ferguson's who could himself play fast and loose with the facts when the occasion demanded it, observed in his notes towards a book that Ferguson 'never re-

gained his kudos' after the McLoughlin scandal. See USA, Yale University Library, New Haven, AC 565, Box 7, Folder 75, Louis Cohen Scrapbooks, manuscript for his work on Johannesburg and Kimberley, p. 17.

62. On Ferguson's dismissal, see W.K. Hancock, *Smuts, 1: The Sanguine Years, 1870–1919* (Cambridge, 1962), p. 80.
63. Rex vs McLoughlin, 1909, p. 70, evidence of J. McLoughlin.
64. McLoughlin later denied this but, on balance, the evidence of Detective Mynott, who heard the tale first-hand from McLoughlin during a relatively relaxed voyage back to South Africa from Australia many years later, seems plausible enough. See Rex vs McLoughlin, 1909, pp. 4 and 71, evidence of Detective Charles Mynott and J. McLoughlin.
65. 'Another Mine Safe Robbery', *Standard & Diggers' News*, 2 Feb. 1895; also 'An Alleged Accomplice' and 'Politics, Parsons and Police', *Standard & Diggers' News*, 5 Feb. 1895.
66. See especially 'An Alleged Accomplice' and 'Politics, Parsons and Police', *Standard & Diggers' News*, 5 Feb. 1895; and 'The Champ Deep Robbery', *Star*, 6 Feb. 1895.
67. There is a good deal of archival material devoted to Jack McCann's 1895 extradition. Among the more important items are: RSA, NASA, Pretoria, TAB, SP Vol. 62, Ref. SPR 1688/95 (28 Feb. 1895); SSA Ref. RA 1875/95 (25 May 1895); SSA Ref. RA 1894/95 (30 May 1895); and SP Vol. 10, Ref. SPR 5259/95 (15 July 1895). On McCann's death – as claimed by McLoughlin – see Rex vs McLoughlin, 1909, evidence of J. McLoughlin, p. 72.
68. See Rex vs McLoughlin, 1909, pp. 5 and 67, evidence of Detective C. Mynott and J. McLoughlin. On G.H. Woolf, who was deeply implicated in the illegal trade in gold and gang warfare at the time, see, for example, 'The Charge Against Treu', *Star*, 12 Jan. 1899.

**CHAPTER 6**

1. See Hobsbawm, *Bandits*, pp. 17–29. Seal, who has reservations about macro-analytical approaches to the phenomenon of 'social banditry', seeks instead to focus on case-by-case studies in the belief that the specificities of individual manifestations of brigandage make excessive generalisations either banal or unhelpful. He identifies 'ten motifs' that characterise the phenomenon of the 'criminal hero'; see Seal, *The Outlaw Legend*, p. 11. In a similar vein, Kooistra, in *Criminals as Heroes*, develops his notion of 'heroic criminals'. It is my view that the notions of 'criminal heroes', 'outlaw legends' and 'social bandits', while focusing at different levels of magnification in various socio-economic settings, offer us concepts that overlap sufficiently for them not to be entire-

ly oppositional. I move freely between 'social banditry' (usually when discussing the structural dimensions of the problem of brigandage) and 'outlaw heroes' or 'outlaw legends' (when dealing with individual bandits).

2. 'Doodvonnis Bekrachtig', *Land en Volk*, 3 Nov. 1891.
3. D.P. McCracken, *Forgotten Protest: Ireland and the Anglo-Boer War* (Belfast, 2003), pp. 114–115 (emphasis added).
4. Kooistra, *Criminals as Heroes*, p. 32 (emphasis in the original).
5. Hobsbawm, *Bandits*, p. 40.
6. 'By one of his Pals', *Standard & Diggers' News*, 2 Feb. 1895.
7. As quoted in the chapter on 'Avengers' in Hobsbawm, *Bandits*, p. 63 (emphasis added).
8. Rex vs McLoughlin, 1909, pp. 63–70 (emphasis added).
9. 'Where is McLachlan?', *Standard & Diggers' News*, 5 Feb. 1895.
10. Bulpin, *Storm over the Transvaal*, p. 219.
11. 'A Sensational Saturday Night', *Star*, 28 Jan. 1895.
12. USA, Yale University Library, New Haven, AC 565, Box 7, Folder 75, Louis Cohen Scrapbooks, manuscript for his work on Johannesburg and Kimberley, pp. 12–13.
13. Bulpin, *Storm over the Transvaal*, p. 218.
14. In this regard it might be noted how McLoughlin meets most of the twelve requirements of an outlaw legend as suggested by R.E. Meyer, 'The Outlaw: A Distinctive American Folktype', 267 pp. 94–124. In a similar vein, McLoughlin and J.L. McKeone meet the ten motifs suggested by Seal, *The Outlaw Legend*, p. 11.
15. *Standard & Diggers' News*, 7 Feb. 1895.
16. 'The Desperado at Large' and 'Letter from McLachlan', *Standard & Diggers' News*, 2 and 7 Feb. 1895.
17. A. Lezard, *The Great Gold Reef: The Romantic History of the Rand Goldfields* (New York, 1937), p. 58.
18. See D.P. McCracken, 'Alfred Aylward: Joubert's Fenian', in McCracken, *Forgotten Protest*, pp. 119–123.
19. See R. Turrell, 'The 1875 Black Flag Rebellion on the Kimberley Diamond Fields', *Journal of Southern African Studies* 7 (2), April 1981, pp. 194–235.
20. Lezard, *The Great Gold Reef*, pp. 58–59.
21. John Louis McKeone to the Secretary of the Executive Council, Pretoria, written from 'Whereabouts Unknown', 1 April 1890, as reproduced in the *Star*, 16 April 1890.
22. See the letter from J.L. McKeone to B. McKeone, written from 'Maama's Village' on 1 April 1890, as reproduced in the *Star*, 16 April 1890.

23. Ibid.
24. On the broader significance of absent fathers for social bandits, see the comments in Kooistra, *Criminals as Heroes*, pp. 15–21.
25. Lezard, *The Great Gold Reef*, p. 60.
26. 'Recapture of McKeone', *Star*, 16 April 1890.
27. *Standard & Diggers' News*, 18 April 1890.
28. *Diamond Fields' Advertiser*, 26 March 1890.
29. *Standard & Diggers' News*, 18 June 1890.
30. 'McKeone', *Diamond Fields' Advertiser*, 13 March 1890. On invisibility and the 'noble bandit' see Hobsbawm, *Bandits*, p. 51.
31. 'Return of the Police', *Star*, 9 March 1890. On the 'noble robber' and magic see Hobsbawm, *Bandits*, pp. 51–53.
32. 'The Chase After McKeone', *Star*, 8 March 1890.
33. That was after their escape from prison in Bloemfontein – see 'McKeone and Cooper' in *De Express*, 10 Nov. 1891.
34. See W.J. De Kock (ed.), *Die Suid-Afrikaanse Biografiese Woordeboek, Deel 1* (Cape Town, 1968), pp. 458–461.
35. 'This is very warm', *Star*, 7 Nov. 1891.
36. 'Transvaal Justice', *Natal Witness*, 4 and 7 Nov. 1891.
37. 'Transvaal Justice', *Natal Witness*, 4 Nov. 1891.
38. The first observation is drawn from 'Reprieved', *Cape Argus*, 6 Nov. 1891, and the second from the leader in the *Natal Witness*, 30 Oct. 1891.
39. For an Afrikaans-Dutch perspective on the McKeone-Cooper case and its consequences as presented in a bilingual journal, see, for example, the following items in *De Express* (Bloemfontein): 'Death Sentence Approved Of' and 'Highwaymen', 27 Oct. 1891; and 'Eere van de Hoofdrechter' and 'The McKeone Sentence', 10 Nov. 1891. As viewed from Pretoria, see the following in *Land en Volk*: 'Een Familie van Skelms', 13 Oct. 1891; 'De Doodvonnis', 27 Oct. 1891; 'Cooper en McKeone' and 'De Doodvonnis', 10 Nov. 1891; and 'De Doodvonnis', 17 Nov. 1891. Also from Pretoria, *De Volksstem*: 'Ter Dood Gevonnis', 24 Oct. 1891; 'Gevraagd een Strafwetboek', 29 Oct. 1891; 'Praatjes van den Dag', 3 Nov. 1891; 'Voet bij Stuk Houden', 5 Nov. 1891; 'Kracht of Zwakheid', 7 Nov. 1891; and 'Hoofdrechter Kotze', 12 Nov. 1891.
40. RSA, NASA, Pretoria, TAB, UR Vol. 10, p. 503, and Vol. 52, p. 28, entries for 2 Nov. 1891. See also, for example, 'Transvaal Condemned Men', 'Cooper and McKeone's Fate' and 'Cooper and McKeone' in the *Cape Argus*, 28 and 30 Oct. and 2 Nov. 1891. Also 'Cooper and McKeone: Their Sentence Confirmed', *Natal Witness*, 3 Nov. 1891.
41. See, among others, 'Kimberley Before the Reprieve', *Cape Argus*, 7 Nov. 1891; 'Kimberley's Petitions', 'Outlying Opinion', 'Petition at Kimberley' and 'Pub-

lic Meeting Suggested' – all items carried in the *Star* of 5 and 9 Nov. 1891. Significantly, the Beaconsfield Town Council, representing arguably the most important element of the white working class on the diamond fields, led the way by passing a resolution appealing for the sentences to be commuted to penal servitude. See RSA, NASA, Pretoria, TAB, SS Vol. 3070, Ref. R 14391/91, Telegram from the Mayor and Town Council, Beaconsfield, 4 Nov. 1891, requesting reprieve for Cooper and McKeone; also, 'Cooper and McKeone', *Cape Argus*, 4 Nov. 1891.

42. RSA, NASA, Pretoria, TAB, SS Vol. 3075, Ref. R 13227/91, American Consul to State Secretary, re Cooper and McKeone, 2 Nov. 1891; and SS Vol. 3071, Ref. R 13592/91, High Commissioner, Cape Town, to State Secretary, plea for reprieve of Cooper and McKeone, 5 Nov. 1891.
43. RSA, NASA, Pretoria, TAB, SS Vol. 3070, Portuguese Consul, Kimberley, to State Secretary, plea for commutation, 4 Nov. 1891. See also 'Cooper and McKeone', *Cape Argus*, 6 Nov. 1891, and 'De Doodvonnis', *Land en Volk*, 10 Nov. 1891. The figure of 10 000 signatories is taken from 'Cooper en McKeone', *Land en Volk*, 10 Nov. 1891.
44. RSA, NASA, Pretoria, TAB, SS Vol. 3070, Ref. R 13500/91, plea by L.J. Vigneron and others for reprieve for Cooper and McKeone, 30 Oct. 1891; and SS Vol. 3069, Ref. R 13472/91, Request by L.J. Vigneron to be present, without other witnesses, at the execution of Cooper and McKeone, 5 Nov 1891.
45. See also 'Cooper and McKeone', *Cape Argus*, 4 Nov. 1891, and 'The Petitions Presented', *Star*, 9 Nov. 1891.
46. See, for example, 'Cooper en McKeone', *Land en Volk*, 10 Nov. 1891.
47. On J.W. Leonard, the Political Reform Association and the National Union, see Mawby, *Gold Mining and Politics*, pp. 100–101.
48. See, among others, 'McKeone and Cooper: The Doomed Men', *De Express*, 10 Nov. 1891; 'The Condemned Men's Appeal', *Star*, 9 Nov. 1891; and 'News from Pretoria', *Natal Witness*, 6 Nov. 1891.
49. See 'Cooper and McKeone's Fate', *Cape Argus*, 30 Oct. 1891; and 'The Death Sentence', *Star*, 31 Oct. 1891.
50. 'Reprieved', *Cape Argus*, 6 Nov. 1891.
51. See, among others, 'McKeone and Cooper', *De Express*, 10 Nov. 1891; 'Cooper en McKeone', *Land en Volk*, 10 Nov. 1891; 'The Sentence Commuted', *Natal Witness*, 7 Nov. 1891; and 'The Right of Appeal', *Star*, 7 Nov. 1891.
52. See especially 'The Death Sentence', *Star*, 7 Nov. 1891. The Afrikaans-Dutch press was quick to point out that the Kruger administration had been confronted by a combination of forces that had proved unstoppable. See, for example, 'Cooper en McKeone' and 'De Doodvonnis' in *Land en Volk*, 10 and 17 Nov. 1891, and especially 'Kracht of Zwakheid', *De Volksstem*, 7 Nov. 1891.

53. See 'To be Framed and Glazed: Comforting the Chief Justice', *Star*, 21 Nov. 1891, which reprints both the original letter and Kotze's reply. See also 'Hoofdrechter Kotze' in *De Volksstem*, 12 and 21 Nov. 1891. The *Star*, however, continued to pursue the Chief Justice; see, for example, 'This Really is the Last', 13 Nov. 1891.
54. William Cooper's request to make a speech from the scaffold – an attempt to be seen to 'die game' in the tradition of the bandit-hero as sketched by Seal in *The Outlaw Legend* and others – is reported on in 'The Condemned Men', *Star*, 31 Oct. 1891, and his threats of revenge on Kotze in 'The Reprieved Men', *Cape Argus*, 7 Nov. 1891.
55. Hugh McKeone 'has the same sort of high-flown theoretical opinion of justice and the wrongs of those in authority to the people, and concentrates in himself all the elements which go to make the socialist of fairly advanced aims' – 'Cooper and McKeone', *Star*, 9 Nov. 1891.
56. 'Reprieved', *Cape Argus*, 6 Nov. 1891.
57. See 'The Transvaal Desperadoes', *Cape Argus*, 22 Oct. 1891, and 'Justice for Kaffirs', *Star*, 22 Oct. 1891.
58. 'Another Meaning to It' and 'At the Eleventh Hour', *Star*, 4 and 7 Nov. 1891.
59. 'More Commutations', *Cape Argus*, 9 Nov. 1891.
60. See 'Second Chamber: The Gallows', *Standard & Diggers' News*, 17 and 21 June 1892.

**CHAPTER 7**

1. *Star*, 27 Jan. 1890.
2. 'The Burglar Brigade', *Natal Witness*, 14 Aug. 1891.
3. C.T. Gordon, *The Growth of Boer Opposition to Kruger, 1890–1895* (Oxford, 1970), p. 17.
4. E.J. Hobsbawm, *Primitive Rebels* (Manchester, 1959), p. 5.
5. In this way, for example, we need to take up the implied challenge in McCracken's observation that 'it is probable that some Irish lads in the Transvaal in the 1890s did have liaisons with black women' (*MacBride's Brigade*, p. 20). It is not just that they probably had relations with African women; we know that they did, but we need to question to what extent Catholicism among Irish males, as with other ethnic minorites such as the Italians or Portuguese, perhaps facilitated the assimilation and/or integration of northern white male 'marginals' into female African or 'coloured' society on the Rand. In this regard it may be helpful to re-examine Brazilian and Latin American historiography on slavery and race relations and compare and contrast it with that on the American South. In this way there may also be fruitful comparisons to be drawn between the role of Islam in the making of the 'coloured'

community in the commercial Cape and the emergence of the 'coloured' communities of the industrialising highveld in the late nineteenth and early twentieth centuries.

6. See Sauer, *Ex Africa*, p. 136.
7. See I.R. Phimister, 'Rhodes, Rhodesia and the Rand', *Journal of Southern African Studies* 1 (1), Oct. 1974, pp. 75–77.
8. All the English equivalents, such as 'dale', 'chasm', 'portal', 'hollow', 'ridge' and 'marsh', are, frankly, quite hopeless descriptors. Consciousness, experience and local geomorphology are, as is well known, all encoded into memory in distinctive ways. See especially S. Schama, *Landscape and Memory* (Toronto, 1996).
9. See Blackburn and Caddell, *Secret Service in South Africa*, p. 4.
10. McCracken, *MacBride's Brigade*, p. 20. See also McCracken, *Forgotten Protest*, pp. 114–118.
11. See *Longland's Johannesburg and South African Republic Directory 1898* (Johannesburg), pp. 752–753.
12. For reports on the founding of or functions involving various Friendly Societies in Johannesburg see, for example, items in the *Standard and Transvaal Mining Chronicle*, 29 Feb. 1888 (Masons); *Standard & Diggers' News*, 27 Feb. 1891 (Buffaloes); *Star*, 7 Aug. 1893 (Oddfellows); and *Star*, 10 Aug. 1893 (Druids). On the functionalities of such societies see, for example, S. Cordery, *British Friendly Societies, 1750–1914* (Basingstoke, 2003), pp. 7–13. See also Chapter 2, note 34.
13. Thus it was later claimed that while among 'Magato's people', in 1894, '[t]he other [McLoughlin] was a man who was always drunk and had an iron hook where his hand should be! He used it to fight with, and many natives bore the marks of it on their faces and bodies' (Blackburn and Caddell, *Secret Service in South Africa*, p. 167). Long before that, another Spring Heel Jack – more prankish than devilish in mode – had, it was said, visited some of the ladies of the diamond fields. See Cohen, *Reminiscences of Kimberley*, pp. 225–226. See also P. Haining, *The Legend and Bizarre Crimes of Spring Heeled Jack* (London, 1977), p. 52; or J. Westwood and J. Simpson, *The Lore of the Land: A Guide to England's Legends, From Spring-Heeled Jack to the Witches of Warboys* (London, 2005), pp. 480–481. As with Friendly Societies, the role played by transplanted English legends and myths in the consciousness and lives of early immigrant miners on the Witwatersrand remains uncharted historical terrain.

**CHAPTER 8**

1. With the exception of 1893 and 1897, the mining and sale of gold attracted new legislation from the Volksraad in every year between 1886 and 1899. The

industry's early desire to criminalise the possession of gold by employees, in 1892–93, drew its inspiration from the Kimberley mine owners, but, in the case of the Rand, they had to wait until after the Jameson Raid had administered its shock to the ZAR for them to achieve their objective on a larger scale. For the legal background to these changes in the 1890s, see L.V. Kaplan, 'The Development of Various Aspects of the Gold Mining Laws in Southern Africa from 1871 until 1967', unpublished D.Phil. thesis, Faculty of Law, University of the Witwatersrand, 1985.

2. Witwatersrand Chamber of Mines, *The Mining Industry, Evidence and Report of the Industrial Commission of Enquiry, with an Appendix* (Johannesburg, 1987), p. 49. (I am indebted to Prof. K. Breckenridge for drawing FitzPatrick's observation to my attention.) On FitzPatrick more generally, see S. Trapido, 'Sir (James) Percy FitzPatrick (1862–1931)', in H.C.G. Matthew and B. Harrison (eds), *Oxford Dictionary of National Biography Vol. 10* (Oxford, 2004), Ref. ODNB/33157, while his reticence on the subject of the illegal trade can be followed in A.H. Duminy and W.R. Guest, *FitzPatrick, South African Politician: Selected Papers, 1886–1906* (Johannesburg, 1976). See also A. Wessels, 'An Irish Gentleman in Africa: The Ambiguous Political and Cultural Identity of Sir Percy FitzPatrick', *English in Africa* 31 (1), May 2004, pp. 5–22.
3. J. Scoble and H.R. Abercrombie, *The Rise and Fall of Krugerism: A Personal Record of Forty Years in South Africa* (New York, 1900), p. 228.
4. See W.K. Hancock and J. van der Poel (eds), *Selections from the Smuts Papers, Vol. 1, Jan. 1886–May 1902* (Cambridge, 1966), p. 50.
5. Scoble and Abercrombie, *The Rise and Fall of Krugerism*, p. 228.
6. See K. Breckenridge, '"Cross of Gold": The Gold, Liquor and Pass Laws and the Problem of Identification, 1895–1899', Paper presented to the Anthropology and Development Department, University of Johannesburg, 8 Oct. 2008, p. 3.
7. These petty-bourgeois roots are noted in M. Kelly, 'Dublin Fenianism in the 1880s: "The Irish Culture of the Future"?', *The Historical Journal* 43 (3), 2000, especially pp. 734–735.
8. See, for example, Coohill, *Ireland*, pp. 115–119.
9. McCracken, *MacBride's Brigade*, pp. 17–18.
10. McCracken, *MacBride's Brigade*, p. 16, and, more pertinently – but not unproblematically – RSA, Pretoria, University of South Africa (UNISA) Library, *The Great Irish Conspiracy*, anonymous pamphlet, circa 1899 (hereafter, *The Irish Conspiracy*). On Gillingham's leading role in corrupt practices on the Rand dating back to at least 1892, see Gordon, *The Growth of Boer Opposition to Kruger*, p. 45, and especially pp. 99–102.
11. McCracken, *Inspector Mallon*, p. 186.

12. Thus, for example, Griffith's biographer-friend Patrick Colum claimed, 'When Arthur Griffith's apprenticeship was over a great trade slump was beginning. After long dreary months of walking about hunger forced him, John MacBride and group of young Dubliners to emigrate to the Transvaal mines' – as cited in P.A. McCracken's 'Arthur Griffith's South African Sabbatical', in D.P. McCracken, *Ireland and South Africa in Modern Times*, p. 227 (hereafter, P.A. McCracken, 'Griffith's Sabbatical'). P.A. McCracken is, on the basis of her own research and sharp analysis, deeply suspicious of Colum's rather trite explanation for Griffith and the rest of the group's move south.
13. McCracken, *MacBride's Brigade*, p. 18.
14. J.R. Whelan, who came from a family of Whelans noted for their activism in Dublin Fenian circles, was, almost certainly, unrelated to his Lancashire, working-class namesake Tommy Whelan – amalgam thief attached to the small but violent Mancunians who formed the inner core of John McLoughlin's Irish Brigade. See also Chapter 5.
15. McCracken, *MacBride's Brigade*, p. 17.
16. McCracken, *MacBride's Brigade*, pp. 17–21.
17. See especially *The Irish Conspiracy*, pp. 4–6, and McCracken, *MacBride's Brigade*, pp. 17–21.
18. See Gordon, *The Growth of Boer Opposition to Kruger*, pp. 234–235.
19. See C. van Onselen, 'The Modernisation of the Kruger State: F.E.T. Krause, J.C. Smuts and the Struggle for the Control of the Johannesburg Public Prosecutor's Office, 1898–1899', *Law and History Review* 21 (3), Fall 2003, pp. 483–526.
20. RSA, NASA, Pretoria, TAB, SP (Secret Minutes) Vol. 193, File GR 6/98; and Hancock and Van der Poel (eds), *Selections from the Smuts Papers, Vol. 1*, p. 50.
21. RSA, NASA, Pretoria, TAB, SP (Secret Minutes) Vol. 193, File GR 6/98, N.L. Sapte to the State Attorney, Pretoria, 6 July 1898, and appendices.
22. RSA, NASA, Pretoria, TAB, SP (Secret Minutes) Vol. 193, File GR 6/98, J.W. Treu to J.C. Smuts, Esq., State Attorney, Pretoria, 11 July 1898.
23. See RSA, NASA, Pretoria, TAB, SP (Secret Minutes) Vol. 193, File GR 6/98, H. Birkenruth to the State Attorney, Pretoria, 29 July 1898.
24. See Van Onselen, 'The Modernisation of the Kruger State', pp. 483–526. For reservations those at Gold Fields held about Krause – and Ferguson in particular – see RSA, NASA, Pretoria, TAB, SP (Secret Minutes) Vol. 193, File GR 6/98, N.L. Sapte to the State Attorney, 18 July 1898.
25. See RSA, NASA, Pretoria, TAB, SP (Secret Minutes) Vol. 193, File GR 6/98, N.H. Sapte to J.C. Smuts, State Attorney, 29 and 30 June 1898 and 6 and 16 July 1898. See also Affidavit by C.J.F. Hartung, 30 June 1898, and C.J.F. Hartung to State Attorney, 4 July 1898.

26. See RSA, NASA, Pretoria, TAB, SP (Secret Minutes) Vol. 193, File GR 6/98, Affidavit by C.J.F. Hartung, 4 July 1898.
27. McCracken, *Inspector Mallon*, p. 186.
28. The only official sources of information on Keller are to be found in RSA, NASA, Pretoria, TAB, SS Vol. 851, Ref. R 8666/97: J. Raaff, T.G. Kieser and Others, Johannesburg, June 1897, forwarding a 'Memorandum requesting remission of sentence for L. Keller and P. O'Reilly'; and SS Vol. 810, Ref. DDM 270/99, Chief Detective, Johannesburg, to Commander of Police, Pretoria, 27 Jan. 1899, 'Attempt to transport gold to Durban aboard the *Dorothea* by Dr. Keller'. There is other, unsourced information on Keller in T.V. Bulpin, *Natal and the Zulu Country* (Cape Town, 1966), p. 489, in which he is referred to as 'Dr. Kelly', suggesting that the information was obtained orally.
29. On Thomas O'Reilly see RSA, NASA, Pretoria, TAB, SP Vol. 35, Refs. SPR 81/93, 207/93 and 253/93, telegrams between the Landdrost, Heidelberg, to State Attorney, Jan. 1893.
30. 'The Pretoria Trio Sentenced, One Year Without Hard Labour', *Standard & Diggers' News*, 22 Jan. 1897.
31. RSA, NASA, Pretoria, TAB, SS Vol. 6501, Ref. R 866/97, J. Raaff, T.G. Kieser and Others, Johannesburg, 'Memorandum requesting remission of sentence for L. Keller and P. O'Reilly'.
32. See especially 'The Trial of Treu' and 'A Man Named Pat O'Reilly' in the *Standard & Diggers' News*, 11 Jan. 1899.
33. See especially 'Abandonment of the "Dorothea"', *Natal Mercury*, 2 Feb. 1898. There is a much fuller account of the history of the ship, but with significant variants that cannot readily be reconciled with the account in the *Mercury*, in Bulpin's *Natal and Zulu Country*, p. 439.
34. 'The Abandoned Barque', *Star*, 4 Feb. 1898.
35. Blackburn and Caddell, *Secret Service in South Africa*, p. 205.
36. See 'Abandonment of the "Dorothea"' and 'The Wreck of the "Dorothea"', *Natal Mercury*, 3 and 4 Feb. 1898. Again, these press reports are at variance with the details supplied by Bulpin in his *Natal and Zulu Country*, p. 439.
37. NASA, Pretoria, TAB, SP Vol. 810, Ref. DDM 270/99, Chief Detective, Johannesburg, to Commandant of Police, Pretoria, 27 Feb. 1899.
38. Ibid. Bulpin, in his *Natal and Zulu Country*, pp. 439–440, provides a great deal of detail about subsequent salvage attempts, but I have been unable to verify their accuracy from contemporary, independent sources. See also J.C. van der Walt, *Zululand True Stories, 1780–1978* (Richards Bay, 2007), pp. 106–107, on the supposed gold discovery of 1980.
39. RSA, NASA, Cape Town, CAD, Governor's Correspondence 1896, GH 15/48, Minutes from the Prime Minister's Office, Cape Town, dated 28 May 1896.

40. RSA, NASA, Cape Town, CAD, Governor's Correspondence 1896, GH 15/48, Report by Acting Chief of Police, Cape Town, Lancelot Harrison, 15 June 1896.
41. RSA, NASA, Pretoria, TAB, SP (Secret Minutes) Vol. 193, Ref. GR 12/98, J.W. Treu to J.C. Smuts, State Attorney, 2 Aug. 1898.
42. D.P. McCracken, 'John MacBride, 1868–1916', in Matthew and Harrison, *Oxford Dictionary of National Biography*; McCracken, *MacBride's Brigade*, p. 19.
43. See *The Irish Conspiracy*, p. 12, and McCracken, *MacBride's Brigade*, p. 19. McCracken appears to have elided the Robinson Mine and the Langlaagte 'Block B' Mines; compare his entry on MacBride in the *Oxford Dictionary of National Biography* above with his observation in *MacBride's Brigade*, p. 19. A plausible explanation would seem to be that MacBride and Griffith at first both worked at the H. Eckstein-owned Robinson Mine, where the latter operated a cyanide vat, and that, after Griffith's departure, MacBride assumed a new and more senior position as 'Chief Assayer' at the Langlaagte Mine – see *The Irish Conspiracy*, p. 12.
44. See D. Harker, *The Real Story of 'The Ragged Trousered Philanthropists'* (London, 2003), pp. 1–10, and J. Hyslop, 'A Ragged Trousered Philanthropist and the Empire: Robert Tressell in South Africa', *History Workshop Journal* 51, 2001, pp. 65–86. (I am indebted to Paul La Hausse de Lalouvière for drawing my attention to Noonan's role in helping to organise the 1898 centennial celebrations.)
45. P.A. McCracken, 'Griffith's Sabbatical', pp. 227–262.
46. Note, for example, D.P. McCracken's hesitancy in accepting financial reasons as the primary motivation for Griffith's migrations south in McCracken, *MacBride's Brigade*, pp. 19–20.
47. P. Colum, *Arthur Griffith* (Dublin, 1959), p. 9. There is, however, no connection to be discerned between Arthur Griffith and 'One-Armed Jack' McLoughlin's close friend Tommy Whelan, a Mancunian who, as a member of the Irish Brigade, also took a great interest in Rand gold refineries. See Chapter 5.
48. This paragraph is based almost entirely on P.A. McCracken's 'Griffith's Sabbatical', pp. 227–228; but see also D.P. McCracken, *MacBride's Brigade*, pp. 17–18.
49. P.A. McCracken, 'Griffith's Sabbatical', p. 232.
50. Ibid., p. 229.
51. P.A. McCracken, as ever, is alert to this slightly paradoxical situation; see her 'Griffith's Sabbatical', p. 232, as well as pp. 248–249.
52. P.A. McCracken, 'Griffith's Sabbatical', pp. 249–250.
53. Blackburn and Caddell, *Secret Service in South Africa*, p. 128.
54. As cited in P.A. McCracken, 'Griffith's Sabbatical', p. 251.
55. See Colum, *Arthur Griffith*, p. 39.
56. See McCracken, *MacBride's Brigade*, p. 21.

57. P.A. McCracken, 'Griffith's Sabbatical', p. 252.
58. Ibid., p. 232.
59. J. Stephens, 'Arthur Griffith. President of Dáil Éireann', from the *Review of Reviews*, as reprinted in *The Republic* 2 (38), 22 April 1922, pp. 7–9. (I am indebted to Patricia McCracken for making a copy of this available to me.)
60. See *Longland's Johannesburg and South African Republic Directory for 1897 and 1898*, pp. 365 and 419.
61. P.A. McCracken, 'Griffith's Sabbatical', p. 253.
62. See Colum, *Arthur Griffith*, pp. 9–10.
63. As cited in P.A. McCracken, 'Griffith's Sabbatical', p. 238.
64. See P.A. McCracken, 'Griffith's Sabbatical', p. 239.
65. D.P. McCracken, 'The Troublemakers: Part 1: Insurgents and Adventurers, 1806–1899', in D.P. McCracken (ed.), *The Irish in Southern Africa, 1795–1910, Southern African-Irish Studies Vol.* 2 (Durban, 1991), p. 46 (hereafter, McCracken, 'The Troublemakers'). Interestingly, Colum suggests that the former gangsters Griffith met were comprised not only of Irishmen but of 'Americans' and 'Germans' who had held up mine managers; see Colum, *Arthur Griffith*, p. 42. I have found no evidence to suggest the presence of so cosmopolitan an element in the early Irish Brigade.
66. RSA, NASA, Pretoria, TAB, SP Vol. 884 (loose papers without a reference number to file), Chief of Police, H.A. Jenner, to Commissioner of Police, Pretoria, 4 Feb. 1898.
67. RSA, NASA, Pretoria, TAB, SP Vol. 884, Ref. GR 83/98, H.A. Jenner, Chief of Police, Cape Town, to Commissioner of Police, Pretoria, 4 May 1898.
68. Ibid.
69. Count De Sarigny's precise status is difficult to determine but it seems clear that he was working for the state and the mining industry as a largely unpaid agent and enjoyed the support of top officials. See especially RSA, NASA, Pretoria, TAB, SP (Secret Minutes) Vol. 193, GR 6/98, Count De Sarigny to State Secretary (with a copy to State Attorney, J.C. Smuts) dated 1 July 1898, in which he requests further instructions. It is, however, possible that at that stage – when the main IGB syndicate was unravelling rapidly and there was treachery afoot at every turn – De Sarigny, too, was playing a double game and that not all his covert dealings were above suspicion.
70. See various items of correspondence in RSA, NASA, Pretoria, TAB, SP (Secret Minutes) Vol. 193, Ref. GR 6/98, and especially, 'Confidential', Birkenruth to State Attorney, 29 July 1898.
71. RSA, NASA, Pretoria, TAB, SS Vol. 7287, Ref. R 80-94/98, Hoff-Meintjes Motion seeking clarification on the criminal proceedings in the State vs Count De Sarigny and J. Spittle, 25 June 1898.

72. See, for example, Scoble and Abercrombie, *The Rise and Fall of Krugerism*, p. 228.
73. See RSA, NASA, Pretoria, TAB, SP (Secret Minutes) Vol. 193, Ref. GR 6/98, handwritten letter from J.W. Treu to J.C. Smuts, State Attorney, marked 'Confidential' and dated 11 July 1898. On Treu and Ferguson see, among others, 'The Trial of Treu', *Standard & Diggers' News*, 11 Jan. 1899. The prosecution of Treu was unsuccessful but he continued to feel vulnerable to threats, which he considered to be coming from Ferguson and others. See RSA, NASA, Pretoria, TAB, SP Vol. 221, GR 51/ 99, J.W. Treu to J.C. Smuts, State Attorney, Pretoria, 1 May 1899. On Ferguson's threats to Treu, see 'Ferguson and Treu', *Star*, 26 and 27 Jan. 1899.
74. See, among others, the following items in the *Star*, 1899 : 'The Charge Against Treu', 10 Jan.; 'The Charge Against Treu', 11 Jan.; 'Ferguson vs Treu', 14 Jan.; 'The Charge Against Treu', 12 Jan.; 'Ferguson and Treu', 26 Jan.; 'The Case Against Treu', 27 Jan.; 'The Treu Trial: Another Alleged Assault', 28 Jan.; 'Treu against Ferguson', 28 Jan.; 'Treu's Tribulations', 31 Jan.; and 'Treu and Ferguson', 3 Feb. In the *Standard & Diggers' News* of 1899 see, among others, especially 'The Trial of Treu', 11 Jan. Treu, who appears to have been assaulted on at least three occasions, lived in fear of his life. His appeals for state protection can be traced in Smuts's 'Secret Minutes', which are held in the state archives.
75. On Griffith's remarkable memory, see Colum, *Arthur Griffith*, pp. 9–10.
76. RSA, NASA, Pretoria, TAB, SP (Secret Minutes) Vol. 193, Ref. GR 12/98, Confidential letter from J.W. Treu to J.C. Smuts, Esq., State Attorney, Pretoria, 30 July 1898.
77. RSA, NASA, Pretoria, TAB, SP (Secret Minutes) Vol. 193, Ref. GR 13/09, loose letter, unfiled, N.L. Sapte to His Honour, The State Attorney, Pretoria, 29 June 1898.
78. RSA, NASA, Pretoria, TAB, SP (Secret Minutes) Vol. 193, Ref. GR 12/98, loose letter, unfiled, N.L. Sapte to His Honour, The State Attorney, Pretoria, 30 June 1898.
79. RSA, NASA, Pretoria, TAB, SP (Secret Minutes) Vol. 193, Ref. GR 16/98, Secretary to the State Attorney's Department, M.J.A. Watermeyer to N.L. Sapte, 7 July 1898.
80. RSA, NASA, Pretoria, TAB, SP (Secret Minutes) Vol. 193, Ref. GR 6/98, N.L. Sapte to His Honour, The State Attorney, 18 July 1898.
81. P.A. McCracken, 'Griffith's Sabbatical', p. 254.

## CONCLUSION

1. McCracken, *MacBride's Brigade*, p. 32.

2. See F. McGarry and J. McConnel, *The Black Hand of Republicanism: Fenianism in Modern Ireland* (Dublin, 2009), p. xix.
3. As quoted in McCracken, *MacBride's Brigade*, p. 36.
4. D.P. McCracken, 'From Paris to Paris via Pretoria: Arthur Lynch at War', *Études Irlandaises* 28 (1), Printemps 2003, p. 130.
5. McCracken, *MacBride's Brigade*, pp. 35 and 170.
6. Hans Sauer, who encountered 'Groot Adriaan' de la Rey along the West Rand in the late 1880s, described him as a well-known 'filibuster' – see Sauer, *Ex Africa*, p. 138. By then De la Rey's doings in Stellaland had already been the subject of questions in Westminster. See UK, *House of Commons Debates*, Vol. 281, columns 1213–1215, 12 July 1883. In the best tradition of setting a thief to catch a thief, Adriaan de la Rey was, in 1887, offered the position of Commandant of Police on the goldfields. It would appear that, amidst a public outcry about his criminal record, the offer was retracted – see D.W. Kruger, *Paul Kruger, Vol. II* (Johannesburg, 1963), p. 97. De la Rey and other Afrikaner bandits in Goshen and Stellaland are the subject of ongoing research.
7. See D.H. Akenson, 'South Africa: A Small Elite Band', in Akenson, *The Irish Diaspora*, pp. 124–130.
8. See, for example, 'Mustering', *Star*, 4 Jan. 1896, and E. Garrett and E.J. Edwards, *The Story of An African Crisis* (London, 1897), p. 139. There were, of course, also non-anglophone brigades such as those formed by the Germans and Hollanders, whose sympathies lay, very clearly, with the Kruger government.
9. K. Jeffery, 'The Irish Military Tradition and the British Empire', in K. Jeffery (ed.), *'An Irish Empire'? Aspects of Ireland and the British Empire* (Manchester, 1996), p. 95; D.O. Rhoodie, *Conspirators in Conflict: A Study of the Johannesburg Reform Committee and Its Role in the Conspiracy against the South African Republic* (Cape Town, 1967), p. 75; and 'Mustering', *Star*, 4 Jan. 1896. (My thanks to Albert Grundlingh for drawing the Rhoodie reference to my attention.)
10. Such confusion as there was may have been slightly less pronounced than I portray it here – it is difficult to tell from existing primary evidence. See especially McCracken, 'The Troublemakers', pp. 47–48.
11. See Sauer, *Ex Africa*, pp. 274–275.
12. On the raid into Free Town see Metrowich, *Scotty Smith*, pp. 50–51; and on the important albeit short-lived role of the trans-frontier illegal trade in diamonds see J.W. Matthews, *Incwadi Yami: Twenty Years' Personal Experience in South Africa* (Johannesburg, 1976), p. 200.
13. 'The Raid', *South Africa Magazine*, 8 Jan. 1896.
14. See McCracken, 'Rhodes and Parnell', in McCracken, *Forgotten Protest*, pp. 19–30.

15. See M. Meredith, *Diamonds, Gold and War: The Making of South Africa* (London, 2007), pp. 311–322.
16. As quoted in Meredith, *Diamonds, Gold and War*, p. 323.
17. See McCracken, *Inspector Mallon*, p. 148.
18. See Sauer, *Ex Africa*, pp. 156–157.
19. Sauer, *Ex Africa*, p. 136.
20. See R.H. MacDonald, *The Language of Empire: Myths and Metaphors of Popular Imperialism, 1880–1914* (Manchester, 1994), p. 113.
21. See J.E.S. Green, *Rhodes Goes North* (London, 1936), pp. 180–181, and B.A. Kosmin, 'Ethnic and Commercial Relations in Southern Rhodesia: A Socio-Historical Study of the Asian, Hellenic and Jewish Populations, 1898–1943', unpublished D.Phil. thesis, University of Rhodesia, 1974, p. 35. (I am indebted to Ian Phimister not only for this observation but for directing me to the sources.)
22. Mark Twain, *Following the Equator: A Journey Around the World, Vol.* 2 (New York, 1899), pp. 358–359.
23. A reading of the relevant chapters in Cohen, *Reminiscences of Kimberley*, in which there are several references to Christiana and Free Town as centres of illegal trade, offers a good start.
24. Kruger visited Johannesburg in February and September 1887, in December 1888 and again in May 1890. Most of these visits were marked by truculent displays of imperialist sympathies by sections of the immigrant population. Kruger, in turn, let them know that he considered them to be potentially hostile 'rebels'. These visits and the 'murderers and thieves' observation can be tracked in Kruger, *Paul Kruger, Vol. II*, pp. 92–107.
25. As seen, for example, by Mawby in *Gold Mining and Politics*, pp. 90–91.
26. Functioning literate societies tend to have expanding repertoires of thoughtful historical works and established – if not thriving – historical professions served by an occasionally buoyant and diversified retail trade in books. Illiterate societies, faced with ongoing identity problems and uncertain futures (but filled with prospects for 'economic development' and brimming with 'potential'), have 'heritage industries' that 'market' historical personalities and places for local and international tourist consumption through displays, exhibitions, guide books, museums, tours, talks and the sale of cheap quasi-historical artefacts. The former try to puzzle over the ever-changing past and struggle with the printed word, while the latter, filled with false confidence, use smoke and mirrors to distract the eyes and ears to sell a vision of the future based on what is considered to be an acceptable past. Those wiser than Solomon will point out that in the 'real world' things are seldom so clear-cut,

and that both paths could and should be used when approaching the past. It is a view which suggests that the routes ultimately lead to the same destination. They do not. The one – respecting time and the past – points to the gradual emergence of a critical public opinion and an informed citizenry; the other tends towards instant gratification and partial political mobilisation of the sort that benefits those who control the 'heritage industry' and their paymasters. The former makes for considered caution; the latter encourages brash bravado. Take your choice, but confuse the two at your peril.

# Index